THE
FRAUD
OF THE RINGS

By the same author, published by LPS publishing:

Buchanan's Dictionary of Quotations for Conservatives (for when only the right quotation will do)
(2010)

Harriet Harman Drove me to France
(2010)

Two Men in a Car (a businessman, a chauffeur, and their holidays in France)
(2008)

Guitar Gods in Beds. (Bedfordshire: a heavenly county)
(2008)

By the same author, published by Kogan Page:

Profitable Buying Strategies: How to Cut Procurement Costs and Buy Your Way to Higher Profits
(Kogan Page, 2008)

THE
FRAUD
OF THE RINGS

Mike B

mike buchanan

lps publishing

publisher's note
every possible effort has been made to ensure that the information contained in this
book is accurate, and the publisher and author cannot accept responsibility for any
errors or omissions, however caused. no responsibility for loss or damage
occasioned to any person acting, or refraining from action, as a result of the material
in this publication, can be accepted by the publisher or the author

first published in great britain in 2009 by lps publishing, this paperback edition first
printed in 2010

lps publishing
1 goodrich avenue
bedford mk41 0de
united kingdom
www.lpspublishing.co.uk

copyright © mike buchanan 2009

the right of mike buchanan to be identified as the author of this work has been
asserted by him in accordance with the copyright, designs and patents act 2008

isbn 9780955878473

british library cataloguing-in-publication data
a cip record for this book is available from the british library

printed in great britain by mpg books group, bodmin and king's lynn

® mbti, myers-briggs type indicator and myers-briggs are registered trademarks of
the myers-briggs type indicator trust. opp ltd is licensed to use the trademarks in
europe

to realism

CONTENTS

ACKNOWLEDGEMENTS

My first thanks must go to the authors and publishers of the splendid works that I cite in this book. I should make it clear that not one of the authors makes the central thesis of this book: that most adults in the developed world in the modern era are unsuited to the institution of marriage as it is currently structured, based upon a traditional and religious paradigm. That thesis is mine alone.

My thanks to the cover designer Mr D, and to the staff at the printer, especially the ever-patient Mr M.

My thanks to the diligent Ms W, my copy editor and proofreader, for finding so many flaws in my flawless manuscript.

My thanks to the people who gave me their views about the institution of marriage, their own marriages, and the marriages of people they know and have known.

A particularly warm 'thank you' to the politician who is the very personification of political correctness in the United Kingdom today, for the material she provided for this book: the unfortunately energetic Rt Hon Harriet Harman QC MP, Minister for Women and Equality. I was sure she would have interesting views on a number of the issues covered by this book, so I wrote to her, requesting a meeting. A copy of the letter is in appendix two. Unfortunately, she declined to meet, so we shall never know her take on my exploration of marriage in the modern era.

I'm grateful to (divorced) Mr W, the finance director of a company in the United Kingdom, for the wonderful title *The Fraud of the Rings*. Never again shall I comment on accountants' lack of a sense of humour.

My final thanks go to a good friend and business associate in Yorkshire who, having suggested I write a book about the subject of unhappiness in marriage, then gave me a good deal of his time and advice over the period it took to write. Mr X, will you *please* stop earning so much money as a business consultant, and start devoting yourself to your writing. You'd be happier, if a little poorer. But then *we* would be a little richer.

INTRODUCTION

When two people are under the influence of the most violent, most insane, most delusive, and most transient of passions, they are required to swear that they will remain in that excited, abnormal, and exhausting condition continuously until death do them part.

(George Bernard Shaw, Preface to *The Doctor's Dilemma*)

Welcome to *The Fraud of the Rings*. I should start by making a point about the scope of the book, which is limited to the institution of marriage in the increasingly individualistic and secular societies of the developed world. I know nothing about the institution of marriage in the developing world, nor indeed in tightly-knit communities linked to individual religions in the developed world, and it follows that I have nothing to say about them. I do not intend to cause offence to people of traditional religious persuasions, nor indeed to anyone else. I do recognise that any attempt at reviewing the institution of marriage will cause offence in certain quarters, but it needs to be done. The divorce statistics demand that it be done.

Isn't it about time we were more honest and admitted what has been blindingly obvious for so many years? That in the developed world in the modern era, marriage is a source of unhappiness – rather than happiness – for many people. Maybe even *most* people. And isn't it also about time we considered whether the issue of personal unhappiness might largely explain the ever-rising divorce rates, rather than the loss of 'traditional values'? If so, it follows that we should make a more serious effort to understand the issues of unhappiness in marriage and what causes so many marriages to be unhappy or to fail altogether. This book represents the outcome of my own efforts to understand the issues.

We live in challenging times. Never has the divorce rate been higher – and it's still rising – despite an ever-growing army of marriage guidance and relationship counsellors and therapists, and countless articles and publications offering advice on marriage and other intimate relationships.

Views about the institution of marriage come from 'relationship experts', social commentators, journalists, book writers, politicians, clerics, and organisations with *vested interests* in our marrying and staying married, sometimes with utter disregard for our personal happiness.

We tend to accept their implied message without challenging it. The message is that the institution of marriage *in its traditional form* remains suitable for the majority of adults in the developed world, and that the majority of adults can expect to find happiness and even joy in it. It follows that people who find themselves unhappy in their marriages must be *flawed.* I believe this cruel message, albeit erroneous – as we shall discover – only adds to the misery of countless unhappily married people, and people who have been unhappily married.

For some years over 50% of new marriages in the developed world, where divorce is freely available and there is no major stigma attached to it, have ended in divorce. Or are predicted to do so in the fullness of time. Around 50% of the marriages that do not end in divorce are broadly unhappy. Most people are literally deluded when they marry with any degree of confidence that they will have long and happy marriages. That's the marriage delusion, which I've termed 'the fraud of the rings'.

Some people are clearly 'comfortable' in the married state, while others report themselves uncomfortable, sometimes severely so. In my mid-forties I married for the second time, to a kind and loving woman of a similar age. Her happy first marriage – of over 25 years' duration – had ended with her husband's death. The length of her first marriage helped me believe I might make more of a success of my second marriage than my first. How wrong I was. How *deluded.*

In 2007 the marriage failed, after only three years, for reasons wholly connected with me and not with my wife, and I resolved to understand the problems I had with the institution. For some time it was only a personal quest and I could not then have imagined that I would eventually write a book about marriage.

In my customary introverted manner I turned to books (written by 'relationship experts' this time) to deliver the insights I was seeking. But a problem soon emerged. While I couldn't readily fault what I was reading, much of the material didn't seem very relevant to me or *my* unhappiness. A frequent piece of advice – particularly from female writers – was to *communicate* more about emotions with a partner. That didn't help. I had been unhappy in my marriages but I didn't know *why.* I had nothing to communicate.

After reading a number of these books, I started to realise that the majority of the writers were unlike me in at least two important regards: they were female and extraverted – they clearly derived great pleasure from intimate relationships. And they were often religious, too, which I'm not. The general thrust of their arguments appeared to be that they themselves had enjoyed lengthy and happy marriages, and they attributed this to certain things they did (or didn't do) in their marriages, such as the ways in which they resolved conflict. And the 'ways' would be outlined in the book. The inference seemed to be that if you followed the writers' advice, happiness would surely follow.

My sceptical mind simply *had* to challenge that inference, by testing its logic in another context. Let's imagine that a world record-holding Olympic athlete wrote a book relating in detail how he'd trained on the way to getting a world record. In the book he led the reader to infer that all he or she had to do to achieve their own world record was to adopt the same training regime. The reader would surely regard the inference as absurd, knowing that he or she almost certainly didn't have the physical 'right stuff' to start with.

But what's less obvious is that we might not have the personality type, the temperament, nor the mental and emotional 'right stuff' to improve our relationships through reading books written by 'relationship experts'. And this might explain why those books sell in such high numbers, and the divorce rate keeps on rising anyway. Maybe the same phenomenon accounts for the growth in diet book sales in parallel with the growth of waistlines across the developed world.

I wasn't getting very far trying to understand my unhappiness in my marriages. Then I had a stroke of luck. A business associate was driving past my home town, and had a little time to kill before a meeting. We met for lunch. I outlined the struggle I was experiencing in trying to understand my unhappiness with marriage, whereupon he had a good idea. He said:

> You've been improving major organisations' annual profits by millions of pounds every year, for over 25 years. You do it by analysing and then solving some of their most challenging problems. Here's an idea. Why not apply sound analytical approaches to help you understand the source or

sources of your unhappiness? You might then also discover a range of reasons behind why other people are unhappy in *their* marriages.

Imagine that the government, knowing the negative impacts of marital unhappiness and the high and rising divorce rate, is determined to reduce marital unhappiness and thereby reverse the divorce rate trend. It has charged a number of organisations with making recommendations, and one of them has commissioned you to conduct a two-year-long study. Take your usual professional and disciplined approach and deliver a book at the end, along with recommendations. Oh, and the organisation *demands* that you tell them the facts as they appear to you. The people there don't want their feelings spared, and they're not easily shocked. They'll be perfectly happy for you to report something which differs from 'received wisdom' on the subject.

His advice made sense, and I felt that I'd soon know whether or not this was a worthwhile project. In the event it took only a day or two before I had persuaded myself that the project *did* merit serious attention. My work over the course of two years led me to a thesis which I believe to have structural integrity. And when I interviewed people who were unhappily married, or who had been unhappily married but were now divorced or widowed, the thesis appeared to explain a great deal of their marital unhappiness – although not, of course, all of it.

My central thesis is that there are three *marriage risk factors*, each of which may contribute to the likelihood that an individual will struggle to find happiness in marriage. The *more* of the factors an individual has, the *lower* the prospect of he or she being happily married. The factors are:

- Introversion (about 54% of men and 47% of women are introverted)
- Being of the male gender (50% of marriage partners)
- Not holding strong traditional religious convictions *in common with a spouse* (over 93% of British adults)

The first two risk factors are beyond the power of the individual to change. And the risk factors may or may not manifest themselves quite *independently* of the quality of relationship with a partner. As for the third risk factor, even moderately well-educated people in the developed world in the modern era would generally not be prepared – for reasons of intellectual integrity, if nothing else – to *genuinely* adopt the religion of their spouse for the sake of marital harmony. In my second marriage I had all three risk factors, my wife had one (she was religious, I wasn't).

To the best of my knowledge, no other writer has put forward this thesis. And I'm certainly no 'relationship expert'. So why has no one suggested this thesis before? I believe the answers include social conditioning, psychological defence mechanisms, religious beliefs, political correctness, an army of (mainly female and extravert) marriage guidance and relationship counsellors, and (mainly female and extravert) writers of books and articles about marriage and relationships.

I came to understand that one of the leading causes of unhappiness in marriage is the unrealistic expectation that marriage *will* reliably deliver happiness. It follows that reduced expectations of happiness in marriage should improve happiness. Strange but true.

One of my motivations for writing this book was to give readers the information they need to help them assess their personal aptitude for marriage, and to help them also predict the likely long-term compatibility of their partners and themselves. Or at least direct the reader to the most appropriate resources, which explains why this book contains extracts from so many other books, over 30 others in fact. I could have simply written material along the lines of 'A recent American study concluded that . . .' but I felt strongly that the reader interested in particular topics should know where to go for further information. All the books are worth reading. I should know, as I bought and read them all.

I should like to see couples who are considering marriage replace their optimism with realism. And given how many people suffer from the marriage delusion, I believe the state should help assess whether couples are adequately prepared for marriage, and refuse them wedding licences when they are not. The key to reducing the divorce rate surely lies in reducing the number of marriages with little prospect of success.

We return to the personality trait of introversion, which I believe to be an important risk factor. This book covers the topic at length, because it's widely misunderstood and popularly deemed a 'negative' trait in the more extraverted societies of the developed world.

People can't change their personality traits – they're born with them and they'll die with them – and it makes no sense to encourage introverts to 'work harder' at their marriages. You would as helpfully exhort them to fly by flapping their arms, and when they fail, tell them it's because they're not making enough of an effort. 'Come on, faster! FASTER!!!'

Even when the two partners in a marriage each have the *personal aptitude* for a happy marriage, there remains the issue of *mutual compatibility*. This was less of a problem at the time marriage developed – thousands of years ago – when most people would not expect to live many years longer after they had reared their children. A 30-year-old would have been a village elder. But now we are told we could – we *should* – have happy and sexually active marriages of 50 years' duration or more. It's not natural, and it's not reasonable. Not for the vast majority of us, anyway.

The children of divorced couples are more likely to divorce than the children of couples who remain together. I wondered if there might be a genetic component to the likelihood that an individual will divorce, and discovered that there is.

There are a number of important yet largely 'missing voices' in the popular literature on long-term relationships and marriage. They include:

- People who find marriage difficult – many are cowed by society effectively telling them they are flawed. They're not
- Men with traditionally male characteristics – many of the books written by men are more sympathetic to female than to male perspectives
- Introverts – but we're starting to value ourselves, at long last

The final chapter explores the future of marriage. It starts with the premise that the institution of marriage should be adapted to suit the increasingly individualistic and secular-minded people of the developed world, rather than those people adapt to traditional marriage. The chapter offers a number of recommendations, including the introduction of a second form of marriage contract, of a fixed term.

The idea of a fixed-term marriage contract emerged from what I knew to work well in the business world. But it turned out not to be an original idea as it had already been proposed by others, including John Cleese in 2008. And in 2007 by Dr Gabriele Pauli, a German politician who had posed for a magazine as a dominatrix. You couldn't make it up.

1

THE FRAUD OF THE RINGS AND THE ISSUES UNDERMINING MODERN MARRIAGE

Strange to say what delight we married people have to see these poor fools decoyed into our condition.

(Samuel Pepys, *Diary*, 25 December 1665)

This chapter covers:

- Over 50% of new marriages will end in divorce
- Why so many people are deluded about the likelihood of having a happy marriage
- Why the fiercest advocates of marriage are sometimes those who have had long unhappy marriages themselves
- Marriage and mental health
- Cognitive dissonance and the 'double whammy' of unhappiness
- Bertrand Russell's views on 'received wisdom'
- The people and organisations that earn incomes directly or indirectly from marriage
- The factors undermining marriage in the modern era
- The relationship between individualism and difficulties with marriage and other close relationships
- Boredom inside and outside of marriage – men and women's different experiences
- Are we mentally equipped for the expectations of lengthy marriages in the modern era?
- Marriage risk factors
- 600 plus forthcoming books on marriage and relationships
- *Getting Wild Sex from Your Conservative Woman*

What is the likelihood that a newly married couple in the developed world in the modern era will eventually divorce? Most commentators put the figure at around 50%, and many put it at well above 50%. In his 1995 bestseller *Emotional Intelligence: Why It Can Matter More Than IQ*, Daniel Goleman wrote the following about the position in the United States:

The rate *per year* of divorces has more or less levelled off. But there is another way of calculating divorce rates, one that suggests a perilous climb: looking at the odds that a given newly married couple will have their marriage *eventually* end in divorce. Although the overall rate of divorce has stopped climbing, the *risk* of divorce has been shifting to newlyweds.

The shift gets clearer in comparing divorce rates for couples wed in a given year. For American marriages that began in 1890, about 10% ended in divorce. For those wed in 1920, the rate was about 18%. For couples married in 1950, 30%. Couples that were newly wed in 1970 had a 50% chance (of divorce). And for married couples starting out in 1990, the likelihood that the marriage would end in divorce was projected to be close to a staggering 67%!

It can be argued that much of this rise is due not so much to a decline in emotional intelligence as to the steady erosion of social pressures – the stigma surrounding divorce, or the economic dependence of wives on their husbands – that used to keep couples together in even the most miserable of matches. But if social pressures are no longer the glue that holds a marriage together, then the emotional forces between wife and husband are that much more crucial if their union is to survive.

Given that most marriages will either end with divorce or be unhappy anyway, what might explain the optimistic expectations – the marriage delusion – that couples hold on their wedding days? The question is even more pertinent for people embarking on their second or subsequent marriages, surely a triumph of optimism over experience.

The British clinical psychologist Oliver James wrote a remarkable book, *Britain on the Couch*, published in 1998. The book seeks to explain 'why we're unhappier than we were in the 1950s – despite being richer'. One of the reasons he cites is the impact of social comparisons, people comparing themselves with those better off, including individuals on television programmes. After explaining the ways in which people can – and *do* – protect their self-esteem, he continues:

The boundless ingenuity we display in dealing with uncomfortable social comparisons and turning them to our advantage is supported by the fascinating finding that most people manage to paint themselves a far rosier picture of their circumstances than is actually the case. At least 121 separate studies have shown that in general we view ourselves in unrealistically positive terms, that we believe ourselves to have far more control over the external events which dominate our lives than is truly the case, and that we hold views of the future which are far more optimistic than is warranted by statistical probability. Furthermore, the evidence shows that these 'positive illusions' are crucial in sustaining mental health.

To give just one (extraordinary) example from the many, a study found that men who had tested positive for HIV were significantly more optimistic that they would not go on to develop the AIDS illness than men who had tested negative! What is more, men with HIV who Think Positive about their prospects may take longer to develop AIDS than men who do not.

It is worth mentioning in passing that the 'positive illusions' body of evidence is perhaps the strongest single empirical basis for accepting the Freudian, psychoanalytically founded view of humans as highly defended against the truth about themselves and their world – ie that 'humankind cannot bear much reality' – and that these psychic defences against reality are essential to mental health, a point which, to my knowledge, has never been made by the academic psychologists who did this research, perhaps because most of them are hostile to psychoanalytic theory.

The positive illusions evidence does not suggest that we are living in a deluded Cloud Cuckoo Land and it clearly distinguishes normal positive illusions from the full-scale delusions of the psychotically depressed and schizophrenic (eg believing you are someone other than the person named on your birth certificate, or hearing voices). The authors of the theory recently concluded that 'We maintain that self-aggrandising self-perceptions, an illusion of control and unrealistic optimism are widespread in normal human thought. We further maintain that these "illusions" foster the criteria normally associated with mental health.' Although attempts have been made to criticise the theory, these have been successfully rebutted and the consensus among cognitive psychologists is that we really do live in this illusory state.

'We hold views of the future which are far more optimistic than is warranted by statistical probability . . . the evidence shows that these positive illusions are crucial in sustaining mental health . . . humankind cannot bear much reality . . . an illusion of control and unrealistic optimism are widespread in normal human thought.' It's quite a list, and surely explains – at least in part – the marriage delusion, the fraud of the rings. But what if you're made aware of the delusion? Might it move you from optimism to realism, in areas of your life where optimism can all too easily lead to poor decisions and consequent unhappiness? For example, marrying when you don't have the personal aptitude for it, or the predicted long-term mutual compatibility of you and your partner is poor? Your future happiness, the happiness of your partner, and possibly much else, might depend on you exchanging that optimism for realism.

James offers a stark insight into the evolution of personal relationships since the 1950s:

> Since 1950, across the life cycle, dependence within personal relationships has been increasingly frowned upon and denied in practice. At the same time and in total contradiction of this trend, there has been a wholly new valuation placed on personal relationships as a fount of happiness.
>
> Many long-term adverse consequences are related to these paradoxical changes. One is to increase our sense of discontent. Another is the dramatic rise in addictive behaviours of all kinds, including the compulsive use of 'solaces', such as illegal drugs, alcohol and gambling. At least in part, addictions are one of the substitutes for unmet emotional and social needs.

I have often noted and been puzzled by the fact that some of the fiercest advocates of marriage have themselves had long and unhappy marriages, yet they actively encourage others to marry. I raised this paradox with an acquaintance recently – he himself has had a long and unhappy marriage – and he suggested an explanation:

> I think there are two issues here for many long-married couples. When two people have been miserable in each other's company for years, they have to believe – and tell themselves and others – that there has been some merit in remaining together, that all the suffering hasn't been in vain. It helps if they're religious and their religion tells them that there is merit in carrying on together; it helps that they think God has an interest in the whole thing. And when they're in the second half of their working lives divorce could be financially ruinous anyway, so they're trapped together and might as well make the most of it.
>
> And why do these couples so often hide their unhappiness from others, especially from people planning to get married? Because miserable people like to make others as miserable as they are.

When people have suffered, and they want to believe that the suffering has been in the service of something of merit or importance, they are exhibiting a form of cognitive dissonance. A theory first put forward by the American social scientist Leon Festinger in 1957. In his book *Cognitive Dissonance: Fifty Years of a Classic Theory* (2007), Joel Cooper, Professor of Psychology at Princeton University and according to the book's cover 'arguably the scholar most associated with dissonance research in the past few decades', charts the progress of dissonance theory. He writes:

Leon Festinger, whose work on social comparison theory had already made him an influential figure in social psychology, made a very basic observation about the social lives of human beings: we do not like inconsistency. It upsets us and it drives us to action to reduce our inconsistency. The greater the inconsistency we face, the more agitated we will be and the more motivated we will be to reduce it.

Before formalising the definition of dissonance, let us imagine some inconsistencies that can happen in social life. Imagine that you prepared at great length for a dinner party at your home. You constructed the guest list, sent out the invitations, and prepared the menu. Nothing was too much effort for your party: you went to the store, prepared the ingredients, and cooked for hours, all in anticipation of how pleasant the conversation and the people would be. Except it wasn't. The guests arrived late, the conversations were forced, and the food was slightly overcooked by the time all of the guests arrived. The anticipation and expectation of the great time you were going to have are discordant with your observation of the evening. The pieces do not fit. You're upset, partly because the evening did not go well, but also because of the inconsistency between your expectation and your experience. You are suffering from the uncomfortable, unpleasant state of cognitive dissonance. . .

Festinger was adamant about one point. People do not just *prefer* consistency over inconsistency . . . The party host does not just wish the party had gone better; he must deal with the inconsistency between the hopes, aspirations, and effort that he put in prior to the party and the observation that the party did not go well. How can that be done? Surely, if the host changes his opinion about how well the party went, then there is no longer an inconsistency. Perhaps the guests loved a slightly blackened lamb and their quietness at the table reflected their enjoyment of the meal.

Festinger's insistence that cognitive dissonance was like a drive that needed to be reduced implied that people were going to have to find some way of resolving their inconsistencies. People do not just *prefer* eating over starving; we are *driven* to eat. Similarly, people who are in the throes of inconsistency in their social life are *driven* to resolve that inconsistency. How we go about dealing with our inconsistency can be rather ingenious. But, in Festinger's view, there is little question that it *will* be done.

An article which appeared in a Minneapolis newspaper gave Festinger and his students an ideal opportunity to study inconsistency in a real-world setting. Cooper's account of a remarkable example of cognitive dissonance is reproduced in appendix three. It relates how an American 'end of the world' sect dealt with the troubling fact that the world *didn't* come to a watery end on 21 December 1955. From a later section of Cooper's book, *Liking What You Suffer For.*

What does punishment feel like? It makes us feel bad, it discourages us from performing the behavior for which we were just punished, and it serves as a reminder to avoid the stimulus or situation that provoked the punishment. Punishments come in many varieties from severe corporal punishment to the more mundane negative reactions we may suffer from friends, teachers, or relatives who disapprove of something we do. Overall, it is safe to say that, at a minimum, we do not like being punished and that punishments typically produce negative affective states. Words like dislike, harm, aversion, and suffering seem to fit within the general rubric of being punished.

Imagine a situation we might be in that brings us pain and suffering. We are in a group that decides to learn to rock climb. We find an instructor in the Yellow Pages who, it seems, has a somewhat sadistic sense of what it takes to learn to climb a wall. He puts us through a tortuous training program designed to make us confront our fear, toughen our skin, strengthen our legs, all for the purpose of climbing a rather ordinary 20-foot wall. Did the suffering the instructor put us through make us thoroughly dislike the wall-climbing experience? Were we sufficiently punished to refrain from wall climbing in the future, to have a negative reaction to the thought of wall climbing, to hate the instructor and his 20-foot wall?

Although there is logic to predicting that the punishment, suffering, and effort that went into the wall-climbing experience would produce negative reactions, Elliot Aronson and Jud Mills used the theory of cognitive dissonance to predict otherwise. They reasoned that the suffering that goes into a given activity is inconsistent with people's desire not to suffer. In the case of the wall-climbing example, the ordeal that we allowed ourselves to undergo with the instructor is inconsistent with our typical preference not to suffer. These two cognitions are inconsistent and therefore should lead to the experience of cognitive dissonance. In addition, the wall we climbed was a rather ordinary challenge that, to a dispassionate observer, should not have required the suffering the instructor put us through. How can we reduce the dissonance? One effective way would be to raise, rather than lower, our evaluation of the wall climbing. If we thought the wall was an amazing challenge and that wall climbing was an exhilaratingly positive experience, those cognitions would support (ie be consistent with) the suffering we endured. Putting it all together, Aronson and Mills suggested that from the perspective of cognitive dissonance theory, enduring punishing activities such as those our instructor heaped upon us should increase the positivity of our attitudes toward the activity for which we suffered.

Aronson and Mills designed an experiment to test the prediction, and found it to be valid. Might this explain – at least partially – the observation that unhappily married people can be strong advocates of marriage? They can't have been unhappy for many years without it being in the service of something important and even wonderful, can they?

I suspect many unhappily married couples suffer a 'double whammy' of unhappiness due to cognitive dissonance. A person who is unhappy in his or her marriage may still believe that marriage *should* deliver happiness. The two most obvious ways of resolving the inconsistency are to believe in the importance of the institution, as we have seen, and/or to believe there must be something amiss with one of three elements – themselves, their partners, or the relationships. Might this explain the astonishing number of books published on the topics of relationships and marriage in the modern era?

And what if a person reads some of those books, and *still* can't manage to have a happy marriage? Surely this will only *increase* their unhappiness? I have a strong suspicion that the sheer effort of trying but failing to make unsuccessful relationships succeed must be damaging the mental health of countless people, and at the very least causing mild depression. Indeed, recent research – which we'll come to in chapter six – suggests an evolutionary link between persistently trying to attain unrealistic goals and mild depression. It is considered that the phenomenon might even largely account for the fact that the United States – surely the home of the ultimate 'can do' culture in the world – suffers the developed world's highest per capita incidence of depression.

There are many individuals and groups seeking to persuade us of a number of 'facts' about marriage, including:

- Marriage is a noble institution, which confers happiness and contentedness on people.
- It is a sign of maturity to enter into, and then to remain in, the institution.
- God wishes you to enter the institution and remain in it for the rest of your life. The strength of God's wishes varies dramatically between religions, as we shall see – and even between different denominations of the same religion.
- You can reasonably expect to have a long, happy, and sexually active relationship with your spouse, possibly for half a century or more.

- If you find yourself unhappy in the institution you are defective in some way, but effective support is available to return you to a happy state.

The relentless stream of approval for the institution of marriage results in the 'social conditioning' of most unmarried people. Because if enough people tell a person something often enough, that person will start to believe the message even in the absence of supporting evidence, or indeed even in the presence of evidence to the contrary (unhappily married parents, relatives, friends, and acquaintances . . .).

Bertrand Russell, the Nobel Prize-winning British philosopher, author, and mathematician, made some interesting observations about thinking and learning, including:

> Passive acceptance of the teacher's wisdom is easy to most boys and girls. It involves no effort of independent thought, and seems rational because the teacher knows more than his pupils; it is moreover the way to win the favour of the teacher unless he is a very exceptional man. Yet the habit of passive acceptance is a disastrous one in later life. It causes man to seek and to accept a leader, and to accept as a leader whoever is established in that position.

Individuals and groups who would have us all believe that marriage is intrinsically 'a good thing', and that the vast majority of adults in the developed world in the modern era are capable of sustaining a happy and very long-term, sexually active, monogamous relationship with an individual of the opposite sex, are surely asking us to 'passively accept their wisdom', to paraphrase Russell. Well, *I* don't accept their wisdom, and I hope that after reading this book, *you* won't either.

So who are these individuals and groups? Well, their prime interest may be your happiness. But it may not. At the very least, some have a potential conflict of loyalties. Some *directly* earn income through people spending their money when they marry, or later buying anniversary gifts, meals, and the like. Others earn income through counselling married individuals and couples. Yet others simply join in the 'chorus of praise' for romantic love in general, and marriage in particular. They include:

- Religions and their clerics
- Marriage and relationship counsellors

- Therapists
- Authors of books about relationships and marriage
- Writers of articles on these subjects
- Authors of romantic fiction
- Friends and family, acquaintances – whether or not happily married themselves
- Event organisers
- Restauranteurs
- Jewellers
- The suppliers of goods and services for weddings: the venue, the car, attire, flowers, food and drink, music, and so on . . .
- Honeymoon providers

In addition to these individuals and groups there are others who earn money *indirectly* from romantic love and marriage, including small 'c' conservative politicians seeking your vote by being highly supportive of marriage and 'traditional values', thereby improving their prospects of securing your vote and attaining, or remaining in, office.

I'm not suggesting a *conspiracy* here. I'm simply pointing out that there are many individuals and groups who benefit from you marrying, and trying to keep you married even if you're unhappy.

All the evidence indicates that, across the developed world in the modern era, divorce rates increase in line with the *opportunity* to divorce. A number of factors have combined to undermine marriage in the modern era, either by reducing the number of people getting married, or by increasing the number of divorces. They include:

- Increased individualism (sometimes associated with declining religiosity, sometimes not)
- The increasing economic independence of women
- The increasing unwillingness of potential marriage partners – particularly men – to marry in the light of the financial implications of divorce
- Feminist thinking
- Gender rancour
- Boredom with partners (sexual and other)
- A decline in traditional religious beliefs
- Increased levels of depression, particularly among women
- Increasing life expectancies

- Ready availability of divorce, and weak societal disapproval of it
- The gap between expectations of marriage in the modern era, and what we are mentally equipped to handle

We come now to the issue of individualism. It is credited in certain quarters with being the death-knell for traditional marriage. It is equated with selfishness and an inability to be concerned about things at the level of society or even the family. That argument is most frequently put forward by clerics and politicians, but what they're really complaining about is that we're taking guidance from *them* less and less over time, if at all (and with very good reason). But we're replacing them with other guides (e.g. relationship 'self-help' books). There still seems to be a deep conformist streak in most people.

Karen and Kenneth Dion of the University of Toronto wrote about the relationship between individualism and relationship quality in a chapter titled 'Individualism, Collectivism, and the Psychology of Love' for Yale University Press's *The New Psychology of Love* (2006):

> At the psychological level, the relation between individualism and love has been debated. There have been competing claims about the relation between individualism and relationship quality. In part, this debate reflects different conceptualisations about the meaning of the term *individualism*. Wachtel pointed out that this term has been used both to stress the uniqueness and dignity of each person and also to describe excessive preoccupation with one's self-interest, such that the needs of the larger community were ignored.
>
> Waterman proposed that freedom of choice, respect for the integrity of others, and fulfilling one's personal potential are central features of individualism; thus, one might expect a positive relation between individualism and relationship quality. If so, individualism should facilitate the development of love for one's partner.
>
> However, others have conceptualised individualism, or at least one type of individualism, as an extreme belief in one's personal autonomy and control, as seen in Sampson's (1977) term *self-contained individualism*. With this self-construal, people try to be as self-sufficient as possible, regarding dependence on others and others' dependence on them with ambivalence.
>
> A similar point has been made by Bellah and his colleagues (Bellah et al, 1985) in their discussion of the role of individualism in both the public and the private/personal domains of life, noting that the competing pulls of wanting one's freedom and the needs of one's partner can create problems for developing intimacy. Given this wariness concerning interdependence among those endorsing self-contained individualism, we

predicted a negative relation between this form of psychological individualism and the quality of love for one's partner.

Paradoxically, when thinking about individualism at both the societal and the personal level, although in societies characterised as individualistic marriage based on romantic love is a cultural ideal, the presence of some forms of individualism at the personal level can hinder the likelihood of realising this ideal. Our research and that of others has found evidence supporting this hypothesis: namely, that psychological individualism can make it more difficult to develop and maintain the desired love-based marriage.

Several studies have found that self-contained individualism is negatively related to relationship quality. In this section, the main points will be presented from research that we have conducted examining the relation between psychological individualism and the affective quality of love for one's partner, as well as one's beliefs about the nature of love and the nature of marriage.

To assess beliefs about the relation between the individual and the group (individualism and collectivism), we have used items developed by Breer and Locke (1965), sampling both domain-specific content and more global items intended to be more general indicators of each construct. Participants in the research to be described were young adults (university students).

In our first study, using a series of simultaneous regression analyses, we examined the contribution of different components of psychological individualism and collectivism, along with age and sex of participants. The most consistent pattern of findings occurred for one component of psychological individualism, which we characterised as reflecting self-contained individualism. The items comprising this component stressed qualities such as the importance of personal freedom and autonomy, personal control over one's life, and valuing self-sufficiency.

Greater self-contained individualism was related to lesser likelihood of reporting that one had ever been in love. Individualists also endorsed a more 'ludic' [Author's note: dictionary definition of ludic – 'adjective: playful, especially spontaneously and aimlessly'] view of love as described by Lee's typology of ideologies of love. The ludic style is characterised by a noncommittal, permissive view of love, as reflected in the idea of love as a type of game.

Of particular interest, among those who did report ever having been in love, self-contained individualism was also negatively related to the reported quality of the experience of love and love for one's partner. The experience of love was less likely to be described by qualities such as tender, deep, and rewarding as self-contained individualism increased.

To assess reported love for one's partner, we used Ruhin's (1970) measure and analysed its three subscales (caring, need, and trust) identified by Steck and colleagues (Steck, Levitan, McLane, and Kelley, 1982), along with Pam, Plutchik, and Conte's (1975) measure of reported physical attraction to one's partner. On all of these measures, we found the predicted negative relation between self-contained individualism and the quality of love for one's partner. This form of psychological individualism was associated with less reported caring, need, and trust of one's partner as well as less reported attraction.

In our second study we once again looked at the relationship quality correlates of psychological individualism and collectivism. In this study, we included some additional measures: attitudes toward marriage and toward divorce. Once again, using the Breer and Locke (1965) items, the 'self-contained individualism' component emerged. Similar to the first study, greater individualism was related to less likelihood of ever having been in love. As predicted, self-contained individualism was related to more negative attitudes toward marriage and a greater wish to marry later.

Other researchers (Agnew and Lee, 1997; Kemmelmeier, Sanchez-Burks, Cytron, and Coon, 1998, study 2) have similarly found evidence for a negative relation between psychological individualism and relationship commitment among samples of university students in the United States. They used scales constructed from the Breer and Locke (1965) items to assess individualism, and a measure developed by Rusbult and her colleagues (see Rusbult, Martz, and Agnew, 1998) to assess commitment in close relationships. There is thus converging evidence from diverse university samples that some aspects of individualism contribute negatively to love and relationship quality.

Since these studies involved young adults, specifically, university students, it is relevant to ask about the nature of the relation between individualism and love among a more representative group of adults.

We examined this issue by analysing previous survey data from the General Social Survey (GSS), which were collected in 1993. The General Social Survey, a probability survey of English-speaking adults in the United States, is conducted almost annually (Davis and Smith, 1992). In 1993, five questions were included about individualism. One of these items quite clearly captured the core of self-contained individualism with its strong focus on putting one's own needs and goals before those of other people.

Also included in the GSS were questions about satisfaction with different types of relationships, such as marriage and friendship, as well as items about subjective well-being and other items related to the quality of one's life. The pattern of findings across a series of regression analyses found considerable evidence of a negative relation between 'self-first' individualism and reported relationship quality, as well as other aspects of subjective well-being.

For example, the greater the individualism, the less reported happiness in romantic relationships, less reported happiness in marriage, and lower satisfaction with family life and with friends. Reported relationship outcomes also emerged as negatively related to individualism; for example, a lower sense of perceived success in one's family life and more likelihood of having been divorced in the past year or the previous five years.

The important point here is that the relationship quality correlates of self-contained individualism for university student samples in Canada and the United States and for a probability sample of adults in the United

States were similar. Across these different studies, the pattern of results indicated that psychological individualism negatively contributed to the quality of close relationships and to the experience of love.

The authors then write about the issue of individualism with respect to other personal relationships:

Our and others' work on individualism and love has focused for the most part on its role in the development, quality, and maintenance of heterosexual relationships in adulthood. Recent evidence also suggests, however, that the problematic aspects of individualism are evident in other important close relationships and the manifestation of love in those relationships. Although not undertaken to study the psychology of love, research on adult children's attempts to care for their ageing parents and their parents' responses to this care, conducted by Pyke and her colleagues, identified several themes consistent with our hypothesis that some forms of psychological individualism have a negative relation to relationship quality.

Using a qualitative research methodology based on interviews with members of three generations (ageing parents, midlife adult children, and adult grandchildren), Pyke and Bengtson (1996) identified both individualistic and collectivistic systems of beliefs concerning the family. Families whose orientation was largely individualistic stressed the value of personal autonomy of family members, voluntary association, and looser kinship ties among family members. Interestingly, family relations were frequently described in more negative or ambivalent terms.

Pyke and Bengston pointed out that among the families whose prevailing ideology was individualism, the adult children were more likely to delegate the physical caregiving to others (nonfamily hired help, nursing homes) and focused on help managing parents' finances and arrangements for eldercare. The underlying motivation when caring for ailing parents seemed to be one of duty rather than affection; hence, caregiving was seen as a burden.

From the individualist perspective, ageing parents valued their own autonomy and neither expected nor wanted intervention in their lives by their adult daughters and sons. To ask for or need help might threaten the parent's relation with the adult child since autonomy was so highly valued. The following statement poignantly reveals this dilemma. An 89-year-old mother said of her 53-year-old daughter: 'I don't want her to have to be burdened with me. Because I want her to keep on liking me, and if they have to take care of you, you never know if they are going to like you or not.'

Older parents thus received relatively little direct help from their children who endorsed a view of the family as supporting the individual autonomy of each member. Pyke (1999) subsequently examined the implications of an individualistic family orientation for eldercare for the power dynamics in a family. By adhering to individualism, older adults could preserve their sense of independence and not yield any of their parental authority to their children.

Although this system of beliefs and related behaviors was functional for older adults in good health, with the dependencies related to poor health Pyke found that endorsing an individualistic view of the family was related to problems for both ageing parents and their adult children, who now had to provide a level of care-related behavior that conflicted with these beliefs and often was resented by their parents. Moreover, the previous stress on self-sufficiency meant that adult children would not always be able to provide the most sensitive caregiving since they were unaware of their parents' preferences and wishes, and inexperienced in providing caregiving.

In essence, adult children might be least able to be fully emotionally responsive to the needs of ageing parents when their parents' needs were the greatest. In some cases, Pyke pointed out, aging parents who were individualists might prefer to forgo closer relationships with their adult children if that meant acknowledging increasing dependency and deferring to their children's wishes, resulting in less companionship and less instrumental assistance from their sons and daughters.

The research conducted by Pyke and her colleagues looked at the relation between individualism and family functioning in a domain different from the one we have been studying. It was independently designed to address other issues than those which have guided our thinking, and used a different research approach. Nonetheless, their results provide striking converging evidence consistent with the pattern of findings in our own program of research on the challenges that individualism poses for the expression of love in close relationships.

On to a topic which I think causes a problem in many long-term relationships: boredom. Quite apart from sexual boredom – which we shall explore later – there's the issue of the boredom that can naturally arise when two people know each other very well. All too often, familiarity *does* breed contempt. We shall later see that the level of contempt in a relationship is important, and can help predict the likelihood of divorce in individual couples.

I've often heard women comment on the superior patience of women compared with men. But there's another way of looking at patience: that it's not necessarily a virtue, but merely evidence of a high boredom threshold. Over the course of two years, when I was 20 to 21, I saw first-hand evidence of the relative patience of men and women.

In 1977, a 20-year-old student, I earned money in my holidays by working 12-hour-long night shifts (6pm to 6am) in a bakery, six nights per week. It was a continuous production operation, so the ovens disgorged loaves of hot just-baked bread at a constant rate, even when downstream operations (eg bread cutting) were not working for some reason.

The boredom of the bread packing jobs was such that there was a longstanding tradition among the (all male) night workers that to alleviate the boredom something must be done to stop one of the downstream operations. The favourite method was to hurl something (a small stone or block of wood did nicely) into the slicing machine, thereby breaking a few of the metre-long steel slicing blades. The engineer would then be woken up (this was in the late 1970s) and asked to sort out the mystery of the loaves that were not fully sliced. After glaring at the operators and cursing us, he would replace the broken blades. In the meantime the operators would have to build substantial stacks of the hot loaves emerging from the ovens, which were later fed back into the newly operating slicing machine. Everyone's spirits were remarkably improved after such an event. Well, not the engineer's spirits, to be fair. One operator claimed these events helped him retain his sanity.

A year later, I graduated from university with an honours degree in Chemistry. The university was one of the three most elite universities in the United Kingdom – Oxford, Cambridge, and Reading. My first job was as a graduate manufacturing trainee in the largest toiletries factory in Europe, operated by Beecham Toiletries. More than 120 operators worked on the 'packing lines' where the products were filled into bottles, jars, tubes, aerosol cans, etc. The operators worked on filling machines, labelling machines, carton erection machines, and the like. The work could best be described as light and repetitive. All the operators were female, and this had apparently always been the case.

I asked the two (female) supervisors why there were no men working on the filling lines. They laughed and one said, 'You have to be joking! Men would be bored rigid by lunchtime on their first day, and probably be on strike within a week.'

How might the issue of boredom play out in marriage? Might it be that if a husband and wife are equally bored with one another, the husband suffers more? I believe so. Of the divorced people I interviewed for this book, boredom was cited as a cause of marital disharmony by more men than women. One husband had been asked countless times over many years by his wife, after she had spoken at great length about the minutiae of her day, why he hadn't been listening to her. One evening he snapped and replied, 'Because I'm trying to retain my damned sanity!' They separated not long afterwards and later divorced.

Could it even be that we are not mentally equipped to meet the common expectations of lengthy modern marriages? This brings us on to the interesting topic of the evolution of the human brain. Unless you're a creationist, you would probably be convinced by the strong and growing evidence supporting the 'Out of Africa' hypothesis of the spread of humans around the world. Barrett, Dunbar, and Lycett in their book *Human Evolutionary Psychology* (2002) cover the topic, and its implications, at length. Research since the book's publication has only supported the hypothesis. The authors write:

> This hypothesis argued that all living humans share a recent common ancestor (or a very small number of ancestors) that lived in Africa some time between 100,000 and 200,000 years ago. After occupying virtually the whole of sub-Saharan Africa, one population crossed the Levant landbridge around 70,000 years ago and, over the next 30,000 years, spread rapidly across Eurasia and into Australia, finally breaching the Bering Strait to cross into the New World by around 15,000 years ago.

Working on the assumption that expectations from love-based marriage – dating back only some 200 to 300 years, as we shall see in the next chapter – differ from intimate relationship expectations in Africa between 100,000 and 200,000 years ago, what might we learn about the adaptiveness of the human brain to cope with such modern expectations? The authors of *Human Evolutionary Psychology* report two schools of thought:

APPROACHES TO THE STUDY OF HUMAN BEHAVIOUR

The broad field of study that we characterise as human evolutionary psychology (that is, the evolutionary-oriented study of human behaviour and cognition) is currently divided into two quite distinct camps which disagree fundamentally on some key issues. In this section, we summarise their basic positions. . .

Human Behavioural Ecology

On one side of the fence, there are those individuals who take a functional perspective and consider a trait to be biologically adapted if it increases the fitness (the number of genes passed to future generations) of those who bear the trait relative to those who do not. Individuals working in this field adopt an approach that is virtually identical to that taken by behavioural ecologists who study non-human animals (see, for example, Krebs and Davies 1997). That is, human behavioural ecology (HBE) focuses on measuring differences in reproductive success between individuals in relation to differences in the behavioural strategies that they follow (Smith et al 2000). Because many of those who adopt this perspective were originally trained in anthropology, they are sometimes referred to as 'Darwinian anthropologists'. . .

Evolutionary Psychology

On the other side of the fence from the human behavioural ecologists – and facing in an entirely different direction – are those who consider themselves to be practising evolutionary (or Darwinian) psychology (EP). As might be expected, workers in this area study human adaptation from a largely psychological perspective and their parent discipline is not behavioural ecology but cognitive psychology. The aim of EP is to identify the selection pressures that have shaped the human psyche over the course of evolutionary time, and then test whether our psychological mechanisms actually show the features one would expect if they were designed to solve these particular adaptive problems (for example, choosing mates or detecting cheats). . .

Environment of Evolutionary Adaptedness

One important source of disagreement between the two approaches centres around the concept of the Environment of Evolutionary Adaptedness (EEA). This issue arises out of the fact that EP and HBE disagree about the extent to which we can expect humans to be adapted to current environments due to a capacity for rapid shifts in phenotype as a consequence of increases in brain size and a capacity for flexible 'off-line' planning of action (Smith 2000). EP on the other hand takes the view that the massive cultural changes that have taken place in the last 10,000 years have occurred at a pace that is simply too fast to allow human brains (and hence behaviour) to adapt. The psychological adaptations we possess today were selected for in our past environment of evolutionary adaptedness (EEA) (Bowlby 1969, 1973) and are not geared for the modern world. Consequently EP argues that, a priori, there is no reason to expect any modern behaviour to be adaptive since present environments are so different from those in which the behaviour evolved (Cosmides and Tooby 1987).

If the EP school of thought is correct, does it follow that the modern human mind has simply not *evolved* to be comfortable with modern expectations of marriage? I believe so. Might *this* explain the countless publications about relationships and marriage, and the army of marriage and relationship counsellors seeking to keep relationships from falling apart? In a sense, marriage is deeply *unnatural* for modern humans. And monogamy is even more unnatural than polygamy, for both genders. Breathing and walking are *natural*. And we seem to manage those activities without the support of breathing counsellors and walking counsellors.

If we accept that marriage as promoted in particular by 'relationship experts' and clerics is challenging for modern humans, what proportion of the modern British population might we expect to find marriage *particularly* challenging? My central contention is that, all else being equal, at least three major groups can reasonably expect to find marriage more challenging than their 'opposite numbers':

- Introverts rather than extraverts
- Irreligious or moderately religious people rather than people who believe strongly in an 'organised' religion and have spouses who do likewise
- Men rather than women

I call these three factors *marriage risk factors* and contend that – all else being equal – the more of them an individual faces, the *lower* will be his or her prospect of a happy marriage. So how do these marriage risk factors play out in the population of the United Kingdom in the modern era? Table 1.1 seeks to answer the question.

Table 1.1 Proportion of British men and women with marriage risk factors

Risk factor	Men	Women
Introversion	54%	47%
Not a strong believer in an 'organised' religion in common with a spouse (1)	93%	93%
Male gender	100%	n/a

(1) Over 93% of the population of the United Kingdom do not regularly attend religious services. I do not know the male/female split but it is known that more women than men are religious.

Given these numbers, maybe we should be less surprised that the divorce rate exceeds 50%. The first two factors can differ by degree: a person can be (a) mildly or highly introverted, (b) an atheist, an agnostic, mildly or highly religious. I believe that the more introverted a person is, the more likely it is that he or she will struggle to find happiness in marriage. And the bigger the difference in married partners' religious convictions, the less likely they will be to find happiness. Introversion and extraversion are covered at length in chapter four, religion in chapter eight.

It seems we don't already have enough advice about relationships to draw upon, because new titles just keep on coming. To illustrate the point, in April 2009 I searched Amazon's website for relationship- and marriage-related books *yet to be published.* The search revealed well over 600 books, including the following random selection:

What Women Want: Getting What You Need – and What You Deserve – Out of Your Relationship by M Gary Neuman (8 September 2010)

Living Successfully with Screwed-up People by Elizabeth B Brown (1 March 2010)

To Have and to Hold: A Personal Handbook for Building a Strong Marriage and Preventing Affairs by Peggy Vaughan (2 February 2010)

The Complete Marriage Counsellor: Relationship-Saving Advice from America's Top 50 Couples Therapists by Sherry Amatenstein (18 January 2010)

Romance Rehab: 10 Steps to Rescue Your Relationship by Jan Hoistad (5 January 2010)

The Wisdom of a Broken Heart: Stop the Pain and Learn to Love Again by Susan Piver (29 December 2009)

Who's That Sleeping in My Bed? The Art of Successful Relationships at 50+ for Men and Women by Keren Smedley (10 December 2009)

Change Your Mindset, Not Your Man: Focus on What's Right Rather Than How to Fix What's Wrong by Sally B Watkins (18 November 2009)

The 'Trouble and Strife' Reader by Deborah Cameron and Joan Scanlon (1 November 2009)

Five Simple Steps to Take Your Marriage from Good to Great by Terri L Orbuch (27 October 2009)

Stop Marrying Mistakes: Proven Principles to Claiming a Healthy Relationship by Lisa J Peck (October 2009)

Have a New Husband by Friday: How to Change His Attitude, Behavior and Communication in 5 Days by Kevin Leman (October 2009)

The Sixty Minute Marriage by Rob Parsons (17 September 2009)

Women Are Crazy, Men Are Stupid: The Simple Truth to a Complicated Relationship by Lee & Morris (15 September 2009)

The Superior Wife: Why Women Wear the Pants in the Family, Why It's Bad for Marriage, and How to Restore Equality in Your Relationship by Carin Rubenstein (8 September 2009)

September Songs: The Good News about Marriage in the Later Years by Maggie Scarf (September 2009)

The Complete Idiot's Guide to Finding Mr Right by Josie Brown and Martin Brown (September 2009)

From Ashes to Beauty: Spiritual Truths for Rebuilding and Revitalizing Your Marriage by Jeff Colon (September 2009)

It's Not Me, It's You by Charlotte Ward (20 August 2009)

Attracting Genuine Love: A Step-by-Step Program to Bring a Loving and Desirable Partner into Your Life by Gay Hendricks and Kathlyn Hendriks (1 August 2009)

Ten Things You Aren't Telling Him: How to Help the Man in Your Life Love You Better by Julie Clinton (August 2009)

Reclaiming Desire: Four Keys to Finding Your Lost Libido by Andrew Goldstein and Marianne Brandon (August 2009)

Building a Marriage That Really Works (40-Minute Bible Studies) by Kay Arthur, David Lawson, and BJ Lawson (21 July 2009)

The Secrets of Happy Families: Eight Keys to Building a Lifetime of Connection and Contentment by Scott Haltzman MD (8 July 2009)

Marital Bliss in a Box: Wisdom and Well-Wishes for Newlyweds by Potter Style (1 July 2009)

To Understand and Be Understood: A Practical Guide to Successful Relationships by Erik Blumenthal (1 July 2009)

Your Intercultural Marriage: A Guide to a Healthy, Happy Relationship by Marla Alupoaicei (July 2009)

The 'Everything' Guide to a Happy Marriage: Expert Advice and Information for a Happy Life Together by Stephen Martin and Victoria Costello (July 2009)

Beat the Bitch: How to Stop the Other Woman Stealing Your Man by Tess Stimson (19 June 2009)

Why Men Fear Marriage: The Surprising Truth Behind Why So Many Men Can't Commit by R M Johnson (9 June 2009)

Smart Girls Marry Money: How Women Have Been Duped into the Romantic Dream – and How They're Paying for It by Daniela Drake (4 June 2009)

The Wholehearted Marriage: Fully Engaging Your Most Important Relationship by Dr Greg Smalley, Dr Shawn Stoever, and Greg Smalley (2 June 2009)

Unlocking Matrimonial Assets on Divorce by Simon Sugar and Andrjez Bojarski (1 June 2009)

Marriage at the Crossroads: Couples in Conversation about Discipleship, Gender Roles, Decision-Making and Intimacy by William Spencer, Aida Spencer, and Steve Tracy (June 2009)

90 Days to a Fantastic Marriage: How to Bring Out the Soul Mate in Your Mate by David Hawkins (June 2009)

The Marriage Checkup: A Program for Sustaining and Strengthening Marital Health by James V Cordova (28 May 2009)

Easy Wedding Planning by Elizabeth Lluch and Alex Lluch (16 May 2009)

The Ring Can Wait: 10 Keys to Getting a Life in Your Twenties Before Saying 'I Do' by Celeste Liversidge and Shannon Fox (12 May 2009)

Passionate Marriage – Keeping Love and Intimacy Alive in Committed Relationships by David Schnarch PhD (5 May 2009)

The Purpose for Marriage: The Spiritual Implications of the Covenant by Gemma Valentine (5 May 2009)

Sacred Marriage: Participant's Guide: How Marriage Can Help You Love God and Reflect Christ More by Kevin G Harney, Sherry Harney, and Gary L Thomas (1 May 2009)

Helping Couples Get Past the Affair by Donald H Baucom, Douglas K Snyder, and Kristina Koop Gordon (30 April 2009)

Amazing Weddings by Bianca Maria Oller and Patricia Masso (27 April 2009)

What Women Want Men To Know by Barbara De Angelis (21 April 2009)

Getting Wild Sex from Your Conservative Woman by Brandi Love (May 2009)

The sheer number of books about relationships and marriage yet to be published, adding to the existing mountain of them, is surely one of the best indicators we have that modern high expectations of happiness from marriage are unrealistic. At least for many people and, I firmly believe, *most*.

The titles of most of the forthcoming books suggest content similar to many of the books already on the market, especially those coming from a traditional and/or religious perspective. But one title caught my eye, and looks to have an original thesis. It was *Getting Wild Sex from Your Conservative Woman*, written by one Brandi Love. I imagine it will be a bestseller in the bookshop at the next Conservative Party annual conference.

2

MARRIAGE AND TRADITIONAL FAMILIES

Those who talk most about the blessings of marriage and the constancy of its vows are the very ones who declare that if the chain were broken and the prisoners were left free to choose, the whole social fabric would fly asunder. You can't have the argument both ways. If the prisoner is happy, why lock him in? If he isn't, why pretend that he is?

(George Bernard Shaw, *Man and Superman*)

This chapter covers:

- The significance of the wedding ceremony
- Social acceptance of alternatives to marriage
- Why women are at particular risk in unhappy marriages
- The long history of a crisis in the institution of marriage
- Love-based marriage as a historically recent development
- The divorce revolution at the end of the 20th century
- Why long life expectancy poses a problem for marriage
- Staying together for the sake of the children
- Myths about traditional family life

We start with an explanation of the significance of the wedding ceremony, from a book written by Pascal Boyer when he was professor of anthropology at Washington University. *Religion Explained: The Human Instincts that Fashion Gods, Spirits and Ancestors* was published in 2002. Boyer provides an anthropological explanation:

Marriages (as well as baby recognition ceremonies) are intensely public and publicised events. Again, the details of wedding celebrations vary a lot with differences in family organisation, in the relative status of men and women, in the degree of autonomy of women and in the particular rules of marital exchange. However, *some* ritual is felt to be necessary in most human groups and virtually everywhere it is made as evident as possible. The cheapest way of celebrating a marriage is to make a lot of noise. Where resources allow, using visual pageantry is another common way of making sure the new union is noticed by all and sundry. To consider marriage a 'private' arrangement between two individual parties is the exception rather than the rule.

A simple reason is that any marriage produces a situation that changes the whole sexual and reproductive landscape for the rest of the group, by removing two persons from the pool of possible mates, and by creating a unit where sexual access and parental investment as well as economic co-operation are bundled up together in a stable pact. This means that people's co-operation with each of the individuals concerned, in terms of sexual access, economic co-operation, social exchange or coalitional loyalty, must be 'realigned' to take account of this situation.

This creates problems of co-ordination. First, at what point should other members of the group change the way they interact with the individuals concerned? Stable couples may be the outcome of a long and gradual process, so there is no clear cut-off point at which others should start to reorient their behavior. Also, if other members of a group modify their behavior to take into account the new solidarity that exists between two people, they should all do it at the same time in the same way.

If you start treating the new family precisely as a family when others are still treating one of the members as if there was no marriage, you may for instance miss out on sexual opportunities. Or if you mistakenly think a person's resources will now be principally geared to their stable monogamous union you may miss out on occasions to borrow or use some of these resources.

So it is convenient that there should be a clear-cut distinction between before and after, as well as a convention that the group's behavior should change at that precise moment. Even in the West, people immersed in an intensely individualistic ideology still have the intuition that social interaction is what makes the ritual relevant.

The American historian and writer Stephanie Coontz is a faculty member of The Evergreen State College in Olympia, Washington. She was the author of *Marriage, a History: From Obedience to Intimacy, or How Love Conquered Marriage* (2005). The book is full of detailed information about marriage in former eras and in the modern era, with some highly nuanced arguments, which can be in short supply in the literature about marriage. There is also a real generosity of spirit in her writing.

Coontz herself is happily married, she tells us, but she is refreshingly clear about the institution, its benefits and pitfalls. The following is from the conclusion:

If we withdrew our social acceptance of alternatives to marriage, marriage itself might suffer. The very things that make marriage so potentially satisfying are for the most part inseparable from the things that make less satisfying marriages less bearable. The same personal freedoms that allow people to expect more from their married lives also allow them to get more out of staying single and give them more choice than ever before in history about whether or not to remain together.

There are those that believe that because married people are, on average, better off than divorced or single people, society should promote lifelong marriage for everyone and lead a campaign against divorce and cohabitation. But using averages to give personal advice to individuals or to construct social policy for all is not wise. On average, marriage has substantial benefits for both husbands and wives. That's because most marriages are pretty happy. [Author's comment: no comment]. But individuals in unhappy marriages are *more* psychologically distressed than people who stay single, and many of marriage's health benefits fade if the marriage is troubled. . .

Women are at particular risk in a bad marriage. A man in a bad marriage still gets some health benefits compared with single men, because even a miserable wife tends to feed her husband more vegetables, schedule his medical checkups, and shoulder much of the housework and the emotional work that makes life function smoothly. But there are no such compensations for an unhappily married woman. Unhappy wives have higher rates of depression and alcohol abuse than single women.

Many people think of marriage as an age-old largely unchanged institution, and that marriages were more 'successful' in the past. In the introduction to the book, Coontz makes the reality clear:

> For thousands of years people have been proclaiming a crisis in marriage and pointing back to better days. The Ancient Greeks complained bitterly about the declining morals of wives. The Romans bemoaned their high divorce rates, which they contrasted with an earlier period of family stability. The European settlers in America began lamenting the decline of the family and the disobedience of women and children almost as soon as they stepped off the boats.
>
> Worrying about the decay of marriage isn't just a Western habit. In the 1990s, sociologist Ann Kaler, conducting interviews in a region of southern Africa where divorce had long been common, was surprised to hear people say that marital strife and instability were new to their generation. So Kaler went back and looked at oral histories collected 50 years earlier. She found that the grandparents and great-grandparents of the people she was interviewing in the 1990s had also described their own marital relations as much worse than the marriages of *their* parents' and grandparents' day. 'The invention of a past filled with good marriages,' Kaler concluded, 'is one way people express discontent with contemporary life.'

Coontz has numerous surprising facts to relate about marriage, among them:

Some things that people believe to be traditional were actually fairly recent innovations. This is the case for the 'tradition' that marriage has to be licensed by the state or sanctified by the church . . . Even the Catholic Church long held that if a man and woman said they had privately agreed to marry, whether they said those words in the kitchen or out by the haystack, they were in fact married. For more than 1,000 years the church just took their word for it.

Coontz points out that love-based marriage is a historically recent development:

In the 18th century, people began to adopt the radical new idea that love should be the most fundamental reason for marriage, and that young people should be free to choose their marriage partners on the basis of love. The sentimentalisation of the love-based marriage in the 19th century and its sexualisation in the 20th each represent a logical step in the evolution of this new approach to marriage.

Until the late 18th century, most societies around the world saw marriage as far too vital an economic and political institution to be left entirely to the free choice of the two individuals involved, especially if they were going to base their decision on something as unreasoning and transitory as love.

Coontz has the following to say about the 'divorce revolution', the impact of increasing life expectancies on marriage, and 'staying together for the sake of the kids':

In 1977, sociologist Amitai Etzioni warned that if present trends in divorce continued, 'not one American family' would be left intact by the 1990s. By 1980 the divorce rate stood at 50%. Half of all people who married could be expected to divorce.

The divorce revolution, as some people have called it, transformed the lives of millions of people. But the surge in divorce was only an early precursor of the bigger storm that swept across marriage and family life between the late 1970s and the end of the century.

As long as rates of marriage and remarriage remained high, the increase in divorce did not threaten the universality of marriage, however disruptive and painful those divorces and remarriages were to the particular families involved. But at the end of the 1970s the impact of high divorce rates was accelerated by a plunge in the number of remarriages and a whole flood of new alternatives to marriage.

After 1981, divorce rates levelled off and began a slow decline, despite the fact that by then no-fault divorce was ubiquitous. But fewer people remarried after divorce. A generation earlier, in the 1950s, two-thirds of divorced women in the United States married again within five years. By the end of the century only half of divorced women were married or even living with partners five years later. . .

For better or worse, people decide what they will and won't put up with in a relationship today on a totally different basis from before. Now that most husbands and wives earn their livings separately, rather than from a jointly run farm or business, it is much easier, though not less painful, for couples to go their separate ways and to survive economically if the union dissolves. Women still generally face a drop in their standard of living after divorce. But never before in history have so many women been capable of supporting themselves and their children without a husband.

The dramatic extension of adults' life expectancy since 1970 has also changed the terms of marriage. An American who reaches age 60 today can expect to live another 25 years. The average married couple will live for more than three decades after their kids have left home. This extension of life expectancy makes staying together 'till death do us part' a much bigger challenge than ever before. What might seem an acceptable relationship when you expect to spend most of your married life raising kids together may seem unbearable when you realise that you will still have 30 years of one-on-one time once the kids are gone. No previous generation has ever been asked to make such a long-term commitment.

Many dissatisfied couples grit their teeth and try to tough it out until the children leave home. But the stress of raising children puts a strain on even the happiest of marriages and can wreak havoc on an unstable union. An older divorced student of mine wrote in her autobiographical essay: 'I really tried to make it last for the sake of the kids. But then I started thinking, "What if I come down with cancer right after they leave? Would it be worth it to be so unhappy for so long and then never even get the pay-off? Or what if I hit 50 and it was too late to find a decent relationship or build a rewarding life for my next 30 years?" After a while I was so miserable that I wasn't even a good parent anymore, which sort of spoiled the point of trying to stick it out.'

Coontz was also the author of another excellent book, this one published in 1992, *The Way We Never Were: American Families and the Nostalgia Trap*. I recommend the 2000 edition, with its lengthy and highly illuminating introduction. From the back cover:

The Way We Never Were is an examination of two centuries of family life that shatters the myths that burden modern families and make them long for the past. In an incisive new introduction, Coontz examines events since the original 1992 publication – from Bill Clinton's sexual transgressions to high school shootings across the nation – and re-examines the myths that continue to compel the American people to long for a time that never was.

From the introduction:

In 1992, during the presidential election campaigns of George Bush and Bill Clinton, then Vice President Dan Quayle made headlines across the country by denouncing a fictional television character, Murphy Brown, for having a child out of wedlock. This book came out that same year, right in the middle of the ensuing debate over changing family values and structures.

Although I could not have anticipated Quayle's now famous Murphy Brown speech, I wrote the book because for several years discussion about America's changing families had been growing increasingly heated. As a family historian, I was concerned that the polemics, on all sides, were based on misconceptions about the past.

My hope was that by exposing many 'memories' of traditional family life as myths, I could help point the discussion of family change and family policy in a more constructive direction. I wanted to show that families have always been in flux, and often in crisis. Knowing that there was no golden age of family life, I believed, would enable people to deal more effectively with the problems facing today's families than if they continued to romanticise the 'good old days.'

In the original introduction, for example, I pointed out that 'traditional' two-parent families had never guaranteed women and children protection from economic deprivation or physical abuse. Budget studies and medical records reveal that many families of the past had two standards of living, with male household heads spending money on beer or recreation while women and children went without needed food and medical care.

Modern statistics on child support evasion are certainly disturbing, but prior to the 1920s, a divorced father didn't even have a legal child support obligation to evade. Until that time, children were considered assets of the family head, and his duty to support them ended if he wasn't in the home to receive the wages they could earn. Wife beating was routinely tolerated by police and social service agencies well into the second half of the twentieth century and spousal rape was legal in most states right through the 1970s.

Similarly, drug abuse was more widespread at the end of the 1890s than at the end of the 1990s, and the rate of alcohol consumption was almost three times higher in the early nineteenth century than it is currently. Prostitution and serious sexually transmitted diseases were also more prevalent in America one hundred years ago than they are today.

In many ways, the response to my book exceeded my expectations. I received hundreds of speaking invitations from groups who wanted to know more about what had and had not changed in American family life. Employed mothers and stay-at-home mothers, as well as single parents of each sex, wrote to me about the stresses and stigmas they faced.

I presented my findings to the House Select Committee on Children, Youth, and Families, debated Pat Buchanan on *Crossfire*, and appeared on the *Oprah* and *Leeza* television talk shows. Most important, I got in touch with many other researchers, policymakers and concerned citizens whose interests lay not in romanticising the past but in working with today's families, in all their diversity, to help each of them succeed.

In other ways, however, the years since 1992 have been disappointing, because of the stubborn persistence of the myths that are discussed in this book. Despite ever mounting evidence that families of the past were not as idyllic and families of the present not as dysfunctional as they are often portrayed, many political leaders and opinion makers in the United States continue to filter our changing family experiences and trends through the distorted lens of historical mythologising about past family life. The contemporary family behavior or value that is unfavourably contrasted with 'the way things used to be' may vary. But the myths themselves remain remarkably resistant to change.

The Way We Never Were contains a good deal of information that exposes as unsound many commentators' conclusions that the breakdown of marriages and families in the modern era are unmitigated disasters.

3

THE DIFFERENT NATURES
OF MEN AND WOMEN

Hogamus, Higamous,
Man is polygamous.
Higamus, Hogamous,
Woman monogamous.

(William James, *Oxford Book of Marriage*)

This chapter covers:

- 'What does a woman want?'
- God and the big question
- Why women are always right in debates about relationships
- The modern denial of human nature
- Why men and women are so frequently at odds with each other
- The different attitudes of the sexes to sex
- Fairytale weddings and honeymoons
- 1:20,000 plus (ratio of wedding day to the number of days of marriage that might follow)
- Women as emotional managers in marriage
- Women and men's physiological responses to stress in marriage
- Gender bias among people working in the 'relationship industry'
- Relate, a highly 'feminised' organisation
- The 'battle of the sexes'
- Why is there no *Men's* Institute?
- Men-only members clubs
- *Woman's Hour* and the 'gender pay imbalance' debate
- 'Why can't a man be more like a woman?'
- Surrendered wives
- Women's search for 'Mr Right'

Sigmund Freud wrote the following in a letter to a female acquaintance:

> The great question that has never been answered and which I have not yet been able to answer, despite my 30 years of research into the feminine soul, is 'What does a woman want?'

Which gives me an excuse to relate one of my favourite jokes:

> A frail old English cleric had led a blameless life, and had been a very active and much-loved man of God. God appeared to him in a vision and told him he'd grant him any wish he wanted. The man thought for a time, then said he'd always wanted to visit New York, but he was scared of flying. So could God arrange for a bridge to be constructed across the Atlantic, so he could be driven from England to New York?
>
> God spluttered, frowned deeply, and after considering the request for a time he declared that the request was unreasonable, as it would take up half of the world's engineering resources for a number of years. Did the man not have a more modest request? The man thought for a moment, then said that throughout the course of his long life he'd never understood women, so could God explain the nature of women to him? God considered the question for a long before replying, 'Let me get back to you about the bridge.'

Women are seemingly always right in any debate about relationships. Women are right, men are wrong, end of debate. When did we vote on this? I must have been out of the country that day. In the debate about relationships the happiness of men does not merit much consideration. The nature of women should be cherished and celebrated. The nature of men should be denigrated and its exercise ideally made illegal. At the very least men need to be controlled by institutions, and marriage is the ultimate institution for controlling them. Little wonder that so many women are so keen on it.

The majority of books written by men about relationships tend to come from a viewpoint similar to that of most women. I think there might be two explanations for this:

- The writers genuinely accept women's perspectives on relationships, and are therefore untypical of their gender; or
- They are mindful that the majority of readers of books about relationships are women, and to be critical of women would be to markedly reduce sales of their books.

The Canadian-American psychologist Steven Pinker is the author of a number of remarkable books including *The Blank Slate: The Modern Denial of Human Nature* (2002). He starts the book with the following passage on 'The Blank Slate, the Noble Savage, and the Ghost in the Machine':

> Everyone has a theory of human nature. Everyone has to anticipate the behavior of others, and that means we all need theories about what makes people tick. A tacit theory of human nature – that behavior is caused by thoughts and feelings – is embedded in the very way we think about people.
>
> We fill out this theory by introspecting on our own minds and assuming that our fellows are like ourselves, and by watching people's behavior and filing away generalizations. We absorb still other ideas from our intellectual climate: from the expertise of authorities and the conventional wisdom of the day.
>
> Our theory of human nature is the wellspring of much in our lives. We consult it when we want to persuade or threaten, inform or deceive. It advises us on how to nurture our marriages, bring up our children, and control our own behavior. Its assumptions about learning drive our educational policy; its assumptions about motivation drive our policies on economics, law, and crime. And because it delineates what people can achieve easily, what they can achieve only with sacrifice or pain, and what they cannot achieve at all, it affects our values: what we believe we can reasonably strive for as individuals and as a society. Rival theories of human nature are entwined in different ways of life and different political systems, and have been a source of much conflict over the course of history. . .
>
> Every society must operate with a theory of human nature, and our intellectual mainstream is committed to one. The theory is seldom articulated or overtly embraced, but it lies at the heart of a vast number of beliefs and policies. Bertrand Russell wrote, 'Every man, wherever he goes, is encompassed by a cloud of comforting convictions, which move with him like flies on a summer day.'
>
> For intellectuals today, many of those convictions are about psychology and social relations. I will refer to those convictions as the Blank Slate: the idea that the human mind has no inherent structure and can be inscribed at will by society or ourselves.
>
> That theory of human nature – namely, that it barely exists – is the topic of this book . . . the Blank Slate has become the secular religion of modern intellectual life. It is seen as a source of values . . .

The Blank Slate theory of human nature has been described as the intellectual foundation of feminism. Pinker convincingly outlines how the theory has been found to be deeply flawed. From the same book:

> Contrary to popular belief, parents in contemporary America do not treat their sons and daughters very differently. A recent assessment of 172 studies involving 28,000 children found that boys and girls are given

similar amounts of encouragement, warmth, nurturance, restrictiveness, discipline, and clarity of communication. The only substantial difference was that about two-thirds of the boys were discouraged from playing with dolls, especially by their fathers, out of a fear that they would become gay. (Boys who prefer girls' toys often do turn out gay, but forbidding them the toys does not change the outcome.)

Nor do differences between boys and girls depend on their observing masculine behavior in their fathers and feminine behavior in their mothers. When Hunter has two mommies, he acts just as much like a boy as if he had a mommy and a daddy.

Things are not looking good for the theory that boys and girls are born identical except for their genitalia, with all other differences coming from the way society treats them. If that were true, it would be an amazing coincidence that in every society the coin flip that assigns each sex to one set of roles would land the same way (or that one fateful flip at the dawn of the species should have been maintained without interruption across all the upheavals of the past 100,000 years).

It would be just as amazing that, time and again, society's arbitrary assignments matched the predictions that a Martian biologist would make for our species based on our anatomy and the distribution of our genes. It would seem odd that the hormones that make us male and female in the first place also modulate the characteristically male and female mental traits, both decisively in early brain development and in smaller degrees throughout our lives.

It would be all the more odd that a second genetic mechanism differentiating the sexes (genomic imprinting) also installs characteristic male and female talents. Finally, two key predictions of the social construction theory – that boys treated as girls will grow up with girls' minds, and that differences between boys and girls can be traced to differences in how their parents treat them – have gone down in flames.

Of course, just because many sex differences are rooted in biology does not mean that one sex is superior, that the differences will emerge for all people in all circumstances, that discrimination against a person based on sex is justified, or that people should be coerced into doing things typical of their sex. But neither are the differences without consequences.

By now many people are happy to say what was unsayable in polite company a few years ago: that males and females do not have interchangeable minds . . . But among many professional women the existence of sex differences is still a source of discomfort. As one colleague said to me, 'Look, I know that males and females are not identical. I see it in my kids, I see it in myself, I know about the research. I can't explain it, but when I read claims about sex differences, *steam comes out of my ears.*'

So logic and facts are trumped by emotion, as so often in the modern era. In his 1993 bestseller *Men Are from Mars, Women Are from Venus*, John Gray wrote tellingly about the differences between men and women:

Without the awareness that we are supposed to be different, men and woman are at odds with each other. We usually become angry or frustrated with the opposite sex because we have forgotten this important truth. We expect the opposite sex to be more like ourselves. We desire them to 'want what we want' and 'feel the way we feel'.

We mistakenly assume that if our partners love us they will react and behave in certain ways – the ways we react and behave when we love someone. This attitude set us up to be disappointed again and again and prevents us from taking the necessary time to communicate lovingly about our differences.

Men mistakenly expect women to think, communicate, and react the way men do; women mistakenly expect men to feel, communicate, and respond the way women do. We have forgotten that men and women are supposed to be different. As a result our relationships are filled with unnecessary friction and conflict. Clearly recognising and respecting these differences dramatically reduce confusion when dealing with the opposite sex.

The end of the first chapter concludes with:

Falling in love is always magical. It feels eternal, as if love will last forever. We naively believe that somehow we are exempt from the problems our parents had, free from the odds that love will die, assured that it is meant to be and that we are destined to live happily ever after.

But as the magic recedes and daily life takes over, it emerges that men continue to expect women to think and react like men, and women continue to expect men to feel and behave like women. Without a clear awareness of our differences, we do not take the time to understand and respect each other. We become demanding, resentful, judgmental and intolerant.

With the best and most loving intentions love continues to die. Somehow the problems creep in. The resentments build. Communication breaks down. Mistrust increases. Rejection and repression result. The magic of love is lost. We ask ourselves:

How does it happen?

Why does it happen?

Why does it happen to us?

To answer these questions our greatest minds have developed brilliant and complex philosophical and psychological models. Yet still the old patterns return. Love dies. It happens to almost everyone.

Each day millions of individuals are searching for a partner to experience that special loving feeling. Each year, millions of couples join together in love and then painfully separate because they have lost that loving feeling. For those that are able to sustain love long enough to get married, only 50% stay married. Out of those who stay married, possibly another 50% are not fulfilled. They stay together out of loyalty and obligation or from the fear of starting over again.

Very few people, indeed, are able to grow in love. Yet, it does happen. When men and women are able to respect and accept their differences then love has a chance to blossom.

Through understanding the hidden differences of the opposite sex we can more successfully give and receive the love that is in our hearts. By validating and accepting our differences, creative solutions can be discovered whereby we can succeed in getting what we want. And, more importantly, we can learn how to best love and support the people we care about.

Love is magical, and it can last, if we remember our differences.

Gray really hits the nail on the head with his descriptions of men and women in the second chapter of the book, 'Mr. Fix-It and the Home-Improvement Committee':

The most frequently expressed complaint women have about men is that men don't listen. Either a man completely ignores her when she speaks to him, or he listens for a few beats, assesses what is bothering her, and then proudly puts on his Mr Fix-It cap and offers her a solution to make her feel better. He is confused when she doesn't appreciate this gesture of love. No matter how many times she tells him that he's not listening, he doesn't get it and keeps doing the same thing. She wants empathy, but he thinks she wants solutions.

The most frequently expressed complaint men have about women is that women are always trying to change them. When a woman loves a man she feels responsible to assist him in growing and tries to help him improve the way he does things. She forms a home-improvement committee, and he becomes her primary focus. No matter how much he resists her help, she persists – waiting for any opportunity to help him or tell him what to do. She thinks she's nurturing him, while he feels he's being controlled. Instead, he wants her acceptance.

These two problems can finally be solved by first understanding why men offer solutions, and why women seek to improve. Let's pretend to go back in time, where by observing life on Mars and Venus – before the planets discovered one another – we can gain some insights into men and women.

LIFE ON MARS
Martians value power, competency, efficiency, and achievement. They are always doing things to prove themselves and develop their power and skills. Their sense of self is defined through their ability to achieve results. They experience fulfilment primarily through success and

accomplishment. A man's sense of self is defined through his ability to achieve results.

Everything on Mars is a reflection of these values. Even their dress is designed to reflect their skills and competence. Police officers, soldiers, businessmen, scientists, cab drivers, technicians, and chefs all wear uniforms or at least hats to reflect their competence and power.

They don't read magazines like *Psychology Today*, *Self*, or *People*. They are more concerned with outdoor activities, like hunting, fishing, and racing cars. They are interested in the news, weather, and sports and couldn't care less about romance novels and self-help books.

They are more interested in 'objects' and 'things' rather than people and feelings. Even today on Earth, while women fantasise about romance, men fantasise about powerful cars, faster computers, gadgets, gizmos, and new more powerful technology. Men are preoccupied with the 'things' that can help them express power by creating results and achieving their goals.

Achieving goals is very important to a Martian because it is a way for him to prove his competence and thus feel good about himself. And for him to feel good about himself he must achieve these goals by himself. Someone else can't achieve them for him.

Martians pride themselves in doing things all by themselves. Autonomy is a symbol of efficiency, power, and competence. Understanding this Martian characteristic can help women understand why men resist so much being corrected or being told what to do. To offer a man unsolicited advice is to presume that he doesn't know what to do or that he can't do it on his own. Men are very touchy about this, because the issue of competence is so very important to them. To offer a man unsolicited advice is to presume that he doesn't know what to do or that he can't do it on his own.

Because he is handling his problems on his own, a Martian rarely talks about his problems unless he needs expert advice. He reasons: 'Why involve someone else when I can do it by myself?' He keeps his problems to himself unless he requires help from another to find a solution. Asking for help when you can do it yourself is perceived as a sign of weakness.

However, if he truly does need help, then it is a sign of wisdom to get it. In this case, he will find someone he respects and then talk about his problem. Talking about a problem on Mars is an invitation for advice. Another Martian feels honored by the opportunity. Automatically he puts on his Mr. Fix-It hat, listens for a while, and then offers some jewels of advice.

This Martian custom is one of the reasons men instinctively offer solutions when women talk about problems. When a woman innocently shares upset feelings or explores out loud the problems of her day, a man mistakenly assumes she is looking for some expert advice. He puts on his Mr. Fix-It hat and begins giving advice; this is his way of showing love and of trying to help. He wants to help her feel better by solving her problems. He wants to be useful to her. He feels he can be valued and thus worthy of her love when his abilities are used to solve her problems.

Once he has offered a solution, however, and she continues to be upset, it becomes increasingly difficult for him to listen because his solution is being rejected and he feels increasingly useless. He has no idea that by just listening with empathy and interest he can be supportive. He does not know that on Venus talking about problems is not an invitation to offer a solution.

LIFE ON VENUS

Venusians have different values. They value love, communication, beauty, and relationships. They spend a lot of time supporting, helping, and nurturing one another. Their sense of self is defined through their feelings and the quality of their relationships. They experience fulfilment through sharing and relating.

A woman's sense of self is defined through her feelings and the quality of her relationships. Everything on Venus reflects these values. Rather than building highways and tall buildings, the Venusians are more concerned with living together in harmony, community, and loving cooperation. Relationships are more important than work and technology. In most ways their world is the opposite of Mars.

They do not wear uniforms like the Martians (to reveal their competence). On the contrary, they enjoy wearing a different outfit every day, according to how they are feeling. Personal expression, especially of their feelings, is very important. They may even change outfits several times a day as their mood changes.

Communication is of primary importance. To share their personal feelings is much more important than achieving goals and success. Talking and relating to one another is a source of tremendous fulfilment.

This is hard for a man to comprehend. He can come close to understanding a woman's experience of sharing and relating by comparing it to the satisfaction he feels when he wins a race, achieves a goal, or solves a problem.

Instead of being goal oriented, women are relationship oriented; they are more concerned with expressing their goodness, love, and caring. Two Martians go to lunch to discuss a project or business goal; they have a problem to solve. In addition, Martians view going to a restaurant as an efficient way to approach food: no shopping, no cooking, and no washing dishes. For Venusians, going to lunch is an opportunity to nurture a relationship, for both giving support to and receiving support from a friend. Women's restaurant talk can be very open and intimate, almost like the dialogue that occurs between therapist and patient.

On Venus, everyone studies psychology and has at least a master's degree in counselling. They are very involved in personal growth, spirituality, and everything that can nurture life, healing, and growth. Venus is covered with parks, organic gardens, shopping centres, and restaurants.

Venusians are very intuitive. They have developed this ability through centuries of anticipating the needs of others. They pride themselves in being considerate of the needs and feelings of others. A sign of great love is to offer help and assistance to another Venusian without being asked.

Because proving one's competence is not as important to a Venusian, offering help is not offensive, and needing help is not a sign of weakness. A man, however, may feel offended because when a woman offers advice he doesn't feel she trusts his ability to do it himself.

A woman has no conception of this male sensitivity because for her it is another feather in her hat if someone offers to help her. It makes her feel loved and cherished. But offering help to a man can make him feel incompetent, weak, and even unloved.

On Venus it is a sign of caring to give advice and suggestions. Venusians firmly believe that when something is working it can always work better. Their nature is to want to improve things.

When they care about someone, they freely point out what can be improved and suggest how to do it. Offering advice and constructive criticism is an act of love.

Mars is very different. Martians are more solution oriented. If something is working, their motto is don't change it. Their instinct is to leave it alone if it is working. 'Don't fix it unless it is broken' is a common expression.

When a woman tries to improve a man, he feels she is trying to fix him. He receives the message that he is broken. She doesn't realise her caring attempts to help him may humiliate him. She mistakenly thinks she is just helping him to grow.

Gray's book then provides sections giving advice to men ('Learning to Listen') and women ('Give Up Giving Advice').

I am surely not alone in being struck by the different reactions men and women elicit from their same-sex friends when they announce they've just become engaged. When women tell their female friends, the result is invariably happy excitement. When men tell their male friends, the result is gloomy resignation – 'another one bites the dust!' – comradely arm slapping, and supportive comments like, 'Er, well done, she's a great woman, it's about time you did the right thing!' What's behind the different mindsets of the sexes, in these days when equality of the sexes is supposed to be all-encompassing?

From an evolutionary and genetic perspective, men should want to scatter their genes as widely as possible, i.e. have unprotected sex with as many women as possible. And of course in certain periods of history powerful men have been able to satisfy this want, with harems. Some cultures and religions, even those that are very strict morally and have harsh penalties for moral transgression, still permit individual men to have a number of wives.

Of course there are numerous restraints on the number of women that individual men are likely to have unprotected sex with over the course of their lives. They include:

- The scarcity of women prepared to allow them to exercise their desires
- The improved life chances of their progeny if they 'stay around' to support the mother and child
- The institution of marriage

When men are unfaithful to their partners, visit a prostitute, or watch pornography, they are guilty of nothing more than failing to suppress their natural urges, whatever anyone might think of them *morally*. And what are many sexual morals other than a set of rules designed to stop men acting on their natural urges?

It is only natural that men should become bored with having sex with just one woman for years, even decades. And vice versa, to be fair. In which other area of life are modern humans expected to display such a lack of interest in variety? We wouldn't expect a person to eat the same dinner every day for half a century, no matter how well-prepared and well-balanced the meal might be nutritionally.

Simon Andreae, in his 1998 book *The Secrets of Love and Lust*, explores in detail men and women's different perspectives. He cites the work of two evolutionary psychologists, John Tooby and Leda Cosmides:

> They suggest that, as all human hearts, or hands, or ears share a similar design, whether they belong to labourers or leaders, so all human minds are created with a similar set of programmes. This set of programmes has evolved according to the same selection pressures that have shaped every other organ of every other human body: chiefly, the pressure to reproduce as effectively as possible.
>
> In the case of the human male, where the primary strategy for reproductive success would seem to be frequent mating with a large number of female partners, Tooby and Cosmides expected to find evidence of mental programmes, or 'adaptations' as they called them, which encouraged them to do just that, no matter what their race, status,

colour, or creed. And their colleagues have not been slow at collecting the evidence.

Andreae describes two researchers (Russell Clark and Brian Gladue) as being 'particularly active' in exploring male mental programmes, and they reported an interesting experiment:

> Clark's experiment was extremely straightforward. He simply wished to test in practice the findings that researchers like Buss had found in theory: namely, that men possess an adaptation for minimising the time they wish to spend with a woman before going to bed with her. To this end, he and his colleague Elaine Hatfield assembled a group of attractive female students and positioned them at discreet intervals on his college campus in Florida.
>
> The students were to approach male passers-by and start a conversation by saying, 'Hi, I've been noticing you around town lately and I find you very attractive.' Then, they were to ask them one of three questions, 'Would you go out tonight?', 'Will you come over to my apartment?' or 'Would you go to bed with me tonight?' In response, almost 50% of the men agreed to go on a date; 69% agreed to go back to their questioner's room; while fully 75% agreed to head straight for bed. More men were willing to have sex with a total stranger than to spend a social evening with her. All the findings pointed to powerful mechanisms which motivate men to grasp every possible sexual opportunity.

The results of the experiment when the sexes switched roles were perhaps predictable:

> What Clark and Hatfield had tried on men, they now tried on women too, asking male students to position themselves around the campus and asking the same questions of female passers-by. They were careful to ensure that the male students were neatly turned-out and that they would seem as unthreatening as possible. The results were extremely clear-cut.
>
> While approximately half the women agreed to go on a date (the same as for the men), the numbers plummeted for anything more immediate or suggestive. Only 6% of those asked agreed to go back to the male student's apartment, and none at all consented to immediate sex. Furthermore, when Clark and Hatfield looked at the nature of the negative responses made by both sexes, they found an even clearer divide, with men much more likely to express regret, and women much more likely to express scorn. 'I can't tonight, but tomorrow would be fine' was a typical response from a man, while 'you've got to be kidding' was more characteristic of the women.

The shelves of the women's magazine section of my local newsagent's are groaning under the weight of numerous glossy magazines about weddings and honeymoons, containing articles with titles such as 'Be a princess for a day!', and 'Book that fairytale honeymoon in the Caribbean now!'.

What are we to make of this? Belief in fairytales surely belongs to childhood, and it's unfortunate that women are being encouraged to marry through the use of images and articles appealing to that side of their natures. A wedding day takes up just one day of a person's life, while a 54-year-long marriage will take up about 20,000 days, and some last even longer. Given that 1:20,000 plus ratio, shouldn't we be spending a lot more time preparing for our marriages than we spend preparing for our wedding days?

John Gottman is co-founder of the Gottman Institute, and an emeritus professor of psychology at the University of Washington. His book *Why Marriages Succeed or Fail: And How to Make Yours Last* (1997) is based on his study of 2,000 married couples over two decades, and is an excellent read. In the chapter on gender differences within marriage, 'The Two Marriages: His and Hers', Gottman starts on familiar territory:

> Let's begin with the widely held belief that women are more comfortable in intimate relationships – that they can easily swim in an ocean of intense emotions while men are more likely to feel 'lost at sea.' I have seen this assumption hold true over and over again.
>
> Can you remember the last time you and your spouse discussed a problem in your relationship? Who brought up the hot topic? I'd be willing to bet it was the woman. Though traditionally described as less assertive in the world at large, in marital relationships women tend to be the emotional managers. They are usually better attuned than men to the changing emotional climate in their relationships and more willing to confront problems . . . it's usually the wife who insists that issues get talked about, while the husband tries to avoid talking.

Gottman provides a compelling account of how gender differences in handling emotions start in childhood and develop in men and women's same-sex friendships. He summarises this as follows:

> From early childhood, boys learn to suppress their emotions while girls learn to express and manage the complete range of feelings. Small wonder that by the time they grow up, meet and marry, men and women are so often at opposite ends of the spectrum when it comes to the importance

they place on expressing feelings. A man is more likely to equate being emotional with weakness and vulnerability because he has been raised to *do* rather than to voice what he feels.

Meanwhile, women have spent their early years learning how to verbalise all kinds of emotions . . . sometimes the differences between men and women become a bane rather than a benefit in marriage. When a woman looks for the same intimacy with her husband that she has experienced with her females friends, she may be sorely disappointed.

Likewise, a man who hopes to duplicate his 'buddy' relationships with his wife may feel overwhelmed by her need to talk about feelings or for emotional intimacy. Finding she demands more intensity than he can comfortably offer, he may withdraw. In a happy marriage, a couple can usually sort out these differences. But in an unstable marriage where negativity has the upper hand, these two emotional styles can clash wildly.

Gottman then points to a physiological as well as a psychological basis for men and women having divergent emotional styles, which lead to so much marital strife. And this is evident even among young children, where boys are more likely to have lengthier – and more intense – tantrums than girls. Gottman explains that, when they become adults, the male of the species is more vulnerable to stress:

We've see this in our own laboratory: during difficult marital discussions, a man's blood pressure and heart rate will rise much higher and will stay elevated longer than his wife's . . . There are two primary explanations for these physiological differences between the sexes. First, the male's autonomic nervous system, which controls much of the body's stress response, may be more sensitive and take far longer to recover from emotional upset than does the average female's. I'm not implying that women are 'invulnerable' to marital stress, but that compared with men it may take more intense conflict before women experience its harmful effect. This may explain why women are so much readier than men to dive directly into potentially explosive issues.

Second, men may be more reactive because even when they withdraw from an argument they are more likely to repeat negative thoughts that keep them riled up. If you could read their minds, you might hear phrases like, 'I don't have to take this crap', or 'It's all her fault', or 'I'll get her back for this.' Such inner scripts, whether of righteous indignation or innocent victimisation, are clearly not self-soothing. Compared with a woman, it seems to be much harder for a man to relax his guard and say, 'Honey, let's talk about it.'

Gottman identifies a number of gender differences that can damage a marriage, and explores them in detail. In another chapter he writes convincingly about four factors that set marriages on the path to destruction, and terms them 'The Four Horsemen of the Apocalypse'. They are criticism, contempt, defensiveness, and stonewalling. We'll return to Gottman's book in chapter six.

The organisation Relate is well known in the UK. Relate offers advice, relationship counselling, sex therapy, workshops, mediation, consultations, and support to couples and families. They also publish a number of books about relationships, which brings us to one of them, *Better Relationships: Practical Ways to Make Your Love Last*, written by Sarah Litvinoff. Litvinoff thanks 39 people in the acknowledgements, only four of whom are men. She actually goes to some trouble to avoid gender bias in the book but nevertheless it comes through in places. I wanted to meet her to explore questions concerning long-term relationships and marriage, and accordingly went onto the website of the book's publisher. Her name appeared on a list of experts on the topic of 'Sex and Relationships', but unfortunately it was made clear on the website that no interviews were available with her. I was disappointed, and then noticed an astonishing gender bias among the 'experts' on the topic in question. Of the 14 individuals, just three were men. One of the men was an 'astrological consultant'. It wasn't made clear whether this alone qualified him to be an 'expert' on sex and relationships. You couldn't make it up.

Moving swiftly on. I looked up another topic, 'Pregnancy and Parenting'. Of the 25 experts, 21 were women. A gender bias towards women on the topic of pregnancy I can understand – other women have been through the same experience etc – but *parenting?*

The Relate Institute is a training academy for Relate counsellors. A faculty of Doncaster College, its academic programme is validated by the University of Hull, and over 300 students a year undertake the programme at five locations across the country. The students include those new to counselling and qualified counsellors extending and developing their skills by undertaking advanced study at postgraduate level.

I was curious about the gender balance of trainee Relate counsellors. They informed me that of the 667 students currently enrolled (April 2009) at Doncaster College, 557 (83.5%) were women. When gender biases far smaller than this are in favour of men, women are up in arms, and sometimes with good reason. Can you imagine a 'relationship support organisation', 83.5% of whose counsellors were *men*? Nor me. I also suspect that the small proportion of men among the counsellors would broadly accept the 'female perspective' on relationships. To do otherwise would surely be a living nightmare for them.

I contacted Relate's Head Office to enquire what proportion of their 1,887 'counsellors, sex therapists, and writers' were women. I was directed to the (female) press officer who finally got round to sending me an email consisting of the following gem:

> As a small charity we cannot reply to every media request that we receive and in this case I am not able to help you.

I then wrote a letter to Claire Tyler, the chief executive of Relate, in November 2008 (copy in appendix one), seeking a meeting of one hour's duration. Her (female) executive assistant responded with an email:

> I have passed on your correspondence to our Press Office and as they are always very busy it would be very helpful if you could distil your query into questions that you would find it useful for Relate to answer.

I replied:

> Many thanks. I'm not really looking for 'answers to questions', more to discuss some themes face-to-face with a senior representative of your organisation. The themes were outlined in my original letter which I emailed to you the other day, another copy attached. This really isn't a matter for a Press Office to respond to by way of an email. I'd hoped that Relate could discuss the themes in an open manner, rather than trotting out some 'official line' through a Press Office. I'm only looking for one hour of someone's time, and am happy to travel to London, Doncaster, or wherever for the meeting.

A meeting was declined, likewise with the (female) chief executive of Relate Bedfordshire, on the grounds that she also was too busy. She did, however, suggest I might like to contact the (female) head of marketing and communications, but by this time I'd lost the will to live. Relate must surely be a contender for The Harriet Harman Prize For Workplace Gender Balance.

Relate is clearly an overwhelmingly female-dominated organisation, whilst giving advice to couples where half the partners are men. And the majority of books and articles about relationships are written by women. It's no wonder that many women are baffled by their partners' perspectives on relationships. Many men won't meekly become the paragons of virtue that women are seeking. Although enough men *do* become those paragons for women to compare the rest of us unfavourably against them. 'John took his wife out for another candlelit dinner last night, and it wasn't her birthday, or their anniversary. Isn't that romantic? I have no plans for Saturday evening.'

Men have become accustomed to women aiming criticisms – witty and otherwise – at them. One of my favourites is the saying attributed to Gloria Steinem, 'A woman without a man is like a fish without a bicycle.' But the reality of many women's desperate search for a life partner, obsession with relationships in general and marriage in particular, surely gives the lie to a lot of the jibes.

Women aren't too happy when even the mildest of criticisms come in their direction. A personal example: I had barely started to explain the content of this chapter to a lady acquaintance when she sneered, 'Oh right – so all men are perfect!' And so any debate is quashed at the outset.

On to the 'battle of the sexes', where women in the developed world fought to win equal rights with men. Women conclusively won the battle many years ago, and yet they keep fighting it. Or at least some of them do. Some women deem themselves qualified to speak for women in general – their elections to these positions are held in secret, one imagines – as if women were a feeble-minded lot who needed such representation. But these stalwart ladies keep fighting the good fight, even though their targets become ever fewer in number as the years roll by.

The combined membership of Women's Institutes in the United Kingdom is around 205,000. They 'play a unique role in providing women with educational opportunities and the chance to build new skills, to take part in a wide variety of activities and to campaign on issues that matter to them and their communities'. Membership is, not unnaturally, restricted to women.

If men had an equivalent body to the Women's Institute – the Men's Institute, say – and excluded women from its membership, doubtless the body would face demands to admit women, and change its name to the People's Institute. But I've never met a man even slightly bothered by the fact that he can't join the Women's Institute. Indeed, I can't recall any man even mentioning the matter.

Men happily recognise that while men and women enjoy the company of the opposite sex, at times they welcome just the company of their own sex, which is why they have no problem with bodies such as the Women's Institute. Or with phenomena such as women-only book competitions, or women-only competitions in sports even when men do not have an advantage on physical strength grounds (snooker, darts . . .).

But do women accord men the same courtesy? No. Readers of *The Independent* might have become a little agitated by the following articles in December 1999. The first is by Paul Waugh and Gary Finn, entitled 'Men-only clubs will not be outlawed', published 7 December 1999:

> The Government last night denied reports that it has secret plans to ban men-only members clubs following admissions from ministers that clubs that barred women from membership were 'anachronisms'.
>
> The moves were said to be being discussed by at least four ministers, including the Cabinet Office Minister, Mo Mowlam. They would lead to the end of membership restrictions from every body ranging from the 17th century St James's Club in London to golf clubs and the traditional Labour bastion, the working men's club.
>
> It was claimed that private clubs, exempted by the Sex Discrimination Act, would be modernised under an amendment to the Equal Opportunities Bill in the next session of parliament. Senior Labour figures are said to be heartened by recent about-turns by men-only stalwarts such as the MCC which last year voted to admit women after 211 years.
>
> A Government spokesman rejected reports of new laws in the pipeline. Many topics were covered in ministerial discussions on equality but Government plans for anti-discrimination legislation did not extend beyond public bodies.
>
> Last night Nicholas Soames MP, the former Tory defence minister, who is a member of White's, Pratt's and the Turf, said: 'This is another sign that living under New Labour is like living in Soviet Russia. What sensible woman wants to be a member of a men's club?'

A good point Mr Soames, and well made. Now there's a man you can imagine tucking enthusiastically into his rhubarb crumble and custard at his club. The following was written by Joan Smith for the paper the next day, entitled 'The Irritations of Modern Life: Men-only Clubs':

I have often wondered what men do in all-male clubs. Million-pound deals? Homosexual rituals? Men, especially if they belong to the Garrick Club, are reticent, giving the impression that it involves little more than long lunches, at which they get slightly squiffy and eat nursery food. Yet, as soon as someone proposes changing the law to force such clubs to admit women, it is as if the very foundations of civilisation had begun to shudder.

'A grotesque curtailment of freedom of association – an almost totalitarian assertion that the state should be able to decide with whom you can spend your own free time on property private to you . . .' is how *The Daily Telegraph* greeted the news that the Government is thinking of banning men-only establishments. Yikes! Next thing you know, Tony Blair will be personally knocking on *Telegraph* readers' doors, pushing a female across the threshold and instructing them to talk to her.

Of course, there are few subjects so likely to fire up a right-wing leader-writer. The age-old right of the British upper classes to exclude outsiders is slowly being whittled away. The Reform Club has admitted women for years; even Lord's is not the bastion it was. What's left for the man who sometimes feels the need to be with people who, not to put too fine a point on it, aren't going to go all funny and exhibit symptoms of pre-menstrual tension?

Men's clubs are an anachronism. Their very existence institutionalises discrimination, draping it with a veil of respectability. When I witnessed the reaction to this mild move towards equality, I felt as if I'd been transported back to a time when misogyny was so firmly taken for granted that most people didn't even have a name for it. Now we do, and it's not acceptable. The bad news for club bores, tucking into bread-and-butter pudding in Covent Garden – or, indeed, a working men's club in Halifax – is that the time has come to grow up.

Ah yes. 'An anachronism.' 'The time has come to grow up.' I don't suppose Ms Smith is quite so agitated by the Women's Institute, even ten years on. And with such reasoning women seek to hide the real reasons why they don't want men to associate freely with one another. Whatever they are. Maybe they've learned about the campaign to withdraw voting rights from them. Damn. We've managed to keep that under wraps for *years*.

On to BBC Radio's *Woman's Hour*, a staple of BBC Radio since shortly after the Second World War. From their website: 'October 7 1946 was the start of something big – it was the first broadcast of a programme designed to celebrate, entertain and inform women.' I have never heard a man say that there should be a programme for men, *Man's Hour*, never mind that it should be 'a programme designed to celebrate, entertain and inform men'.

I often hear *Woman's Hour* when driving around the country on business, and did so on 27 April 2009. It's often an interesting programme but some topics do come up with monotonous regularity, one being the so-called 'gender pay imbalance', annoyingly – to some – still a reality nearly 40 years after the 1970 Equal Pay Act. Today's report concerned The Rt Hon Harriet Harman MP QC who is putting forward the 2009 Equality Bill, which will include provisions to require organisations to publicise wage rates etc.

But the gender pay imbalance *probably doesn't exist* once a number of factors are taken into account, such as choice of profession, career breaks for having children, and many women preferring part-time work. Not that you'll ever hear this mentioned on *Woman's Hour.* Or at least *I* haven't heard it in the past 30 years of listening occasionally to the programme.

A later discussion in the same episode concerned women giving up highly paid stressful jobs to enable them to work for themselves, often on low incomes, or to do jobs they found more fulfilling. One of the women had been a 'high-flying lawyer'. The general tone of the discussion was a celebration of women who decided to forsake lucrative but demanding jobs in favour of more job satisfaction. One woman made the following observation:

> So many women I know are crying themselves to sleep on a Sunday night, because they really can't bear the thought of going to work the next day.

Needless to say, no connection was made between the 'gender pay imbalance' and women voluntarily opting out of highly paid, stressful, unfulfilling jobs. Nor was it even considered worth raising that even if a gender pay balance does still exist, it might be attributable to men being more willing than women to continue with such jobs. And so the myths of the 'gender pay imbalance' and the 'glass ceiling' roll on year after year.

The enthusiasm with which politicians – both female and male – keep perpetuating the myth of the gender pay imbalance is surely a testimony to their enduring vote-delivering powers among female voters. Anyone who believes that the gender pay imbalance is still attributable to male discrimination against women should read a remarkable book written by a Canadian-American psychologist, Susan Pinker. The book is *The Sexual Paradox: Men, Women, and the Real Gender Gap* (2008).

I've heard it said that one of the reasons women tend to be poorly represented at senior levels in many professions is that they don't like to compete. But competition is surely nothing other than proving oneself more capable than one's peers. On what basis other than competition *could* or *should* promotion be made? Women are perfectly capable of vigorous competition when they are pursuing something (or someone) they *really* want. Go to any upmarket city wine bar in the evening and you'll see plenty of young women performing Olympic standard hair-tossing and eyelash-batting in the presence of men with highly paid careers.

Why do some women remain convinced (at least in their public utterances) that female 'under-representation' is attributable to discrimination on the part of men in positions of authority, regardless of all the evidence to the contrary? Maybe it's because feminism has become a religion of an increasingly secular age, with women as its gods. All women. And just as religions over the ages have persecuted people for defying their authority, so feminists try to persecute non-believers – mainly but not exclusively men – whenever and wherever they can. They have become very ingenious at the game, and few men appear to be conscious of the persecution. Maybe it's because men don't want to be accused of that most heinous crime of the modern era, sexism.

When you look for it, it's not difficult to find examples of women working together to advance their interests at the expense of men. Let's start with The Rt Hon Harriet Harman QC, Member of Parliament for Camberwell and Peckham, Deputy Leader of the Labour Party, Labour Party Chair, Minister for Women and Equality, Leader of the House of Commons, and The Lord Privy Seal. She must have the largest business card on the planet.

In the foreword of the paper *Women's Changing Lives: Priorities for the Ministers for Women – One Year On Progress Report*, presented to Parliament in July 2008, Harriet Harman wrote the following:

A modern democracy must be fair and equal. The government has fought for equal representation and it's because of this that we have record levels of women MPs, as well as more black and Asian MPs and councillors than ever before. But we need more women and more black, Asian and minority ethnic MPs and councillors to make our democracy truly representative.

That's why in March I announced that political parties will be able to use all-women shortlists for the next five elections . . .

Wow. So through government diktat, for the next 22 years or so I – and every other man in the United Kingdom – could be stopped from becoming a prospective MP *solely on the ground of our gender*, regardless of our fitness for the office. And the least competent female candidate will *automatically* be deemed more worthy of public office than the most competent otherwise electable male candidate.

To ban *either* of the sexes merely on the grounds of gender would surely and inevitably reduce the pool of competent people willing to stand for public office. Which can only lead over time to Parliament being filled with even fewer competent MPs and ministers. Still, in Hattieworld that's a small price to pay for equal representation. Equality is clearly now far more important than quality.

The possible prospect of women-only MP candidate shortlists is so extraordinary that even the Labour Party must surely have mentioned the matter in its 2005 General Election manifesto. Sorry, I couldn't resist that little joke. Of course it didn't. But it did contain the following gem (one of many):

The EU now has 25 members and will continue to expand. The new Constitutional Treaty ensures the new Europe can work effectively, and that Britain keeps control of key national interests like foreign policy, taxation, social security and defence. The Treaty sets out what the EU can do and what it cannot. It strengthens the voice of national parliaments and governments in EU affairs. It is a good treaty for Britain and the new Europe. We will put it to the British people in a referendum and campaign whole-heartedly for a 'Yes' vote to keep Britain a leading nation in Europe.

British readers will need no reminding that we're still waiting for that referendum. For £0.01 plus postage and packaging you can order the

2005 Labour Party General Election manifesto from Amazon resellers. I can't wait for the 2010 manifesto. It should be a real hoot.

From *The Daily Telegraph* of 13 July 2009:

> Discrimination against northerners by public bodies could be banned under plans being considered by Harriet Harman, the Equalities Minister. Her office is looking at how it can ensure that the boards of national organisations are not dominated by Londoners and other southerners, her deputy disclosed. The remarks were made by Michael Foster, an equalities minister, in a parliamentary debate on 'diversity in public appointments' when replying to Meg Munn, a Labour MP.

Marvellous. That's yet another clipping for my file *Harriet Harman MP (stuff you couldn't make up)*. It's nearly full. I've noticed myself that short fat people with beards – both men and women, I'm not making a sexist point here – are under-represented as bar staff in upmarket wine bars. I must alert Ms Harman to this shocking reality.

Where *does* the woman get her energy from? Is she plugged into an electrical supply while she sleeps? Maybe she's haunted by the knowledge that after the next General Election – in May or June 2010 – she'll have a lot more time on her hands. I do hope she becomes the next leader of the Labour Party after that election.

Am I becoming a little obsessed with Harriet Harman? Possibly. But I'm not alone. A friend told me he once had a dream in which he was a Cabinet minister, and Harriet Harman was chairing a Cabinet meeting, the first in her new role as Prime Minister. The meeting took place in the context of a national emergency. As the meeting was about to begin, in an effort to lighten the mood my friend remarked out loud to Miss Harman, 'Harriet, may I kick off proceedings by remarking on how very *pretty* you're looking this morning?' Whereupon she frowned and drew a .44 Magnum revolver [Author: The gun used by Clint Eastwood in *Dirty Harry*] from her handbag, slowly took aim, and shot his right arm clean off his shoulder. She then glared at the other ministers and growled, 'Does anyone *else* think I'm looking pretty this morning?' They all stared glumly at their papers and mumbled, 'No, Prime Minister.'

A wonderful article by *The Daily Telegraph* columnist Liz Hunt in the 5 August 2009 edition of the paper:

Harriet Harman once cracked a joke. Yes, I know, it's hard to believe. Humour is not one of Miss Harman's chief attributes, nor is self-awareness – and this, remarkably, was a joke against herself. Asked, at the height of the leadership crisis last summer, about her own chances of becoming prime minister, Miss Harman said: 'It will not be possible, because there aren't enough airports in the country for all the men who would want to flee.'

One year on, she could confidently rewrite the line to include all the women who would join the stampede, too: desperate to escape a Britain shaped by her politically correct zealotry. The news that she has been slapped down by No 10 over a policy announcement is the culmination of a disastrous few days for Labour's deputy leader, although an entertaining time for the rest of us. As an end-of-pier turn, she is starting to rival John Prescott in his gaffe-prone heyday.

Topics of national and international import – the swine flu pandemic, doctors' hours, bankers' bonuses, the war in Afghanistan, turbulence in Iran – are of no concern to the woman in charge while Gordon (Brown) chews his nails in a sodden Lake District and rues the political necessity of having to take a holiday at home. Instead, Miss Harman's fixation with 'equality' continues – although her ranting has taken on a disturbing shrillness of the 'all men are rapists' school of feminism.

She does 'not agree with all-male leaderships' because men 'cannot be left to run things on their own', she told an interviewer at the weekend. This eye-popping statement came alongside reports that, after winning the deputy leadership in 2007, she tried to change Labour's rules to ensure that a woman was always in a top job.

Undeterred by the ridicule this generated – not least from many prominent women – she turned her fire on the bankers, suggesting that if the girls, rather than a horde of testosterone-fuelled Gordon Gekkos, had been in charge, the global turndown might not have been as serious. I think she has a point about the macho culture of high finance, but she negated it almost immediately with a crass reference to 'Lehman Sisters rather than Lehman Brothers'. It prompted one minister to say that 'Harriet has literally gone bonkers'. [Author's note: it also prompted a comedian to quip that a similar point could have been made in favour of 'Gay Men Brothers'.]

Yet it is the timing of these ill-judged headlines that really shows how out of touch she is with the public mood. Under Labour, we have had more women MPs than ever before, and more women in government. Yet their success rate in high office has been abysmal, largely through their own ineptitude. The demeaning departure of Jacqui Smith (porn and sink plugs), Hazel Blears (flipping houses) and Caroline Flint ('female window dressing') is kept fresh in our minds by the vengeful recriminations that continue to surface on chat shows or in interviews.

Even the old guard – Patricia Hewitt, Estelle Morris, Margaret Hodge, Clare Short – displayed a general lack of achievement that lingers in our consciousness. So what made Miss Harman think that either sex would sympathise with her renewed demand that a woman should be guaranteed one of the top jobs in the party for reasons of equality rather than ability?

In fact, it rather throws the spotlight on Harriet herself – and makes you wonder what, other than a thick skin and a bludgeoning tenacity that wears others down, she brings to the Cabinet table.

To me, she belongs to a particular breed of Labour women who claim to have the best interests of other women at heart. In reality, their concern is rooted in a blinkered ideology that panders to a particular faction of their party, and is ultimately self-serving.

There is no question that Miss Harman has her eye on a forthcoming vacancy. But she may come to regret her outburst this week. It has alienated a majority of women who know, instinctively or through experience, that without merit there can never be a meritocracy.

I wrote a letter to Harriet Harman in the hope of securing a meeting (see appendix two) but unfortunately she was too busy to meet with me. It was only later that it came to my attention that she had written a book published in 1993, *The Century Gap (20th Century Man, 21st Century Woman)*. I looked for the book on Amazon and found 22 used copies available for £0.01 (plus postage and packaging). At that price, I couldn't resist ordering a copy. From the back cover:

> Women have arrived ahead of time in the 21st century – then, as now, they will have an important role in the workforce as well as at home. But this revolution in women's lives has not yet been matched by men, who remain firmly stuck in the 20th century. That is the Century Gap.

The book contains two chapters on marriage. The following extract is taken from just three successive paragraphs in a section titled 'Men Contributing More':

> What must men do . . . They will have to . . . They will have to . . . Then they will feel able to . . . They must begin to . . . They must dramatically increase . . . They must . . . Men must . . . They must . . . They must . . . they must . . .

On behalf of men everywhere, might I respond feebly with, 'But *why* must we, Mistress Harriet?'

In *The Daily Telegraph* of 6 August 2009 there was a typically insightful piece by columnist Judith Woods, titled 'Are we taking the man out of our men? (Judith Woods wonders if women need to have a rethink)':

Take a long hard look at the man in your life. Yes him, the one lounging on the sofa, half-comatose in front of *Midsomer Murders*. Do you ever find yourself wishing he had a little more get-up-and-go, showed a bit more testosterone-fuelled drive, was – dare I say it – a touch more, you know, *manly*?

Is he passive rather than active? Does he leave most decision-making to you? Do you feel irritated that he happily fusses around in the kitchen when guests come for supper, but expects you to remember to take out the bins and fill the car with petrol?

If so, then chances are, you only have yourself to blame. A new study by Oxford University has revealed that women are attracted to men they believe will help out with household chores and childcare. British men came third, after Swedes and Norwegians, in an international egalitarian index.

The survey concluded that our menfolk make the best husbands – which doesn't quite tally with the fact that 45% of marriages end in divorce. But, according to a leading relationship coach, a great many relationship disasters stem from the fact that modern women are turning their husbands hermaphrodite.

No longer sure of their role, these 'egalitarian' men have been left straddling the gender divide and are becoming male-female hybrids, in some cases displaying far more feminine characteristics than their partners.

'Some women have become ball-breakers,' says Francine Kaye, known professionally as The Divorce Doctor, with an eponymous website. 'It's not entirely our fault, because the demands of the workplace have changed us, and brought out our more masculine side. But unfortunately we're taking that home with us every evening into the domestic sphere, and often bullying our men into submission.'

Harriet Harman's remarks earlier this week, that men can't be trusted to run the Government on their own, appear to chime with a growing female consensus that we are somehow superior.

'Many of us are so focused, decisive and assertive, that the only role left for our husbands is one where they comply and let us take charge – traditionally feminine traits. But the irony is, we don't actually want men like that, and we end up eventually resenting them for not being more dominant and fearless.'

Where once men's clearly defined role was simply to hunt and gather, they are now faced with women who do exactly the same in their careers, and who, once they get back from the office, demand total equality at home. It's by no means an unreasonable expectation – but it is an unwise one.

If you require your partner to take the kids shopping for new ballet kit, take his turn at doing the laundry and make sure the fridge is stocked with Petit Filous, then you are effectively domesticating him to the point where his own instincts – to protect and provide in the broader sense – wither away, and with them, any desire to put up a shelf, relag the boiler or do anything that might fall into the category of man's work.

And as for a thrilling sex life, forget it. He probably has a headache – again. Alarming figures from Relate reveal a 40% increase in married men who are perfectly capable of having sex, but no longer want to. The mooted reason for this chronic loss of libido among men between 30 and 50? Changing roles for men and women in the workplace and the bedroom.

'The unfashionable truth is that men and women are different,' says Kaye, who works with couples trying to save their relationships, as well as those who are set on splitting up and want to do so amicably. 'Male and female employees might be interchangeable in the office, but at home, couples – and women in particular – need to acknowledge, respect and indeed celebrate their differences, otherwise men feel sidelined and retreat into themselves.'

When Kaye examines the traits that each partner displays, she routinely finds that the traditional female and male roles are completely reversed. When questions are asked such as 'Who books the holidays? Who pays the bills? Who calls a tradesman when something breaks down?' the answer is invariably the woman. The same generally goes for 'Who is more aspirational? Who is more decisive? Who is more powerful in the relationship?'

'Men are shocked when they see the results of the test,' says Kaye. 'But, interestingly, they don't seem to mind so much that they have female characteristics; they're far more appalled that their wives have so many male characteristics, because that's what effectively emasculates them. When I tried it out on my own partner I was 70% male and 30% female and he was 50% each way, which we could both live with, but if I am honest I would have preferred to reverse the score.' Under the circumstances, I am grudgingly impressed that my husband is merely 40% female, as it turns out he is actually married to a man – I might have two children but, terrifyingly, I'm 90% male in my bullish attitudes and bossy behaviour. And I'm not the worst.

One of my friends, an attractive blonde events organiser, is 100% male. She claims that her live-in boyfriend's sole contribution to their partnership is paying half the mortgage.

'Sometimes I look at James and find myself wondering what the point of him is,' she says. 'He never suggests anything – not even an evening in the pub – he just relies on me, and so I end up doing everything, or it just wouldn't get done. I'm even the one who instigates sex.'

It's a pattern that Kaye recognises in couples where one partner is particularly dominant. By taking over every household task, women are effectively colluding in their partner's lack of involvement.

'Women are better multi-taskers, and so when our partners don't come up to scratch we complain bitterly, as a parent would, and end up doing the job ourselves, infantilising them in the process,' she says. 'We end up labelling our men lazy, because they have to be nagged into doing things, but the truth is we have pushed them to the point where they are afraid to take the initiative, because they feel they can never get anything right.'

Kaye's views chime with a growing mood of concern about a worrying imbalance in 21st-century relationships. In her controversial book *Save the Males: Why Men Matter, Why Women Should Care* published earlier this year, American columnist Kathleen Parker decried the fact that men were suffering a crisis of identity as a result of the conflicting and often confusing messages they receive from women and society, which often make them feel irrelevant.

'We want them to be providers and protectors – except when we don't,' she writes. 'We want them to count our contractions and share baby's midnight feeds, but then we want them out of the picture when we tire of them.'

One of my single male friends, a divorced surveyor in his early 40s, admits to being all at sea when it comes to wooing 21st-century women, who set the agenda and seem to have little patience. 'I tried online dating and I was shocked by the way these tough women presented me upfront with a list of what they expected from a relationship without seeming to care what I might want,' he says. 'It was like they were brokering a work deal rather than looking for love. By and large, they came across as a bunch of shopping-obsessed hyenas and it was a complete turn off.'

It's little wonder, then, that men's libidos are flagging. Adrian Lord, a psychiatrist and medical director of Cygnet Health Care, says that political correctness means today's chaps are mired in confusion. 'You get branded an ignorant pig if you don't give a woman a seat and a sexist pig if you do,' he says. 'You're damned if you do and damned if you don't. Everything that men stand for has been denigrated and run down over the past few decades, and we've become a bunch of lily-livered, pansy-picking wimps in order to survive.'

It comes as no surprise that sex lives are suffering; or that internet porn is booming, says Lord. 'Evolution hasn't caught up with the sexual politics of the boardroom, and never will; men are still biologically programmed to be attracted to women with curves who look and act feminine, not androgynous women who stride about like men to forge ahead in their go-getting careers,' he says. 'Many men seek sexual gratification online because the women they come across fulfil their fantasies and it's safer than dealing with the hard-bitten females they come across in real life.'

So if emasculation is the problem, what is the solution? According to Kaye, men grow in confidence – and manliness – when they receive the three As: Appreciation, Acknowledgement and Adoration. Women, on the other hand, crave the three Cs: to be Cherished, Complimented and Communicated with.

To get our relationships back on track, we women must try to rein in our control-freakery and rediscover our femininity, which will (theoretically) reawaken our partner's dormant masculinity. We must praise our partners, thank them for taking us out to dinner (even if we split the bill) and generally massage their tattered egos.

It's a bitter pill to swallow for those of us who have spent our working lives striving for parity, while scorning the eyelash-batting treachery of women who played on their gender.

If you find yourself slack-jawed in horror at the prospect of letting your partner off the hook so easily, then welcome to the club. Kaye's female clients often have the same initial reaction, but she claims that once they put her advice into practice they discover that a subtle shift in wording – and mindset – can have a major effect. 'My female clients are invariably amazed at how much impact an appreciative approach can have on their partner, and how quickly he responds when they show their more feminine side,' she says.

'It's not a case of being all helpless and girlie, but of being more feminine. If you behave more like a woman, your partner will act more like a man.'

I think Ms Woods is saying that some modern wives are rather too much in touch with their masculine sides. She is surely right. And she considers the issue of men's unhappiness in much the same way as many women. Men's unhappiness is of interest to them only when it impacts on *women's* happiness – 'Do you feel irritated that . . .', '. . . we end up eventually resenting them . . .', 'As for a thrilling sex life, forget it.'

The quiz referred to in the article is the following:

GENDER BENDERS: TAKE OUR QUIZ

How masculine are you?
Score 10% for each question when the answer is 'me'.

1. **Dominant**: Which of you tends to take over the running of the household?
2. **Fearless**: Which of you is more inclined to suggest new activities or a lifestyle change?
3. **Aspirational**: Which of you is more likely to suggest moving, building work, or a better school for the children?
4. **Possesssive**: Who is more likely to feel jealous?
5. **Focused**: Who takes care of the household bills and joint finances?
6. **Powerful**: Whose opinions tend to be stronger and have the most weight?
7. **Leader**: Which of you organises your joint social life?
8. **Driven**: Which of you is the more determined to get your own way?
9. **Decisive**: Who books the holidays?

10.   **Assertive**: Which of you is more likely to kick up a fuss about shoddy service or a poor restaurant meal?

How feminine are you?
Score 10% for each question when the answer is 'me'.

1.   **Protective**: Who worries more about the welfare of other family members?
2.   **Nurturing**: Who is more sympathetic when the other partner falls ill?
3.   **Trusting**: Which of you is happy to trust your partner's judgment?
4.   **Considerate**: Who is more likely to show respect for the other's viewpoint?
5.   **Appreciative**: Which of you is more likely to voice their appreciation and give positive feedback?
6.   **Co-operative**: Who is happier to defer to the other partner's opinions?
7.   **Encouraging**: Who tends to offer support and a pep-talk when the other partner is feeling at a low ebb?
8.   **Pleasing**: Who seeks to placate the other when tempers get frayed?
9.   **Accommodating**: Which of you hates confrontation more?
10.   **Open**: Which of you is happier talking about your feelings?

As I'm writing this – early August 2009 – numerous high-profile women are bemoaning the 'shortage' of women in Gordon Brown's cabinet. Which brings me neatly to a remark made a few weeks ago on BBC Radio by Diane Abbott, a Labour MP. It followed the 'resignation' of her fellow Labour MP Hazel Blears, widely regarded as an incompetent minister:

> Some weeks ago, before Hazel Blears resigned, a number of us went to a minister very close to Gordon Brown and told him Hazel just *had* to be fired. The minister responded with, 'But who could we replace her with?' I laughed and told him, 'Just about anyone with a pulse, to be honest!'

Daniel Goleman had some interesting points to make about the sexes' different perspectives in his 1995 bestseller *Emotional Intelligence*. After outlining how the sexes develop differing perspectives over the course of their school lives, he continues:

> These differing perspectives mean that men and woman want and expect very different things from a conversation, with men content to talk about 'things', while women seek emotional connection.

In short, these contrasts in schooling in the emotions foster very different skills, with girls becoming 'adept at reading both verbal and nonverbal emotional signals, at expressing and communicating their feelings,' and boys becoming adept at 'minimising emotions having to do with vulnerability, guilt, fear and hurt' . . . women, on average, experience the entire range of emotions with greater intensity and more volatility than men – in this sense, women *are* more emotional than men. . .

All of this means that, in general, women come into a marriage groomed for the role of emotional manager, while men arrive with much less appreciation of the importance of this task for helping a relationship survive. Indeed, the most important element for women – but not for men – in satisfaction with their relationship reported in a study of 264 couples was the sense that the couple had 'good communication.' Ted Huston, a psychologist at the University of Texas who has studied couples in depth, observes, 'For the wives, intimacy means talking things over, especially talking about the relationship itself. The men, by and large, don't understand what the wives want from them. They say, 'I want to do things with her, and all she wants to do is talk.'

Notice here an unwritten but clear value judgement, one that is repeated in much of the literature on the subject of relationships. The judgement is that men *should* become more communicative about their emotions, and women *shouldn't* need to recognise that their (male) partners are different and act accordingly; for example, not expect them to talk to them (or indeed listen to them) at great length about emotions.

How exactly has this value judgement come to be so universally accepted in the developed world in the modern era? My hunch is that it results from the very high proportion of the following groups of people, who are women:

- Writers of books and articles about relationships
- Readers of material about relationships, in books, women's magazines etc
- Psychologists
- Relationship counsellors
- Literary agents

A relation is a psychologist, and he graduated from Leeds University in 2007. Over 90% of his fellow psychology students were female. I mention literary agents because they are the 'gatekeepers' between writers and publishers, which might help explain the paucity of books about relationships with any sympathy towards masculine perspectives.

In her book *The Relate Guide to Better Relationships* (2001), the author – Sarah Litvinoff – takes up about a quarter of the book's length with a chapter on communication. The chapter includes the following advice:

> Make a date to talk to your partner for one hour specifically about yourselves and your feelings. Toss a coin to see who begins. Take half an hour each to talk about how you feel and what you want in life – as if you are explaining yourself to a stranger. While each person talks, the other must be silent and listen with full attention. On the half-hour you switch roles. During this time you must not talk about your partner or your relationship, though you can talk about your past. . .

Now I know a number of women who could talk for half an hour without interruption about themselves and their feelings, but not one man who could. Most men would, I'm sure, prefer to remove their own teeth with a pair of old rusty pliers, without the benefit of anaesthetic.

A thought prompted by a line from George Bernard Shaw's *My Fair Lady*. The line is Professor Higgins's, 'Why can't a woman be more like a man?' Today we would all think the remark chauvinistic and old-fashioned. But what is the implied question underlying much of the criticism so often aimed by women at men? Nothing less than 'Why can't a man be more like a woman?'. Surely the question that defines female chauvinism in the modern age.

I emailed a copy of the last few pages to a male friend, a fellow businessman and writer, and asked for his comments. He replied:

> If asked about my emotions I don't need half an hour to explain them. Half a minute would do. I'm either happy, relaxed, stressed, tired, pissed off or bored. Very occasionally anxious, but usually only when tired or stressed. Covers everything. Nothing else to say. It's not a big deal. When I'm fed up, I wait until I'm not fed up. I don't want to bloody talk about it. I want a beer.
>
> You have uncovered an interesting broader point. When my wife and I go to our place in Brighton, she and I often walk on the beach for half an hour. She wants to *talk*, I want to look at things – the sea, clouds, pebbles etc – and *think*. I always thought it was me who was weird. Maybe it's simply because I'm a man.

On to an interesting book with a title that would surely make a feminist kick a sickly puppy into a fast-flowing river, which is ironic because it was written by a self-described 'feminist and former shrew', Laura Doyle. It's her 1988 bestseller *The Surrendered Wife: A Step-by-Step Guide to Finding Intimacy, Passion and Peace with a Man.* I couldn't resist ordering it after reading a large number of reviews on Amazon. Most were positive, some extremely so, such as the following five-star review:

> **The best book on saving your marriage that I have read**
> Obviously not for everyone, because nothing is. But my experience reading this was that I recognised myself in 95% of what she described. There's no question in my mind that you can do all this, have a better marriage, and be an incredibly strong woman, both in the world and in your marriage. But with a far far subtler strength in the latter case. By which I DO NOT mean manipulation. But anyone who's tried to be married long-term knows it's a VERY subtle business indeed. This is a smart book for people with control issues who are suffocating their marriages . . . Not at all a retreat to the dark ages. In fact this book is about taking risks. The risk to love without forcing a relationship into a shape that feels safe but is actually dead.

At the other end of the appreciation spectrum was the following one-star review from a reviewer with the unlikely website sobriquet of 'Little Ray of Sunshine':

> The author should be ashamed of herself. Why should a woman have to subvert her personality just to keep her egotistical, fragile and emotionally retarded man happy? Women have been doing that for hundreds of years. Just when we see the light at the end of the tunnel along comes an idiot like Laura Doyle to give men all the justification they need to keep the little woman in her place. Whatever you do, don't buy this book; it will only encourage her.

'Don't buy the book.' No, keep the battle of the sexes going with the help of women like Little Ray of Sunshine. Among the plaudits on the book's cover we find two from well-known authors:

> Forget the rights and wrongs – it works. It's a miracle! A bad day for gender justice but a brilliant day for marriage. (Fay Weldon)

The Surrendered Wife is a practical and valuable tool for women to regain intimacy in their relationships. (John Gray, author of *Men Are from Mars, Women Are from Venus.*)

I'm reminded of a recently divorced acquaintance who said of his marriage to his formerly respectful partner, 'I thought I had married a pleasant and kind woman. How wrong I was. It turned out I had married the military wing of the women's movement. Every day was a battle, a request for a cup of tea an assault against all women over the millennia.'

The book contains deep insights into the nature of men, and what makes so many marriages a misery for both men and women. It is honest about the nature of women, and full of highly nuanced arguments. It covers the topic of sex in marriage, which other books tend to shy away from, or deal with very inadequately.

The following excerpt is from the introduction:

> When I was newly married at 22, I had no idea I would ever call myself a surrendered wife. At that time, the very phrase would have repulsed me.
>
> I did know that marriage was risky because I had watched my parents go through a brutal divorce. Still, I was hopeful that I could do better. I was amazed that my husband, John, could love me as much as he did, and part of me believed we could make our marriage work simply because it was born of so much goodness.
>
> At first our marriage was blissful. Then I started to see John's imperfections more glaringly, and I began correcting him. It was my way of helping him to improve. From my point of view, if he would just be more ambitious at work, more romantic at home, and clean up after himself, everything would be fine. I told him as much.
>
> He didn't respond well. And it's no wonder. What I was really trying to do was *control* John. The harder I pushed, the more he resisted, and we both grew irritable and frustrated. While my intentions were good, I was clearly on the road to marital hell. In no time I was exhausted from trying to run my life and his. Even worse, I was becoming estranged from the man who had once made me so happy. Our marriage was in serious trouble and it had only been four years since we'd taken our vows.
>
> My loneliness was so acute I was willing to try anything to cure it. I went to therapy, where I learned that I often used control as a defence. I read John Gray's *Men Are from Mars, Women Are from Venus*, which gave me some understanding of the different ways men and women communicate and approach life. I talked to other women to find out what worked in their marriages.
>
> One friend told me she let her husband handle all of the finances, and what a relief that was for her. Another one told me she tried never to criticise her husband, no matter how much he seemed to deserve it. I decided I would try to follow in these women's footsteps as an

'experiment' in my marriage. I desperately wanted to save the relationship, and I also hoped to rescue my self-respect, which was fading with each episode of anger and frustration I unleashed on John.

Little did I know that I was taking the first baby steps in surrendering and that doing so would renew our marital tranquillity and my self-respect. Today I call myself a surrendered wife because when I stopped trying to control the way John did everything and started trusting him implicitly, I began to have the marriage I've always dreamed of. The same thing will happen to you if you follow the principles in this book.

None of us feels good about ourselves when we're nagging, critical, or controlling. I certainly didn't. The tone of my voice alone would make me cringe with self-recrimination. Through surrendering, you will find the courage to gradually stop indulging in these unpleasant behaviors and replace them with more dignified ones. . .

Surrendering to your husband is not about returning to the fifties or rebelling against feminism.

This book isn't about dumbing down or being rigid.

It's certainly not about subservience.

It's about following some basic principles that will help you change your habits and attitudes to restore intimacy to your marriage. It's about having a relationship that brings out the best in both of you, and growing together as spiritual beings. Surrendering is both gratifying and terrifying, but the results – peace, joy, and feeling good about yourself and your marriage – are proven.

The basic principles for a surrendered wife is that she:

- relinquishes inappropriate control of her husband
- respects her husband's thinking
- receives his gifts graciously and expresses gratitude for him
- expresses what she wants without trying to control him
- relies on him to handle household finances
- focuses on her own self-care and fulfilment

A surrendered wife is:

- vulnerable where she used to be a nag
- trusting where she used to be controlling
- respectful where she used to be demeaning
- grateful where she used to be dissatisfied
- has faith where she once had doubt

A surrendered wife has abundance where she was once improverished, and typically has more disposable income and more satisfying, connected sex than she did before she surrendered. . .

Long before we fell in love and got married, every controlling wife suffered disappointments. At a young age, some of our most basic needs were unmet. This could be the result of any number of things: the untimely death of a parent or the frustrations of a family member's addiction. It could have been the consequence of relatively small things, like not getting the tennis shoes we desperately needed to fit in at school, or having to adjust to less attention due to the arrival of another sibling. Whatever the cause, we then made an erroneous conclusion that no one would ever take care of us the way we wanted.

We embraced a childish belief that if we were always in charge, things were more likely to go our way.

Some of us were so used to living in fear about not getting what we needed that we never even noticed our quickened pulse and shallow breathing. We normalised this level of terror and our accompanying auto-response: taking control. We believed that the more we could control people around us – husbands, siblings and friends alike – the better off we would be.

Just as fish are always the last to discover they are in the ocean, those of us who survive by trying to control things around us are often the last to recognise our behavior. We tell ourselves that we are trying to instruct, improve, help others, or do things efficiently – never that we are so afraid of the unpredictable that we do everything in our power to ensure a certain outcome.

Of the many topics Doyle covers well, I'll draw on just two more. The first is 'The Mother Complex':

If you feel as if you are the only adult in the family, think about this: Your husband manages to communicate, problem-solve, and produce in his job. Clearly he has the skills to do the same at home. So why doesn't he? Whenever we feel as if we have an extra child instead of a husband, it's because we're treating our husbands as little boys instead of capable men.

When I correct, criticise or tell my husband what to do I automatically become his mother in that moment, which means he doesn't see me as his lover. There's no greater turn-off for me than seeing him as a helpless little boy and there's no bigger intimacy killer for him than feeling he's with his mother. Your husband may not say so, but he feels the same way.

Your husband won't tell you he feels emasculated when you correct his behavior. He won't say that when you use that tone it gives him the same aggravated feeling he used to get when he was a teenager fantasising about going someplace where no one would bother him. He certainly won't tell you when he finds you as sexually unappealing as he finds his mother.

Instead, the cold war begins.

When you let him know you don't think he'll make good decisions, he reverts to his boyhood ways and makes a mental note to give up to some degree, because he can never meet your standards. He may even agree with you subconsciously, and retreat from the activity entirely.

Who can blame him?

When men feel disrespected, they withdraw. Before I surrendered, my husband watched a lot of TV. Yours may find playing golf, working longer hours or fixing up old cars in the garage more appealing than being with you. Sure, there's some satisfaction in letting your husband know what you really think, but the price of that satisfaction is high: You have just isolated yourself from him and created your own bubble of loneliness.

Treating your husband with respect makes him want to be around you more, talk to you more, share more deeply, and make love to you more passionately. It can't hurt to remind him (and yourself) that you've married a clever, capable man.

Doyle on 'Taking a Feminine Approach to Sex':

High gender contrast in a marriage is what makes things exciting in the bedroom. It means that instead of striving for agreement and sameness, you highlight and appreciate each other's unique characteristics and special traits. Just as we can't see stars without the cover of darkness, so the grandeur of our husband's masculinity is obscured without the foil of our femininity. By being feminine, we allow our husband's masculinity to shine. There can be no yin without yang, but the two together are sweet fulfilment – especially when it comes to sex.

Controlling wives are usually in charge of the contrast knobs because we have taken on so many masculine characteristics that our gender contrast is typically set very low. Your husband will respond to you with low contrast too, so that he matches you. That means he's going to be less attractive to you because he'll seem more feminine. For years we've said that we want men to be more sensitive, but as soon as they start talking about their feelings, we're not as attracted to them. I tell men not to fall for this trap, because what women typically want is a manly man – someone with his gender contrast set high. Of course the best way to have that is to adjust your own setting. He'll adjust his to match soon enough.

Most couples start their relationship with plenty of gender contrast, which is part of the reason that sex is so exciting initially. But then not only does the novelty wear off, the gender contrast diminishes as you become more sexually aggressive (a masculine characteristic) and he takes less sexual initiative (a feminine characteristic). Suddenly, even reruns of *Gilligan's Island* are more appealing than lovemaking.

Your physical union will intensify and have greater drama when you set your gender contrast to high. Just as our bodies are perfectly and intricately designed to fit together and bring each other pleasure, a feminine and masculine spirit complement each other brilliantly. Since you're the woman, come to the bedroom as female as possible. That means being soft, delicate, and receptive. Wearing something feminine never hurts either. It also means pretending that you never knew the meaning of ambition, aggression or . . . control. It means that instead of being the aggressor in sex, you are the seductress.

Remember that we're more attractive to our husbands when we're soft, tender, vulnerable and receptive, since those qualities are fundamental to the nature of a woman. Your husband married a woman because it's women – in body, mind, and spirit – who turn him on.

Doyle's approach would clearly suit couples who are traditionally minded in the area of gender roles. And a wife's expectation that her husband take responsibility for some major areas might *possibly* be more motivational than criticism about the uselessness of men in general, or her husband in particular.

The 'surrendered spouse' model has at least one thing going for it from a psychological perspective. It eliminates or at least reduces the frequency of the 'battles of will' that bedevil so many marriages over the years, and lead to considerable rancour. It requires that one partner amicably accept being the 'surrendered' one, whether the wife or the husband. And that the other partner uses his or her power sensitively.

In his 1998 book *The Secrets of Love and Lust*, Simon Andreae had some interesting things to say about women's search for 'Mr Right':

> Handsome men will pass their physical advantages down to the children of whoever they mate with, giving those children a head-start in the race for reproductive success. The indices of conventional male good looks – a rugged jaw, broad shoulders, a full head of hair and a healthy physique – are also indications of genetic health and strength. Yet looks in the opposite sex seem to be less important to women than they are to men, and less important than other factors.
>
> In Douglas Kenrick's study of the percentages required of potential partners before women would consent to dating, having sex, steady dating or marrying them, 'good looks' was the only criterion where women, across the board, were ready to accept a lower percentage value than men. They were even prepared to consider men of below-average physical attractiveness . . . as long as they had other things to offer.
>
> Legend has it that, some years ago, the actor Dustin Hoffman was sitting in a restaurant quietly enjoying dinner when he began to notice the attentions of a number of female diners. They were looking at him, whispering, giggling. Hoffman began to feel a little uncomfortable. Eventually, they approached him and asked for his autograph. One even asked him out on a date. At this point, Hoffman began to grow exasperated and, turning to his audience, uttered in mock dismay: 'Girls, please, where were you when I needed you?'
>
> Hoffman is, by most standards, not conventionally handsome. As a male model, stripped to the waist and lined up next to the Diet Coke hunk, he probably wouldn't have made the grade. But Hoffman, like most famous men, has other attributes. In Glenn Wilson's study of British sexual fantasies, men were found to fantasise more frequently about group sex than any of the other scenarios he presented to them.
>
> But women had a very different fantasy life. For them, by far the most characteristic fantasy was straight, monogamous sex with a famous

personality. The argument runs that famous men today, like village headmen in the past, and successful hunters during the early period in which we evolved, would have acquired the status and resources to furnish a woman and her children with more food and protection than the next man.

Over the incremental advances of time, evolution would therefore have favoured women who developed mental programmes which allowed them to judge the signs of status within their particular environment and culture, and calibrate their desire accordingly.

Fame is not the only indicator of a man who is high in status and rich in resources. In 1986 the American psychologist Elizabeth Hill published the results of an experiment in which she asked her students to describe what sort of clothes they considered high-status men to wear, and what sort of clothes they considered low-status men to wear. Among the former were smart suits, polo shirts, designer jeans and expensive watches; among the latter were nondescript jeans, tank tops and T-shirts.

She then photographed a number of different men in variations of both styles of dress and showed the photographs to a different group of female students, asking them to rate each one for attractiveness. Overall, the same models were found more attractive when wearing the high-status costumes than when wearing the low-status ones.

It's important to note, though, that it's not just status symbols, and resources they indicate, that women find attractive. It's also those personality characteristics which indicate the capacity to acquire such symbols in the future. In most cultures, women rarely have the luxury of being able to wait for a man to achieve all that he sets out to do before pairing up with him; as a result they have to calibrate his desirability partly on unrealised potential.

To find out what these characteristics of future success might be, and to see how they correlated with female desire, psychologist Michael Wiederman examined more than a thousand personal ads placed in various American periodicals between January and June 1992. He speculated that, in an arena where men and women were paying to attract potential mates, they would be more than usually forthright in specifying the attributes they sought, and more than usually direct in how they expressed their priorities.

Taking the various descriptions of what people wanted, and arranging them into categories, Wiederman noticed that terms denoting high status and plentiful resources (terms such as 'business owner', 'enjoys the finer things', 'successful', 'wealthy', 'well-to-do', and 'financially affluent') cropped up ten times as often in the women's wish lists as in the men's.

But there was also a considerable female preference for terms like 'ambitious', 'industrious', 'career-oriented', and 'college-educated'; in other words, for terms which clearly indicated the potential to acquire status and amass resources in the future.

Wiederman's results have been backed up by numerous other studies covering different decades and geographical areas. The American periodical *The Journal of Home Economics* took the sexual temperature of the nation's youth in the 1940s, '50s and '60s and found in each decade that young women rated financial prospects as highly desirable (though not absolutely essential) in men they were considering dating.

Douglas Kenrick, in his study of how intelligent, attractive and so on men and women had to be before they were considered sexually attractive by the opposite sex, found that earning capacity was much more important to women than to men; and David Buss, in a massive study of mating habits which covered 10,000 people in 37 cultures around the world, found that women rated financial resources on average at least twice as highly as men did.

Some researchers argue that an evolutionary explanation is not justified here. Women only desire wealthy men, they say, because most cultures don't allow women to make much money for themselves. But the female preference for wealth seems to exist regardless of the financial status of the women in question.

There is an unprecedented number of independent, self-supporting women with resources of their own in the world today, yet their mate preferences still seem to be following the age-old, evolved pattern of looking for men who can offer more.

One study of American newly-wed couples in 1993 found that financially successful brides placed an even greater importance on their husbands' earning capacities than those who were less well-off. And another, conducted among female college students, reported that those who were likely to earn more in respected professions placed greater importance on the financial prospects of their potential husbands than those who were likely to earn less. Buss's fellow psychologist Bruce Ellis summed up the prospect for future mate choice by saying, 'Women's sexual tastes become more, rather than less, discriminatory as their wealth, power, and social status increase.'

So there you have it. Women are keen that resources such as money flow in one direction only, *to* them *from* men. And what better mechanism to ensure this happens than marriage?

4

PERSONALITY TYPES, INTROVERSION AND EXTRAVERSION, GENETICS, ADULTERY

I try my best to be just like I am,
But everybody wants you to be just like them.

(Bob Dylan, *Maggie's Farm*)

This chapter covers:

- The 'big five' personality dimensions
- The impact of the family environment on children's personalities
- Shifting the blame for our failings onto our parents
- The impact of 'fighting families' on children
- A long-term study on the relationship between personality traits and real-life marital outcomes
- Sigmund Freud's and Carl Jung's different views on introversion
- A self-assessment test for introversion
- Descriptions of introversion and extraversion
- 'America the extraverted'
- In defence of introverts
- Personality traits other than extraversion
- Why extraverts become bored with their partners
- Why introverts become bored with their partners
- In defence of solitude
- In defence of loners
- The genetic influence on the risk of divorce
- Extraversion and adultery
- Why introverts are often avid book readers

An individual's personality type will profoundly influence how he or she will experience marriage. The same can be said for the interaction between their personality type and their partner's personality type. And yet few books offering advice on relationships cover the subject of personality types in any depth, and many ignore it altogether.

David Nettle is a reader in psychology at the University of Newcastle, and the author of *Personality: What Makes You the Way You Are* (2009). He reports a growing consensus around there being a 'big five' of personality dimensions, and offers the following overview:

Dimension	Low scorers are . . .	High scorers are . . .
Extraversion	Aloof, quiet	Outgoing, enthusiastic
Neuroticism	Emotionally stable	Prone to stress and worry
Conscientiousness	Spontaneous, careless	Organised, self-directed
Agreeableness	Uncooperative, hostile	Trusting, empathetic
Openness	Practical, conventional	Creative, imaginative, eccentric

Nettle's stated aim is 'to vindicate the idea that people have enduring personality dispositions which partly predict what they will do, and which stem from the way their nervous systems are wired up'. He stresses that low or high scores on individual traits are neither 'good' nor 'bad' in themselves, but reflect variations which have evolved to enable the human species to cope with differing environments and challenges. He goes on to explain that, 'studies reliably show that about half of the variation in big five personality traits is associated with genetic variation. Thus, people differentiated by high or low scores on the big five are also differentiated by which variant forms of some of the 30,000 or so genes in the human genome they are carrying.'

Nettle explores the impact of the family environment on personality, and more specifically the impact of 'shared family environments' on children brought up in them. He reports that studies have shown that family environments have no influence on the personalities of children:

> Given that this is the case, then we cannot avoid the following rather unsettling conclusions. Parental personality cannot have any measurable effect on child personality (except of course via genetics). Parenting style (to the extent that it is consistent across all children) cannot have any measurable effect on child personality.
>
> Parental diet, smoking, family size, education, philosophy of life, sexual orientation, marital status, divorce or remarriage cannot have any

measurable effect on child personality . . . if any of these had consistent effects, then unrelated children who grew up in the same household would be more alike in personality than randomly chosen pairs of children, and they are not . . . what the studies really show is that across a range of normal family-to-family variation, shared family factors have no effect on adult personality.

This is a stunning finding, and it has caused quite a stir. It is probably the most important discovery in psychology in recent decades, not least because it is counter-intuitive and overturns many entrenched beliefs. Out must go all simple notions about how cold mothers or absent fathers or large families or farm living shape our personalities. If any of these family effects were operative, then they would show up in a non-zero influence of the shared environment.

But what about the various research findings reported from time to time showing that children of divorced couples are more likely themselves to divorce, that maternal depression is linked to offspring depression, that people who are hit as children turn out more violent as adults, and so on?

What studies such as these are actually picking up is genetics. People high in Neuroticism are more likely to become depressed and get divorced, and their kids are more likely than average to do these things too, but not because of the kids learning the behaviour in childhood. Rather, the kids have good odds of inheriting the genetic variants that made their parents like that in the first place. Pretty much all evidence of similarities between parents and children, or of parenting behaviour and behaviour in the offspring once grown up, can easily be explained in this way.

For more insights into childhood and its impact on later life we turn to Martin Seligman, professor of psychology at the University of Pennsylvania, a past president of the American Psychological Association, and a leading expert on motivation and emotion. From his outstanding book *What You Can Change . . . and What You Can't (The Complete Guide to Successful Self-Improvement)* (2007):

THE POWER OF CHILDHOOD
It is an easy matter to believe that childhood events hold sway over what kind of an adult you become. The evidence seems to be right before your eyes. The kids of smart parents turn out to be smart; it must be all those books and good conversations. Kids from broken homes often divorce; they must have lacked good 'role models' for how to love enough. Kids who were sexually abused often become frightened pessimists; little wonder, they found the world a frightful place. Kids of alcoholics often turn out alcoholic; they learned uncontrolled drinking at their father's knee. The kids of authoritarian parents turn out authoritarian. The kids of basketball players and musicians turn out to have these talents. Kids who were beaten by their parents beat up their own kids.

As persuasive as they seem, these observations are hopelessly confounded. Yes, these people did grow up in worlds in which they were nurtured in their parents' image, *but they also have their parents' genes.*

Each of these observations supports a genetic interpretation as much as a childhood interpretation: smart genes, unloving genes, anxious genes, pessimistic genes, alcoholic genes, authoritarian genes, athletic and musical genes, violent genes. Why do the genetic interpretations sound so farfetched to the modern ear while the childhood interpretations sound so comfortably true?

The appeal of the child-rearing explanations has a theoretical dimension and a moral dimension. Freud assumed both that childhood events create adult personality and that their consequences can be undone by reliving – with great feeling – the original trauma. Sound familiar? It should, because the premises are just the same as those of the inner-child movement. Freud's premises may have undergone a steady decline in currency within academia for many years, but Hollywood, the talk shows, many therapists, and the general public still love them. The recovery movement marries Freud's basic premises to the confessional method of Alcoholics Anonymous. The result is the most popular self-help movement of the 1990s.

Childhood trauma and catharsis do make good theatre. But the appeal of the inner-child movement goes much deeper, for there is here a sympathetic moral and political message as well. Its appeal has its modern beginning with the defeat of the Nazis. The Nazis used the respectable science of genetics to bolster their theory of Aryan superiority. Genetically 'inferior' people – Jews, Gypsies, Slavs, the retarded and deformed – were deemed subhuman and were sent to the death camps. In the wake of our victory over the Nazis, anything they used or misused was tainted. Nietzsche's philosophy, Wagner's operas, and authoritarianism all became suspect. American psychology, already environmental, now shunned genetics completely and became wedded to explanations of childhood personality and the dogma of human plasticity.

When stoked by this reaction to Nazism, the logic of the dogma of human plasticity is: Once we allow the explanation that Sam does better than Tom because Sam is genetically smarter, we start our slide down the slippery slope to genocide. After World War II, genetic explanations became explanations of last resort, for they had the fetid odour of fascism and racism about them. All this accorded well with our basic democratic ideal that all men are created equal.

The second aspect of the moral appeal of the inner-child movement is consolation. Life is full of setbacks. People we love reject us. We don't get the jobs we want. We get bad grades. Our children don't need us anymore. We drink too much. We have no money. We are mediocre. We lose. We get sick. When we fail, we look for consolation, one form of which is to see the setback as something other than failure – to interpret it in a way that does not hurt as much as failure hurts. Being a victim, blaming someone else, or even blaming the system is a powerful and increasingly widespread form of consolation. It softens many of life's blows.

Such shifts of blame have a glorious past. Alcoholics Anonymous made the lives of millions of alcoholics more bearable by giving them the dignity of a 'disease' to replace the ignominy of 'failure,' 'immorality,' or 'evil.' Even more important was the civil rights movement. From the Civil War to the early 1950s, black people in America did badly – by every statistic. How did this get explained? 'Stupid,' 'lazy,' and 'immoral' were the words shouted by demagogues or whispered by the white gentry. 1954 marks the year when these explanations began to lose their power. In Brown v. Board of Education, the Supreme Court held that racial segregation in schools was illegal. People began to explain black failure as 'inadequate education,' 'discrimination,' and 'unequal opportunity.'

These new explanations are literally uplifting. In technical terms, the old explanations – stupidity and laziness – are personal, permanent, and pervasive. They lower self-esteem; they produce passivity, helplessness, and hopelessness. If you were black and you believed them, they were self-fulfilling. The new explanations – discrimination, bad schools, lean opportunities – are impersonal, changeable, and less pervasive. They don't deflate self-esteem (in fact, they produce anger instead). They lead to action to change things. They give hope.

The recovery movement enlarges on these precedents. Recovery gives you a whole series of new and more consoling explanations for setbacks. Personal troubles, you're told, do not result as feared from your own sloth, insensitivity, selfishness, dishonesty, self-indulgence, stupidity, or lust. No, they stem from the way you were mistreated as a child. You can blame your parents, your brother, your teachers, your minister, as well as your sex and race and age. These kinds of explanations make you feel better. They shift the blame to others, thereby raising self-esteem and feelings of self-worth. They lower guilt and shame. To experience this shift in perspective is like seeing shafts of sunlight slice through the clouds after endless cold, gray days.

We have become victims, 'survivors' of abuse, rather than 'failures' and 'losers.' This helps us get along better with others. We are now underdogs, trying to fight our way back from misfortune. In our gentle society, everyone roots for the underdog. No one dares speak ill of victims anymore. The usual wages of failure – contempt and pity – are transmuted into support and compassion.

So the inner-child premises are deep in their appeal: They are democratic, they are consoling, they raise our self-esteem, and they gain us new friends. Small wonder so many people in pain espouse them.

DO CHILDHOOD EVENTS INFLUENCE ADULT PERSONALITY?

Flushed with enthusiasm for the belief that childhood had great impact on adult development, many researchers eagerly sought support. They expected to find massive evidence for the destructive effects of bad childhood events such as parental death, divorce, physical illness, beatings, neglect, and sexual abuse on the adulthood of the victims.

Large-scale surveys of adult mental health and childhood loss were conducted. Prospective studies of childhood loss on later adult life were done (these take years and cost a fortune). Some evidence appeared – but not much. If your mother dies before you are eleven, you are somewhat more depressive in adulthood – but not a lot more depressive, and only if you are female, and only in about half the studies. A father's dying had no measurable impact. If you are firstborn, your IQ is higher than your siblings – but by less than one point, on average. If your parents divorce (we must exclude the studies that don't even bother with control groups of undivorced families), there is a slight disruptive effect on later childhood and adolescence. But the problems wane as children grow up, and they may not be detectable in adulthood.

The major traumas of childhood, it was shown, may have some influence on adult personality, but the influence is barely detectable. These reports threatened one of the bulwarks of environmentalism. Bad childhood events, contrary to the credo, do not mandate adult troubles – far from it. There is no justification, according to these studies, for blaming your adult depression, anxiety, bad marriage, drug use, sexual problems, unemployment, beating up your children, alcoholism, or anger on what happened to you as a child.

Most of these studies were methodologically inadequate anyway. They failed, in their enthusiasm for human plasticity, to control for genes. It simply did not occur to their devisers, blinded by ideology, that criminal parents might pass on criminal genes, and that both the felonies of criminals' children and how badly criminals mistreat their children might stem from genes rather than mistreatment. There are now studies that do control for genes: One kind looks at the adult personalities of identical twins reared apart; another looks at the adult personalities of adopted children and compares their personalities with those of their biological parents and of their adoptive parents.

All of these studies find massive effects of genes on adult personality, and only negligible effects of any particular events. Identical twins reared apart are far more similar as adults than fraternal twins reared together for the qualities of authoritarianism, religiosity, job satisfaction, conservatism, anger, depression, intelligence, alcoholism, wellbeing, and neuroticism, to name only a few. In parallel, adopted children are much more similar as adults to their biological parents than to their adoptive parents. These facts are the latest, if not the last, word in the renascent nature–nurture controversy. They come from a convergence of large-scale studies using up-to-date measures. These studies find ample room for non-genetic influences on adult personality because less than half the variance is accounted for by genes. But researchers have not found any specific nongenetic influences yet (nongenetic influences can include foetal events, child rearing, childhood trauma, schooling, adolescent and adult events, and measurement error, among others). Some of these specific factors may yet emerge as important to adult personality, but to date, none have.

> If you want to blame your parents for your own adult problems, you are
> entitled to blame the genes they gave you, but you are not entitled – by
> any facts I know – to blame the way they treated you.

Seligman has some interesting observations to make in the same book on
the venting of anger in the family environment, and the impact of warring
parents on their children. It makes sobering reading for parents who
cannot – or will not – hide their animosity towards one another in front
of their children, yet stay together 'for the sake of the children':

> Serious turmoil between parents is the most depressing ordinary event that
> children witness. We have followed the lives of some 400 children for the
> last five years, focusing on children whose parents fight (20%) and those
> whose parents divorce or separate (15%). We watched these 140 children
> carefully and contrasted them to the rest of the children. What we saw has
> important implications for our society at large and for how married
> couples should deal with anger.
>
> The children of fighting families look the same – that is, just as bad – as
> the children of divorce: These children are more depressed than the
> children from intact families whose parents don't fight. We had hoped the
> difference would diminish over time, but it didn't. Three years later, these
> children were still more depressed than the rest of the children.
>
> Once their parents start fighting, these children become unbridled
> pessimists. They see bad events as permanent and pervasive, and they see
> themselves as responsible. Years later this pessimism persists, even after
> they tell us their parents are no longer fighting. Their worldview has
> changed from the rosy optimism of childhood to the grim pessimism of a
> depressed adult. I believe that many children react to their parents'
> fighting by developing a loss of security so shattering that it marks the
> beginning of a lifetime of dysphoria [Author's note: 'impatience under
> affliction; morbid restlessness; uneasiness; absence of feeling of
> wellbeing'].
>
> It is important to realise that these are averaged results. Some of the
> children do not become depressed, some of the children do not become
> pessimists, and some of the children recover over time. Divorce or
> fighting does not doom a child to years of unhappiness; it only makes it
> much more likely.
>
> Many more bad life events occur to children whose parents divorce or
> fight. This continued disruption could be what keeps depression so high
> among such children. Among these bad events are:
>
> - Classmates act less friendly
>
> - Parent hospitalised
>
> - Child fails a course at school
>
> - Parent loses job

- Child himself hospitalised
- A friend dies

This adds up to a nasty picture for the children of parental turmoil. Parents' fighting may hurt children in such a lasting way for one of two reasons. The first possibility is that parents who are unhappy with each other fight and separate. The fighting and separation directly disturb the child, causing long-term depression and pessimism.

The second possibility is the traditional wisdom: Fighting and separation themselves have little direct effect on the child, but awareness of parents' unhappiness is the culprit – so disturbing as to produce long-term depression.

Only future research can clarify this, but although there is nothing in our data to tell us which of these two is right, I lean toward the first. I don't believe that children are subtle creatures with 'unhappiness in parents' detectors; in fact, I think that most children see their parents in a very positive light and that it takes real upheaval or deprivation to make a child notice how rotten things are. Fighting and violence between the two people the child most depends on for his or her future is just such upheaval.

Many people are, of course, in rocky marriages, filled with strife and conflict. Less dramatic, but more common, is this situation: After several years of marriage, many people don't like their spouses anymore, which breeds resentment and is fertile ground for fighting.

But at the same time, both marriage partners are often overwhelmingly concerned with the well-being of their children. It seems to be a plain fact – at least statistically – that either separation or fighting in response to an unhappy marriage is likely to harm children in lasting ways. If future research tells us that it is parents' unhappiness and not the overt fighting that is the culprit, then I would suggest marital counselling aimed at coming to terms with the shortcomings of the marriage. This sometimes works.

But if future research determines that it is the act of fighting and the choice to separate that are responsible for children's depression, very different advice would follow. All of us save money for our children. We put off the trip to Hawaii now, and perhaps forever, so that our children might lead better lives than we do. Are you willing to forgo separation from a spouse you don't like anymore? An even harder challenge: Are you willing to choose to refrain from fighting – on just the same grounds – for the sake of your children?

There may be something to be said for couples' fighting. Sometimes justice is achieved for you. But as far as your children are concerned, there is very little to be said in favour of parents' fighting. Therefore, I choose to go against the prevailing ethic and recommend that it is not your well-being, as much as it is your child's, that is at stake.

We return to Nettles' book, which has some interesting information on the relationship between personality traits and real-life marital outcomes. He writes about a study of marriages by two psychologists, Lowell Kelly and James Conley, which started in 1935, and the outcomes reported in 1987:

Between 1935 and 1937 Kelly recruited 300 couples, mainly from the US state of Connecticut, who were engaged to be married. Kelly kept in touch with them, collecting data on the state of their marriage – that is, both whether it was intact, and how happy they were within it – in the years immediately after their weddings, again in 1954–5, and again in 1980–1. Back in the 1930s Kelly had asked five acquaintances of each man and woman to rate them on personality scales which were the forerunners of those we use today. From these, he extracted an average personality score for four dimensions, which were basically Extraversion, Neuroticism, Conscientiousness and Agreeableness.

The results show the personality scores – those simplistic ratings, filled out by friends back in the 1930s – are really rather strong predictors of how the marriages turn out. If either the man or the woman is high in Neuroticism, divorce is much more likely, and if they do stay together, the marriage is less happy, as indicated by the average of his and her independent ratings 40 years later. The negative emotions that the high Neuroticism scorer is prone to experience really do make a difference in real life and in the long haul.

There are also other interesting patterns. The man's, but not the woman's, Conscientiousness is a predictor of divorce (the lower the Conscientiousness, the higher the likelihood). The accounts of reasons for divorce that Kelly and Conley collected suggest that low Conscientiousness men are basically bad heads of household. Some of them turned out to be drinkers, others financially irresponsible, or both.

Bear in mind that these are couples married before the war, with what we would now regard as a rather traditional gender division of labour. The lack of effect of female Conscientiousness can be attributed to the fact that women of this period did not generally play a provider role.

What distinguishes those who stay in an unhappy marriage from those who divorce is levels of Extraversion and Agreeableness. Again this makes sense. Extraverts are above all very good at meeting people, so it is likely that, in an unhappy marriage, they would tend to find someone else more often than average, and terminate the marriage.

As for Agreeableness, my interpretation would be that someone high in empathy and the capacity for fellow-feeling would see when a relationship was causing two people to suffer, and try to work it out one way or another. Someone with less mental connection to the mental states of others might just go on despite coldness or even hostility.

I believe one personality dimension, that of extraversion (as least as it manifests itself in introversion), is the cause of unhappiness in many marriages. I'm highly introverted myself, and if given the choice I wouldn't wish to be an extravert. But there's a price to pay for introversion. I have come to believe that while introverts *can* have successful marriages, the institution is *by its very nature* more uncomfortable for them than it is for extraverts. To understand why this is so, it is necessary to understand the introverted personality type in far greater depth than it is commonly understood, particularly by extraverts. This chapter aims to provide that understanding.

The psychoanalysts Sigmund Freud and Carl Jung held very different views on introversion. Freud (an extravert) thought introversion unhealthy and equated it with narcissism, while Jung (an introvert) thought introversion in itself neither healthy nor unhealthy. Jung also concluded that extraverts naturally struggle to understand the nature of introverts, and vice versa. We shall see in due course that approximately half the population is by 'preference' extraverted, half introverted. The term 'preference' is used by psychologists to mean the domain in which individuals are most comfortable. A right-handed person may be *able* to write with his left hand, but that wouldn't be his preference.

Jung's highly influential book *Psychological Types* was first published – in German – in 1921, and translated into English in 1923. Before including material from the book, it may help the reader to understand that in psychoanalytical terminology, somewhat confusingly, the terms 'subject' and 'subjective' relate to the individual whose psychological state is being described, while the terms 'object' and 'objective' relate to the external person or persons with whom that person may interact. From the book's introduction:

> In my practical medical work with patients I have long been struck by the fact that besides the many individual differences in human psychology there are also typical differences. Two types especially become clear to me; I have termed them the introverted and the extraverted types.
> When we consider the course of human life, we see how the fate of one individual is determined more by the objects of his interest, while in another it is determined more by his own inner self, by the subject. Since we all swerve rather more towards one side or the other, we naturally tend to understand everything in terms of our own type. . .

The hypothesis of introversion and extraversion allows us, first of all, to distinguish two large groups of psychological individuals. Yet this grouping is of such a superficial and general nature that it permits no more than this very general distinction. Closer investigation of the individual psychologies that fall into one group or the other will at once show great differences between individuals who nevertheless belong to the same group. If, therefore, we wish to determine wherein lie the differences between individuals belonging to a definite group, we must take a further step. Experience has taught me that in general individuals can be distinguished not only according to the broad distinction between introversion and extraversion, but also according to their basic psychological functions. For in the same measure as outer circumstances and inner disposition cause either introversion or extraversion to predominate, they also favour the predominance of one definite basic function in the individual.

I have found from experience that the basic psychological functions, that is, functions which are genuinely as well as essentially different from other functions, prove to be *thinking, feeling, sensation,* and *intuition.* If one of these functions habitually predominates, a corresponding type results. I therefore distinguish a thinking, a feeling, a sensation, and an intuitive type. *Each of these types may moreover be either introverted or extraverted,* depending on its relation to the object as we have described above.

The American psychotherapist Marti Laney (an introvert) in her 2002 book *The Introvert Advantage: How to Thrive in an Extravert World* writes convincingly of the 'internal world' of the introvert, and the issues it raises in various contexts, including relationships.

Before progressing much further, the reader might like to gain a sense of his or her degree of introversion or extraversion. Laney offers the following 'Self-Assessment for Introverts':

Take the test for introversion on a day when you are feeling relaxed and not stressed out. Pick a cosy nook where you won't be interrupted. Consider each statement in terms of what is generally true or false for you, not how you wish you were or how you are some of the time. Don't analyse or think too deeply about each statement. Your first impression is usually the best. For an outside view of yourself, it can be enlightening to have a partner or friend answer for you. Compare your results with your friend's score. If the two tallies differ, talk about both of your views. Answer the following questions True or False, then add up your True answers and check the scoring at the end of the list to see if you're an introvert, fall in the middle of the continuum, or are an extravert.

- When I need to rest, I prefer to spend time alone or with one or two close people rather than with a group.
- When I work on projects, I like to have larger uninterrupted time periods rather than smaller chunks.
- I sometimes rehearse things before speaking, occasionally writing notes for myself.
- In general, I like to listen more than I like to talk.
- People sometimes think I'm quiet, mysterious, aloof, or calm.
- I like to share special occasions with just one person or a few close friends, rather than have big celebrations.
- I usually need to think before I respond or speak.
- I tend to notice details many people don't see.
- If two people have just had a fight, I feel the tension in the air.
- If I say I will do something, I almost always do it.
- I feel anxious if I have a deadline or pressure to finish a project.
- I can 'zone out' if too much is going on.
- I like to watch an activity for a while before I decide to join it.
- I form lasting relationships.
- I don't like to interrupt others; I don't like to be interrupted.
- When I take in lots of information, it takes me a while to sort it out.
- I don't like overstimulating environments. I can't imagine why folks want to go to horror movies or go on roller coasters.
- I sometimes have strong reactions to smells, tastes, foods, weather, noises, etc.
- I am creative and/or imaginative.
- I feel drained after social situations, even when I enjoy myself.
- I prefer to be introduced rather than to introduce others.
- I can become grouchy if I'm around people or activities too long.
- I often feel uncomfortable in new surroundings.
- I like people to come to my home, but I don't like them to stay too long.
- I often dread returning phone calls.
- I find my mind sometimes goes blank when I meet people or when I am asked to speak unexpectedly.
- I talk slowly or have gaps in my words, especially if I am tired or if I am trying to speak and think at once.
- I don't think of casual acquaintances as friends.
- I feel as if I can't show other people my work or ideas until they are fully formulated.
- Other people may surprise me by thinking I am smarter than I think I am.

Add up the number of Trues. Then read the following to see where you fall.

20–29 True: Pretty darn introverted. As a result, it is extremely important for you to understand how to keep your energy flowing and how your brain processes information. You relate to life through your ideas, impressions, hopes, and values. You are not at the mercy of your external environment. This book can help you use your inner knowledge to create your own path.

10–19 True: Somewhere in the middle. Like being ambidextrous, you are both introverted and extraverted. You may feel torn between needing to be alone and wanting to be out and about. So it's very helpful to notice when and how you consistently feel more energised. You judge yourself by your own thoughts and feelings and by the standards of other people. This gives you a broad view, but at times you may get caught up in seeing both sides of a situation and not know where you stand. It is important to learn to assess your temperament so you can maintain your energy and balance.

1–9 True: You are more extraverted. You judge yourself in the light of the values and reality of others. You work within the bounds of what exists to bring about change. As you reach midlife and your body slows down, you may surprise yourself by wanting to take a break from socialising or needing time to yourself and then not knowing what to do. You can develop techniques to help yourself remember what is best for you to do when you need solitude. To do this you will have to balance your extraverting skills by learning more introverting skills.

From the first chapter of the book:

Introversion is at its root a type of temperament. It is not the same as shyness or having a withdrawn personality, and it is not pathological. It is also not something you can change. But you can learn to work with it, not against it.

The strongest distinguishing characteristic of introverts is their energy source: Introverts draw energy from their *internal world* of ideas, emotions, and impressions. They are energy conservers. They can be easily overstimulated by the external world, experiencing the uncomfortable feeling of 'too much.' They need to limit their social experiences so they don't get drained. However, introverts need to balance their alone time with outside time, or they can lose other perspectives and connections.

Introverted people who balance their energy have perseverance and the ability to think independently, focus deeply, and work creatively.

What are the most obvious characteristics of extraverts? They are energised by the *external world* – by activities, people, places, and things. They are energy spenders. Long periods of hanging out, internal contemplation, or being alone or with just one other person understimulate them. However, extraverts need to balance their time *doing* with intervals of just *being*, or they can lose themselves in a whirlwind of anxious activities. Extraverts offer much to our society – they express themselves easily, they concentrate on results, and they enjoy crowds and action.

Introverts are like a rechargeable battery. They need to stop expending energy and rest in order to recharge. This is what a less stimulating environment provides for introverts. It restores energy. It is their natural niche.

Extraverts are like solar panels. For extraverts, being alone, or *inside*, is like living under a heavy cloud cover. Solar panels need the sun to recharge – extraverts need to be out and about to refuel. Like introversion, extraversion is a hard-wired temperament. It cannot be changed. You can learn to work *with* it, not *against* it. . .

In the early 1900s, psychoanalyst Carl Jung was working with Sigmund Freud and Alfred Adler, two other pioneering psychoanalytic theorists, when he noticed something puzzling. When Freud and Adler discussed the same case histories of patients, they focused on very different information. They also had developed almost opposite theories. Jung thought they had both captured something valuable. Jung gave it some thought and developed his own theory.

Jung thought Freud was extraverted because his personal orientation was outward toward the world of people, places, and things. Many of Freud's theories were developed in conjunction with extensive correspondence and discussions with numerous colleagues. Freud believed that the goal of psychological development was to find gratification in the world of external reality. Jung thought Adler was introverted, since his theory and focus were inward toward one's own thoughts and feelings. Adler's theories were based on the internal struggle to overcome the feelings of helplessness expressed in his term 'inferiority complex.' He saw people as creative artists shaping their own lives.

Freud's theoretical differences with Adler and Jung ended in bitterness. The three parted company and each went his own way. At that point, Freud began to use the concept of introversion as a negative, implying a turning inward away from the world, in his writings about narcissism. This shifted the evolution of the concept of introversion away from healthy and toward the unhealthy, a misconception that remains to this day.

Jung continued to develop his theory, and he surmised that we are born with a temperament endowment that locates us somewhere on a continuum between very introverted and very extraverted. He believed that there was a physiological foundation for these dispositions. Science is now finding his intuition was right. He realised we could adapt best in the world if we could move easily on the continuum, introverting and extraverting when needed. However, he recognised that humans don't seem to work that way. We are oriented or pulled in one direction more than the other. He concluded that we all have a 'natural niche' where we function best. Jung also thought that, apart from either extreme, any place on the continuum is healthy. Jung believed that it is harmful to push a child outside of the natural range of his or her temperament, thinking this would 'violate the individual's innate disposition.' In fact, he thought this was the cause of some mental illness.

Beyond children, what about adults, and married adults in particular? Is it going too far to suggest that for an introvert, and especially for highly introverted adults such as myself, the expectations of 'traditional' marriage – such as being happy in the close and frequent company of the same partner for year after year, decade after decade – are so far out of 'the natural range of his or her temperament' that if he or she is not allowed the 'personal space' they require, the result could be considerable stress, possibly resulting in mental health issues (such as depression) over the medium to longer term? I don't think it is going too far.

Marriages will consist of one of the following three pair options:

- Introvert–introvert
- Extravert–extravert
- Introvert–extravert

Even if we speculate that some mutual attraction between extraverts may lead to more than one-third of marriages consisting of an extravert–extravert pairing, we can still confidently predict that the majority of marriages will contain at least one introvert, a person *who by his/her very nature is likely to feel uncomfortable within the institution.* That's a personal reflection, not Laney's. I believe introverts are more likely than extraverts to be the people feeling themselves 'slowly going insane' in marriages.

Laney covers the issues expected to arise with the following relationships:

- Introvert male with extravert female
- Introvert female with extravert male
- Introvert female with introvert male

A personal reflection on introversion: People sometimes talk about a married couple's 'identity' as being distinct from the partners' identities as individuals. This is baffling to introverts. As an introvert I don't want to share my partner's identity, and I don't want her to share mine.

In 2008 the American clinical psychologist Laurie Helgoe (an introvert) published a very insightful book entitled *Introvert Power: Why Your Inner Life Is Your Hidden Strength*. From the introduction:

AMERICA THE EXTRAVERTED

There's a lot to love about America – freedom, the melting pot of diversity, individualism – all attractive concepts, especially to an introvert. In fact, the introverts were probably the first to feel crowded in England and to daydream about all the space they would find in the New World. Peace! Quiet!

Fast-forward to the new millennium – and it has been a fast trip forward – in which we are more likely to associate America with office space than with 'spacious skies'. We have become an outward and upward society, conquering, building, competing, buying out, improving – extraverting. The squeaky wheels get greased, the ones who snooze lose, the best team wins, and the winner takes all.

In this culture of competition, it is no wonder that those of us who prefer introversion feel anxious. We are expected to 'think on our feet', but we think best when we're still. We're pressured to join and keep up, when we'd rather follow an inner guide. And with the ever-multiplying multimedia – from pop-up ads on the Internet to phones that can reach us *everywhere* – the competition finds us where we live. . .

When introverts sense invasion, we instinctively shut down to protect our inner resources. But in doing so, we lose access to ourselves. From this defensive position we may feel that our only options are to practice extraversion, go underground, or go crazy. . .

INTROVERSION FOR ALL

According to the introverted psychiatrist Carl Jung, introversion and extraversion are two opposing forces within an individual. Jung was the first to identify these personality attitudes, one 'characterised by orientation in life through subjective psychic contents' (introversion) and the other, 'by concentration of interest on the external object' (extraversion). Isabel Briggs Myers and Katharine Cook Briggs, who developed the popular Myers-Briggs Type Indicator ® (MBTI ®), built on the idea that introverts prefer to focus on their own inner world, whereas extraverts prefer to focus on the outer world. But as the concepts of introversion and extraversion gained popularity, they began to lose their dynamic roots. We tend to see ourselves as introverted OR extraverted, rather than as a creative, evolving combination of the two.

It is this dynamism that makes introversion relevant to all of us. Whether the scale tips in the I direction and you call yourself an introvert, or you load up on the side of E, every one of us has some capacity for introversion. When a culture devalues these qualities, we are all reduced.

The way personal growth is supposed to progress, according to Jung, is that we first develop what comes naturally – introversion or extraversion. This specialisation works well until later life, when the individual gets bored and wants to expand his or her range. But what happens when the introvert is discouraged or, worse, prohibited from practicing her specialty?

The introvert may adapt, but she walks around with a nagging sense of homelessness. She won't need to wait until midlife to become bored – she's bored already! It's hard enough to be in a career that doesn't fit, but for many introverts, the *life* doesn't fit.

For these introverts, what is needed is *not* a move toward extraversion, but as a friend of mine put it, an opportunity to 'melt into introversion'. This book is not about finding balance – we are really tired of doing that! Besides, finding balance assumes that we have been *allowed* to be fully introverted. We have not. This book is about embracing the power of introversion. It's about indulging, melting into, drinking in, immersing ourselves in the joy, the genius, and the power of who we naturally are – and not just on the occasional retreat, but in the living of our lives. Ironically, balance will only come to us if we forget about extraversion for a while, and balance will only come to our society when we see and respect the introversion in all of us.

THE BIG LIE

Thanks to Jung and his successors, we have the tools to understand these qualities. We have a personality test to measure introversion and extraversion. The *Myers-Briggs Type Indicator* has generated a vast amount of research on introversion and extraversion. Popular literature has emerged to explain how each of us can understand our personality preferences and use them to our advantage. But lies about introversion are so imbedded in the fabric of our culture that even the literature geared toward correcting misconceptions inadvertently promotes them.

The biggest lie is that introverts are in the minority, making up one-fourth or one-third of the population, depending on what you've read. Any introvert who has done a quick web search, attempting to find some company, has probably run across and even quoted these figures. But not only are these figures floating around the Web, they are also repeatedly quoted in the self-help books many of us use as resources.

When I started my research for this book, I wanted to know where these statistics came from. I wanted to find the research that the books were quoting. So I went to the source: the *MBTI Manual (2003)*, a regularly-updated compendium for the research on introversion, extraversion, and the other personality dimensions measured by the *MBTI*. But what I found was quite different.

The first large-scale population study of the *MBTI* revealed that introverts make up a good *half* (50.7%) of the population (and if you want to split hairs, we seem to be in the *majority*). This study, the largest to date, was conducted in 1998. A more recent population study, reported in the *MBTI Step II Manual*, puts introverts a little further into the majority: 57%, compared to 43% extraverts.

It took me much longer to find the source of the claim that introverts make up only a third of the population. Isabel Myers made this estimate when the *MBTI* was being developed – prior to *1962*!

[Authors note: the reader will find more on the MBTI in Appendix 4.]

How can we be so far off?

As much as research shows the contrary, the belief that introverts are in the minority has stuck. After all, in America, extraversion is *what we value*. And we see what we value, so we see extraverts everywhere, and we no longer notice the introverts everywhere. Sometimes we even miss the one looking back at us in the mirror. We might tell ourselves that *introverts are naturally less visible than extraverts*. This lie is as insidious and damaging as the lie about our numbers. Perhaps a better way to put it is that we are less *seen* in America. Go to Japan, for example, and, despite the massive population, an introverted businessperson is more likely to be noticed than a 'fast talker.'

In America, we think of introverts as withdrawn loners, quiet and scared. We readily diagnose a preference for looking inward as stemming from depression, anxiety, or antisocial tendencies. We don't know what introversion really is, and we interact with introverts all day without realising it.

We've got it all wrong.

REVIVING YOUR INTROVERSION

From a young age, most of us are taught the value of social skills. We learn how to introduce ourselves, how to smile and be polite. We are told to be friendly and make friends. These are all useful abilities to develop. But how many of us are taught the value of solitude skills? How many of us are taught to protect our boundaries, to foster imagination, to be alone? How many of us are encouraged to withdraw from social activity and nurture the life of the mind?

This book is here to provide that missing training and support. We'll examine how introversion may have gotten away from you, and how to get it back. We'll deconstruct the extraversion assumption, and see how it manifests in everyday conversations, judgments, and ideas about work and play. As you are freed to reclaim your preference, you will be amazed at the power you feel. Life will flow in a way you hadn't thought was possible. You may find yourself asking: 'Is this okay?', 'Can things be this easy?'

From the chapter 'The Mistaken Identity':

The stereotyped introvert is often seen as introvert by default when, in fact, introversion is defined as a *preference*. Introverts generally prefer a rich inner life to an expansive social life; we would rather talk intimately with a close friend than share stories with a group; and we prefer to develop our ideas internally rather than interactively.

So how have we jumped from these preferences to images of a cowering, reclusive weirdo? Iris Chang commented, 'Whatever is not commonly seen is condemned as alien.' We have lost our eyes for introversion. As we discussed in the introduction, introverts make up *more than half* of the population, yet we assume that introverts are an occasional deviation – the geeks in the shadows.

Introversion, by definition, is not readily seen. Introverts keep their best stuff inside – that is, until it is ready. And this drives extraverts crazy! The explanation for the introvert's behavior – *and there must be an explanation for this behavior, say the extraverts* – is that he or she is antisocial, out of touch, or simply a snob.

Because introverts are trickier to read, it is easy to project our fears and negative biases onto this preference. And it's not just extraverts who do this. As my informal poll revealed, we often make similar assumptions about other introverts, and – most troubling of all – about ourselves! One of the introverts I polled is a striking beauty. She described her physical appearance as 'OK'. Another very attractive introvert described herself as 'the status quo'. These downplayed descriptions may reflect a tendency to focus less on externals, but we also tend to downplay our very personalities – the style we *prefer*. For example, do you ever jokingly or apologetically admit to being antisocial, or view yourself as boring in relation to your chatty associates? Do you beat yourself up for not joining in? Do you worry that something is wrong with you; that you're missing out; that who you are naturally is a problem needing correction?

Your nature is not the problem. The problem is that you have become *alienated* from your nature – from your power source. As Isabel Briggs Myers discussed in her book, *Gifts Differing*, 'The best-adjusted people are the "psychologically patriotic" who are glad to be what they are.' For introverts this means, 'Their loyalty goes to their own inner principle and derives from it a secure and unshakable orientation to life.'

But we *have* been shaken. To reclaim the power of introversion, we must first deconstruct the assumptions we make about who we are.

THE OPPOSITE OF SOCIAL IS NOT ANTISOCIAL

Of all the assumptions made about introverts, the idea that we are *antisocial* is the most ridiculous. The term 'antisocial' actually refers to sociopathy (or antisocial personality disorder), a condition in which a person lacks a social conscience. This has nothing to do with introversion. Introverts are often deeply concerned about the human condition; they just tend to look within for answers. Ironically, the classic sociopath is quite charming and socially engaging, but lacks the *inner* capacity to feel empathy and guilt.

This is a great example of how our vision tricks us. An introvert deep in thought will *look* self-absorbed, whether he's thinking about world hunger or working out how to hack into someone's bank account. An engaging extravert will *look* friendly, whether he really cares about your day or is trying to pick your pocket. Therapists are reluctant to apply the diagnosis of antisocial personality disorder until there is clear evidence for it, because it is a serious problem with a poor prognosis. Enjoying your own company does not warrant any diagnosis, but this one is especially cruel.

But are we just talking semantics here? When we use 'antisocial' in this way, we really mean not social, or *asocial* – the correct term for someone who does not like to interact with people. So would it be fair to say that introverts are asocial?

Wrong again.

THE OPPOSITE OF SOCIAL IS NOT INTROVERTED

An introvert may *feel* asocial when pressured to go to a party that doesn't interest her. But for her, the event does not promise meaningful interaction. In fact, she knows that the party will leave her feeling *more* alone and alienated. Her social preference may be to stay home and reflect on a conversation with a friend, call that friend, and come to an understanding that is meaningful to her. Or she might indulge in the words of a favourite author, feeling a deep connection with a person she has never met. From the perspective of a partygoer, this introvert may appear to be asocial, when, in fact, the introvert is interacting in a much different way.

Because the introvert is oriented to the inner world, she 'takes to heart' something a good friend says and needs time to reflect before responding. This can happen during a relaxed talk, but, for the introvert, the understanding deepens during the time *between* conversations. If we think of each person as having a finite amount of interpersonal spaces an extravert is more like a hotel – able to accommodate a large number of interactions that come and go. Note that I said *interactions*, not people. Extraverts are often able to accommodate more people as well, but because extraverts wrap up interactions *in the interaction*, even a close friend may check in and check out as needed. An introvert may have the same square footage, but each meaningful interaction is reserved in its own luxury suite, awaiting the follow-up interaction. Bookings are more limited.

A related assumption about introverts is that we are socially incompetent. Are you starting to see a pattern? Assumptions about introversion usually link the preference with some kind of *lack* or disorder. So let's get this one over with too. Just as extraverts can have poor social skills (think of the raucous, obnoxious socialiser), introverts can be socially savvy. Introverts often choose 'people professions' as their life work. I have been wrong too many times to assume that an outgoing social leader is an extravert. The introverted leader may check out for refuelling and relish alone time after work, but be quite 'out there' in her public role. Stories abound of high-profile introverts who chill out to read a book, watch golf on TV or take a walk.

So, being an introvert does not mean you're antisocial, asocial, or socially inept. It does mean that you are oriented to ideas – whether those ideas involve you with people or not. It means that you prefer spacious interactions with fewer people. And it means that, when you converse, you are more interested in sharing ideas than in talking about people and what they're doing. In a conversation with someone sharing gossip, the introvert's eyes glaze over and his brow furrows as he tries to comprehend how this conversation could interest anyone. This is not because the introvert is morally superior – he just doesn't *get it*. As we've discussed, introverts are energised and excited by ideas. Simply talking about people, what they do and who they know, is noise for the introvert. He'll be looking between the lines for some meaning, and this can be hard work! Before long, he'll be looking for a way out of the conversation.

But when an introvert is hanging out with a friend, sharing ideas, he is in his element. The conversation is 'mind to mind' rather than 'mouth to mouth.' Extraverts share ideas too, but the ideas are secondary to the interaction, and develop *between* the two people as they talk. The focal point is external. For introverts, the focal point is internal, with each participant bringing the other inside and working things out there. A good conversation leaves an introvert feeling more connected, but also personally richer.

Understanding the *location* of interactions puts introverts back on the map. Extraverts understandably need more face-to-face time, because that's where the interaction is located. Introverts need more *between* time – between words in a conversation and between conversations – because the interaction is located within.

WE ARE NOT SNOBS

While this is an assumption some introverts like – being a snob is better than being *impaired* – it ultimately hurts us. Think of a group of Extravert Moms gathered together at a Little League game, excitedly chatting and enjoying the action. In comes Introvert Mom who, after a full day of work, wants nothing more than to savour the game – all by herself. She sits off a bit from everyone else, stretching her feet onto the bleacher bench, and may even have a book to indulge in as the team warms up. She might enjoy watching the people around her, but she has no energy to interact.

What are the Extravert Moms thinking? Because they are oriented to people, they will likely assume that Introvert Mom is, too – which means they see Introvert Mom as not liking people (what we know now as asocial) or being a 'snob', thinking she's too good for the Extravert Moms. More likely, Introvert Mom *is not thinking about them at all!* She is just doing something she likes to do.

The snob assumption is an extravert personalisation of the introvert's behavior: she's not just doing something for herself; she's dissing *us*. This misunderstanding may lead to gossip and suspicious looks. If Introvert Mom feels this hostile energy; she may become defensive and further withdraw to protect herself, only confirming to the Extravert Moms that she is indeed a snob.

An introvert who regards herself as a snob, and looks down on extraverts as superficial or shallow *loses*, rather than gains, strength. This is because her focus moves outward, away from her power source. Though she may think she is being unkind to the extraverts around her, she is actually being very unkind to herself. The snob myth perpetuates the idea that her introversion is a snub of those around her, rather than something she enjoys and values. . .

WE ARE INTROVERTS

What constitutes an introvert is quite simple. We are a vastly diverse group of people who prefer to look at life from the inside out. We gain energy and power through inner reflection, and get more excited by ideas than by external activities. When we converse, we listen well and expect others to do the same. We think first and talk later. Writing appeals to us because we can express ourselves without intrusion, and we often prefer communicating this way. Even our brains look different than those of extraverts.

In 1967, psychologist Hans Eysenck published his 'arousal theory' of introversion and extraversion, which predicted that introverts would have higher levels of cortical arousal than extraverts. In other words, introvert brains would be more stimulated on an ongoing basis; extravert brains would be quieter. This would explain why introverts pull away from environmental stimuli while extraverts seek out more.

To test the theory, researchers have looked at various measures of mental stimulation, such as blood flow and electrical activity, in the brains of introverts and extraverts. The consistent finding was that, as predicted, introvert brains were busier than extravert brains. After summarising this research, the writers of the 2003 *MBTI Manual* concluded: 'Introverts appear to do their best thinking in anticipation rather than on the spot; it now seems clear that this is because their minds are so naturally abuzz with activity that they need to shut out external distractions in order to prepare their ideas.' So it is impossible to fully and fairly understand introversion without looking inside. We aren't just going *away*, were going *toward* something. Extraverts may have more going on socially, but we've got more going on upstairs.

The simple preference for inner life, when honored, opens the introvert to a richness and complexity that is highly personal and is indeed *personality* with the exclamation point! Instead of defining – or diagnosing – introversion from the outside, let's look at a description by a man who mined the depths of inner life, Carl Jung:

> For him (the introvert) self-communings are a pleasure. His own world is a safe harbour, a carefully tended and walled-in garden, closed to the public and hidden from prying eyes. His own company is the best. He feels at home in his world, where the only changes are made by himself. His best work is done with his own resources, on his own initiative, and in his own way . . . His retreat into himself is not a final renunciation of the world, but a search for quietude, where alone it is possible for him to make his contribution to the life of the community.

As much as introverts may be misunderstood or devalued, people are drawn to the richness we conceal and enjoy the products we create in our 'tents'. The reclusive songwriter entertains through the computer audio system developed by introverts. Voices of introverts speak through books so varied we can be entertained by just looking at the titles in a bookstore. Introverts make us think and ask questions. We fall silent as the quiet person in the room reveals wisdom from his inner reservoir.

Introverts, it is time for us to claim our space, our time, and our vitality.

From the chapter, 'Showing Up for Relationships':

For introverts, relationships create a paradox. We crave safe, comfortable, intimate, small-talk-free connections. But we also want ample time to ourselves, space of our own, and quiet. Some of us want a relationship at the centre of our lives, and some of us want solitude at the centre. Many of us want both.

How do we work this paradox? How do we maintain relationships – *close* relationships – and still have the alone time that sustains us? What happens if we marry? And what if we want kids?

We are culturally conditioned to want and seek out the relationship side of the paradox, but we get very little validation for the 'alone time' part. I am married, very happily, and we have two boys that I couldn't wait to conceive and bring into our world. I am one of ten children, though, and I needed therapy to help me accept my scandalous wish to stop having children at two. I knew that I would short change the two we had if we added more. I was certain I would short change myself; I had reached my interpersonal maximum. Thankfully, I had the space of my analysis to sort this out and to contend with all my training to believe 'the more the better'. I have never looked back.

But if it was scandalous for me to stop at two, what about the many introverts who prefer not to have kids? What about those who prefer to stay single? In 'America the extraverted,' relationships are good, and even if they are very bad, they are better than no relationship. Introverts don't think this way. Many of us want and have great relationships, but we generally prefer 'no relationship' to a bad one. Quality matters. We conserve our relationship resources, because we know they are limited. We probably see ourselves as having *less* to offer a relationship than we actually do; extraverts generally think they have more to offer. This is not because extraverts are arrogant, but because America is about quantity, and extraverts revel in quantity.

But when an introvert is self-aware enough to say 'no' to a relationship that he is not willing to invest in, we assume he is afraid or selfish. When a woman says 'no' to having babies, we assume she is selfish and 'missing something'. In these assumptions, we neglect what is often missing for the socially preoccupied extravert: the nourishment of the inner life. . .

THE PROBLEM OF FAMILY
In America, the term 'family values' has become a political and social rallying point. We don't really know what it means, but we know it's good – something we should have. Any spin on this theme tends to get

swallowed without question: 'Family comes first', 'Family is the bedrock of society', blah, blah, blah.

Introverts are often very close to family members. We like the familiarity, the shared history, the opportunity to bypass small talk. But the 'family comes first' idea is often foreign to introverts. We are wired to start inside: many of us couldn't start outside if we wanted to. We are centred inside, and we like it that way.

Family was at the centre of my childhood home, and I knew that I was not a part of that centre. I was loved – that wasn't it. I just didn't function that way. The physical structure of our home mirrored this reality. The living room was the 'family room'. This room was the gathering place, the centre. I did not live in the living room. And I still don't. My husband, the extravert, lives in the living room. I do more of my living in *my* room and *visit* the living room, as I did in my childhood home. The exception to this is when I have the house to myself then the entire house is 'my room'. These days are sweet.

My impulse right now, from my cultural programming, is to explain how much I love my boys and my husband, but I really don't want to do that. I don't talk a whole lot about my family, because I don't talk a whole lot about *people*. When I'm with them, I'm really with them, but I don't tell everyone what they're doing, and I won't suffer 'empty nest syndrome'.

My centre will not be torn when my boys go off to college. I will miss them, but my relationship is less dependent on proximity. I hold them inside wherever they are.

It's different for my husband, the extravert. He will be torn, and he knows it. His *interactions* with the boys, and with me, are at his centre. He holds them inside too, but that's not his centre.

Latest estimates suggest that about 54% of men and 47% of women are by 'preference' introverted. As an introvert I am naturally more conscious of what makes marriage difficult for introverts rather than what makes it difficult for extraverts. But extraverts have their own issues. Let's remind ourselves of a characteristic of extraverts raised by Lacey: and let's use the word 'bore' in preference to 'understimulate'. Being alone with just one other person bores extraverts. Given that the state of marriage forces individuals to be with just one person for much of the time, often for many years, can we be surprised that extraverts are likely to become bored by their partners, and therefore find marriage difficult?

Introverts have their own reasons for becoming bored with their partners. Once they know their partners well, and are familiar with their views on every subject imaginable, they no longer receive much fresh mental input from them. No wonder so many long-married couples eating together in a restaurant exchange barely a word from the start of the meal to the end.

An interesting observation on the impact of ageing on introversion, from William Jeffries' *True to Type: Answers to the Most Commonly Asked Questions About Interpreting the Myers-Briggs Type Indicator* (1991):

> **QUESTION 19: My preference for introversion has become stronger the older I have become; is that unusual?**
> No, not at all. There has not been much research done to explore the relationship between ageing and (personality) type. In fact it is one of the real gaps in scholarship that must be corrected as we age as a culture. About all we know is that – all things being equal – our preferences tend to become clearer as we age. The one preference where we notice significant shifts is in introversion. As we age, we seem to become more comfortable with our introversion. Don't forget, introverts live in an extraverted conspiracy. The population seems to be about 70% extraverted. [Author's note: this figure reflects the understanding at the time the book was written, 1991. More recent books have the population 43–50% extraverted.] Thus, there is great pressure to develop extraverted skills. As we mature, we seem to become more comfortable acting on our preferences, particularly, it seems, if one of them is introversion. When this happens with clients it is often exciting to watch them finally give themselves permission to be themselves: just what Jung intended to happen.

I'm Not Crazy (I'm Just Not You) was written by two psychologists, Roger Pearman and Sarah Albritton, and published in 1997. An interesting passage covers the subject of communication with regards not only to the extravert/introvert dimensions, but also the other six dimensions in the MBTI 'personality inventory':

> As a refresher, note the following dimensions from the *MBTI* personality inventory, which is based on Jung's theory:
>
> **Extraverting**   Seeking and initiating in the environment
>
> **Introverting**   Receiving and reflecting on the environment
>
> **Sensing**   Attraction to data from present-oriented experiences, often seeking pragmatic and realistic information

Intuition	Attraction to ideas about future possibilities, seeing patterns, seeking abstract and theoretical information
Thinking	Deciding by logical arguments; often critical and analytical
Feeling	Deciding by value, relational arguments; often accommodating
Judging	Acting in a decisive way, either in an analytical or a value-oriented way
Perception	Acting in an emergent, go-with-the-flow way; primarily conscious of either the present or the imagined future

Communication Effects of Extraversion / Introversion

By habit, Extraverts tend to express themselves freely. They are so comfortable initiating in their environment that they assume everyone else is, too. Further, a lack of immediate reaction from Extraverts usually occurs when they do not trust a situation (or person) or when they feel incapable of making a reasonable response. Aware of this personal discomfort, they often assume that when they see someone else who is not immediately responsive, or who appears cautious, then that person must also be uncomfortable, worried, and possibly slow or only moderately competent in the situation.

Notice the ease with which the Extravert's experience becomes the baseline for judging others' reactions. This is the nature of projection. It is an unconscious process that colours our understanding. It may well be the Extravert's first unspoken prejudice; understanding is based on what the Extravert is comfortable with, rather than what may be true for an Introvert. . .

Missed Associations

Whatever a person's preference, the behavior of a person with the opposite preference seems inconsistent and out of synch with our experience. Never mind that to the second person, the associations the first person is making are all wrong and lead to a complete misjudgment. Given the studies showing that we assess and make up our minds about people within 30 seconds of meeting them, it seems important to keep this kind of cross-preference projection in mind. It is most pronounced between Extraversion and Introversion, but missed associations happen at every level between the individual preferences and among whole types. It is therefore vital to know that the message you intend to send may not be reaching your audience.

With the Extravert's typical hunger for pace, variation, and expressive engagement, it is easy to see how people in committed relationships can get into trouble. The energy they put into engaging in the world may be interpreted by Introverts in their life as leaving little energy for them. Likewise, the Extravert may feel that the energy an Introverted partner puts into internal analysis denies him the important insights needed to solve the problem before them.

It is safe to assume that people engaged in the environment and interacting with others are *expressing* Extraversion. In that mode, their comments may simply be the beginning or middle of thought, not the end. They may be probing for reactions, and if so their comments may have no more significance than to simply spur the conversation. They are constantly misunderstood as meddling, opinionated, and forceful, but if you listen carefully and hold your judgments in tow, you may hear information that reveals the richness of thought and the intent of the message.

When individuals are observant, somewhat disengaged, and seem careful about word choice, it is reasonable to assume they are expressing Introversion. In this mode, their comments are usually the end parts of their thoughts. What comes out verbally is their most complete thought on the topic for the time being. Receptive and appearing cautious, they are simply trying to create space in their environment to let their heads work. Typically oblivious to being seen as guarded, their pace may simply allow their minds to be undistracted as they sort through their experiences. But they generally share what is important to them, and if you listen carefully you will get a very good idea of their mind-set and perspective. They are not holding back, necessarily; they are simply sorting through all the internal static to become clear on what to finally say. Often misunderstood as aloof, condescending, and anxious, they are actually creating the time and space needed to respond to the experience they are having.

Communication Effects of Sensing and Intuition

If the differences between Extraversion and Introversion lead to misunderstandings of the value and meaningfulness of shared information, the differences between Sensing and Intuition hit at the heart of trust and honesty. There is no more profound difference in communication than the projections developed by these preferences, because they are at the root of building our understanding of reality.

The Essence of Sensing

Sensing, by its nature, finds the information of the moment clear, concise, and concrete. A person with this preference is likely to have an appreciation for brief statements describing the who, what, where, when, how, why, and relative status of the situation. Studies of military personnel consistently show that a large proportion of them report having a Sensing preference: Order, precision, focus, and immediate action are hallmark qualities. Military forms must be filled out with exact information; they do not ask what you think was going on in the heads of folks involved in an incident. Fidelity to the facts of the present is bedrock Sensing.

Contrasting the Intuitive

Nothing could be further from the attention of Intuition than fidelity to facts. For intuition, a fact only begins to have meaning in context to situations; thus, from the Intuitive perspective, the interpretation of a fact may change as the context shifts, and more often than not focusing on facts creates barriers to new ideas. Those with an Intuitive preference are more inclined to imagine the potential outcomes, extrapolate about events and people's motives, and look for information that confirms the reigning theory (about people, situations, or other things). More important to such folks than facts is whether certain perceived principles were honored.

Imagine a meeting of a business team in which three members have a Sensing preference and two have an Intuitive preference. The discussion could be filled with a considerable amount of conflict if one cluster wants to focus on the realistic, present-oriented, concrete elements of a problem and the other two seek to develop multiple alternatives to solve the problem at some point in the future. The abstraction and theoretical interests of the intuitive will be evident in the language and the questions used during the discussion. Depending on the critical nature of the situation, the pressures could drive these two groups into heated and difficult conflict as each group believes the other is focusing on the wrong set of issues.

A sense of the pragmatic versus a sense of the possible will always stump interactions between Sensing and Intuitive types until they are cognisant of each other. In fact, each can easily begin to believe the other is idiotic. Sensing types are often baffled at the language used by Intuitives and at their apparent focus on the future, the theoretical and the abstract. 'How can a simple question generate so much stuff?,' Sensing types often wonder. 'Why can't they see more in this information, see its paradoxical meaning?' say the Intuitives about the Sensing types. Because the influence of perception is the fountainhead to the operation of the psyche, these differences are profound. And the profound nature of these differences can be seen in the speed with which distrust can be created among people of goodwill.

Communication Effects of Thinking and Feeling

If Sensing and Intuiting perception are at the heart of trust in communication, then Thinking and Feeling are critical to the communication of mutual respect. Thinking types often show their interest and enthusiasm by critiquing their experiences and the information put in front of them. Feeling types, by contrast, show their interest and enthusiasm by identifying and expressing appreciation for important aspects of their experiences and the information put before them.

'Stepping Out' for Clarity

Trying to step out of the situation in which they find themselves in order to gain clarity, individuals with a Thinking preference seek to find criteria that can frame information and experience in such a way that there is a sense of objective analysis. It seems objective because of the logical, orderly manner in which situations are reviewed. Folks with a Thinking preference put enormous effort into looking at the pros and cons of a situation, analysing how things are related, and proposing principles to guide their thoughts.

'Stepping In' for Awareness

Those with a Feeling preference want to step in to a situation and have a very specific awareness of how people in the situation are affected. Feeling types immediately focus on the consequences of contemplated actions or real choices in terms of the people involved. Acutely aware that reasoned criteria are valuable for decisions, those with a Feeling preference have an automatic personal value system that places specific human well-being above any externally imposed system of analysis. Knowing full well the argument that decisions are made in business to ensure the well-being of the greatest number of employees, the Feeling type's concern for the outcomes on individual human beings nevertheless remains undaunted.

There is often the danger, when exploring Thinking and Feeling, of people taking the definitions too far. Thinking types have feelings and values that inform their analysis; Feeling types use reason and logic to assist their judgment. But the primary basis of the judgment they use is profoundly different.

Define Conflict and Give Three Examples

When people grouped together by preference are asked to define conflict and give three examples, they consistently respond in the following general ways.

Thinking types: Conflict exists whenever two or more people disagree for so long that emotions get involved. It is often very productive and useful and enables us to get to the heart of issues and make better decisions. Take, for example, some wars that are very useful, some corporate actions that are critical to competitiveness, and even some vigorous arguments at home that clear the air.

Feeling types: Conflict exists when we disagree. It is often avoided because of the discomfort created. It is rarely useful and gets in the way. A clear example is the conflict evident when people argue or debate. Can individual realities be so different? Driven by a framework of fair play, those with a Thinking preference are inclined to assume that everyone values that playing field. Focused on a value of avoiding harm to others, those with a Feeling preference naturally assume that anyone choosing to make others uncomfortable simply does not honor other people over their need to be right or correct. Consider this dialogue:

Teacher: I had to fail three students last year in my English class. I've seen those kids since then and I worry about their self-esteem.

Principal: You shouldn't worry about them. They chose not to do the work. We need to be careful not to let our emotions override standards for performance.

Teacher: First of all, I said they failed, so my standards are very much in place. Second, my emotions are not involved with these students, as you're suggesting, but they are getting involved with this discussion.

Principal: I was merely trying to make the point that standards are important.

Teacher: I was merely pondering whether we are attending to the self-esteem of these kids so they will grow up to be caring and productive adults! I don't need to justify my feelings or my standards.

Potential Loss of Respect

The teacher's comments are a fairly typical Feeling reaction, and the principal's are a fairly typical Thinking response. This type of interaction leads to the false conclusion that one does not really respect the other. It would be easy for either one to walk away with the awareness of being misunderstood and perhaps even feeling unappreciated. And as we noted at the beginning of this section, this dimension has the greatest affect on the sense of mutual respect between people during interactions. Often the source of considerable interpersonal pain and discomfort, the language of Thinking and Feeling prompts deeply felt reactions.

If the role of projection is as critical as it seems, the loss of respect between persons with these differences is understandable. Because the Thinking type judgment process relies on logic, it quickly and constructively responds to a logical presentation of information. Thinking types tend to communicate respect to a person whose presentation is elegantly logical, that is, with the conclusion following efficiently from the premise without the static of interpersonal overtones or caveats. We know that a Thinking type is dedicated and even passionate about things when he or she thoroughly critiques them. Thinking types report that they know a person when they receive feedback about what they can do to improve the next presentation or project.

On the other hand, Feeling types have enormous energy associated with the awareness of accepting and being accepted. They tend to communicate respect through acceptance. Often what they most want in an interaction, before continuing a discussion, is an initial indication that the other individual finds them acceptable as persons.

Feeling types say that they know a person respects them when the feedback is initially about the importance of the individual contribution and effort before discussing the range of improvements that could be made in a presentation or project.

Communication Effects of Judgment and Perception

Isabel Briggs Myers carried Jung's theory of types to its fullest extension by focusing on the dynamic within each type. As discussed earlier, we extravert either judgment or perception and introvert the opposite of what is extraverted. Myers had to struggle with how to get at such subtle distinctions when constructing the *MBTI* inventory. We developed the following material about her Judging-Perceiving dimension to identify the preferred mental function in the Extraverted mode. For example, Myers' assumption is that an ENFP extraverts Intuition and introverts Feeling. But like the other dimensions at the core of psychological type, this carries with it another layer of interactional issues. With this exploration we begin wading into the dynamics of the types.

Judgment in the Extraverted mode, whether Thinking or Feeling, is an orientation toward observable decision making. The attraction of closure is strong for those who extravert their judgment function. Often desirous of a methodical and systematic approach, those who sort Judgment on the *Myers-Briggs Type Indicator* instrument are indicating that you are likely to see and hear decisive action from them. The message often received by others who run into Extraverted Judgment is one of impatience and bare tolerance of anything that slows down the action.

Decision Now or Later

Those who extravert Perception give the message that they are concerned about the negative consequences of making premature decisions. Preferring to trust data, they find almost any information useful and tend to seek out interactions that move among several different topics before settling on any given one. This often annoys those who are ready to make something happen now by making a decision.

Unfortunately, given the speed with which decisions about other people are made upon first meeting them, this observable behavior can trigger all kinds of preconceptions. Extraverted Perceptive types often see those with Extraverted Judgment as rigid, dogmatic, and pushy; Extraverted Judgers often see those with Extraverted Perception as ineffectual, inefficient laggards. For example, in a committee meeting where a person who extraverts Judgment (ET, EF) wants a time limit for discussion on each topic, often the Extraverted Perceiver (EN, ES) will object that doing so feels confining and could cause the group to lose out on important late-breaking information. When the Extraverted Perceiver wants to keep the discussion going past the agreed upon time, often the Extraverted Judger feels that the other person is wasting time, looking at irrelevant material, and waiting too long to act.

At the age of 82, the remarkable originator of the Myers-Briggs Type Indicator, Isabel Briggs Myers, collaborated with her son Peter Myers to write *Gifts Differing: Understanding Personality Type*, published in 1980. The following extracts are from the chapter 'Type and Marriage':

Differences in type between husband and wife may give rise to friction, but this can be diminished or eliminated when its origin is understood. Nothing in this chapter is intended to discourage anyone from marrying a person of largely opposite type, but such a marriage should be undertaken with full recognition that the other person is different and has a right to remain different, and with full willingness to concentrate on the virtues of the other's type rather than the defects.

The role of type in courtship and marital choice is subject to some debate. Proverbially, birds of a feather flock together. It seems only reasonable that the greater mutual understanding between couples with more likeness than difference should lead, on the whole, to greater mutual attraction and esteem. Among 375 married couples whose Indicators were obtained in the 1940s, the most frequent situation was for the couple to be alike on three of their four preferences rather than on only two, as would be expected by chance.

On the other hand, Jung said of extraverts and introverts, 'Sad though it is, the two types are inclined to speak very badly of one another . . . they often come into conflict. This does not, however, prevent most men from marrying women of the opposite type' (1971, p. 517). Plattner (1950), a Swiss marriage counsellor, wrote that in most marriages, extraverts marry introverts, and two Jungian analysts, Gray and Wheelwright (1944), advanced a theory of 'complementary mating.'

The apparent conflict of evidence here is itself informative. The observers just cited were testifying about the marriages they saw in their own practices. Their clients were in marital or psychological difficulty or both. Jung is reported to have commented, 'Of course, we analysts have to deal a lot with marriages, particularly those that go wrong because the types are too different sometimes and they don't understand each other at all.' If the marriages seen by analysts have gone wrong because the types are too different, then analysts and marriage counsellors would be expected to encounter more oppositeness than occurs in successful marriages, which may confirm the thesis that having two or three preferences in common contributes to the success of a marriage and lessens the need for counselling.

Among our 375 couples, there was significantly more similarity than difference between husband and wife on each of the four preferences. The most frequent similarity was on SN, which suggests that *seeing things the same way*, whether by sensing or by intuition, does more to make a man and woman understandable to each other than a shared preference on EI or TF or JP.

The percent distribution of the couples was as follows:

Alike on all preferences	9%
Alike on three	35%
Alike on two	33%
Alike on one	19%
Alike on none	4%

Couples who were mainly alike outnumbered those who were mainly opposite by two to one. Among the couples who were alike on all preferences, most were feeling types and may have had harmony as a conscious goal in choosing a spouse. Among the couples who were different on all preferences, nearly all the husbands were thinkers.

The amount of likeness that two people actually find in a marriage may fall far short of what they expected. In this respect the extraverted male before marriage has a decided advantage over his introverted brother. He is more aware of what people are like, he circulates more, and he knows more women. He has a wider circle from which to choose and may have a somewhat clearer idea of what he is choosing. This wider and more informed choice may explain why 53% of the extravert husbands (but only 39% of the introverts) had at least three preferences in common with their wives. . .

Regardless of who is the extravert and who is the introvert in a marriage, the differences in sociability may cause problems. The extravert's wish for active sociability runs counter to the introvert's wish for privacy, especially when the introvert's work is socially demanding. The day's work may use up all the extraversion available; home represents a chance for the peace and quiet needed to regain a balance. If the extravert spouse wants to go out, to have people in, or at least to spend the time at home in conversation, frustration may develop. For the introvert, silence, some chance to think quietly, is essential and requires the partner's cooperation. This need is hard to explain and impossible for the extravert to understand unless it is explained. Once partners understand each other's needs for quiet or sociability, they can usually make constructive adjustments. . .

From the study of this sample (of 375 couples), several conclusions emerge. In these marriages, which were in no apparent difficulty, there is significantly more similarity than difference between husband and wife on each of the four preferences. This finding contrasts sharply with the observations of psychiatrists and marriage counsellors that the marriages they see exhibit more type differences than similarities. Similarity would appear to contribute to the success of a marriage.

Preferences held in common simplify human relations. They furnish a shortcut to understanding people, because it is easier to understand likeness than to understand difference. When people understand and admire someone whose type is close to theirs, they are, in a way, appreciating their own best qualities, which is enjoyable and productive though perhaps not as educational as appreciating someone quite different.

Even with only a single preference in common, a marriage can be wonderfully good (as I can testify) if the man and woman take the necessary pains to understand, appreciate, and respect each other. They will not regard differences between them as signs of inferiority, but as interesting variations in human nature, which enrich their lives. . .

Of course there are problems along the way, for example, the partner's faults. Those faults are probably only the reverse side of the partner's most admirable traits. A feeling man may value very much his thinking wife's strength, presence of mind in a crisis, steadiness in the face of possible disaster. The thinker is not going to take small things very seriously, except to note what should be done or should have been done. A thinker may fall in love with a feeling type's warm, quick response, which nourishes the thinker's own half-starved feeling. The feeling partner is not going to stop to consider the logic of every remark and action. Even the best of qualities tend to have inconvenient side effects, which may annoy those who do not see the reason for them, but the side effects are trivial in comparison with the good qualities from which they spring. . .

It is the appreciation of what is fine in each other that matters, and communication of that appreciation, not necessarily in sentimental words. Some people comfortably assume their appreciation of their partner is understood; they should occasionally make it explicit. If it is too hard to be articulate about the big things, they can speak out about the small ones. 'I like the way you laugh.' 'I looked across the room tonight and was so proud of you.' 'That was the best suggestion anyone made at the meeting.' 'You do think of the nicest things to do for people.' What one says will be remembered. . .

There are several pitfalls to be avoided by a feeling type and thinker married to each other. Feeling types should avoid being too talkative; one can easily talk too much to a thinker. Thinkers should not be too impersonal. They tend to think it obvious that by marrying a person they have demonstrated their esteem once and for all and their useful everyday acts demonstrate their concern for that person's well-being (it would probably be a little sentimental to refer to it as happiness); therefore, it seems to them superfluous to mention either fact. . .

Feeling types want nourishment for their feelings. Thinkers are less concerned with feelings than with cause and effect. In order to avoid mistakes, they look ahead from a proposed action to its probable effect; that is a profitable precaution. They also look back from an unsatisfactory state of affairs to its probable cause, so that they may discover what mistake was made and try to ensure that it will not be made again. When the mistake is their own, they benefit because they can change their own behavior as they see fit. If, however, they try to change their feeling partner's behavior by criticism, there is apt to be no benefit and a high cost. The feeling partner may react defensively, often at greater length than the thinker can tolerate with equanimity, and nothing is accomplished except frustration for the thinker and hurt for the feeling type.

If the thinking partner in a thinking-feeling marriage deeply wants some change in the feeling partner's behavior (something that will really make a difference to the thinker), the thinker's best approach is to avoid criticism altogether and simply express, as well as possible, the need and admiration for whatever it is the thinker desires. The feeling partner then has a valid incentive for making whatever effort is involved and doing it gladly. There is much nourishment for feeling in the thought that 'My spouse likes me to do this!' but none at all in 'doesn't like it if I don't.' The first is an accolade for excellence, the second a reproof for falling below the norm. This approach will probably work better than criticism in any marriage. It makes no demand; it simply appeals for something – much desired – which the partner has the power to give.

Many of the thinkers' criticisms are not uttered with any expectation of producing change. They are just thrown out in moving from one thought to another. Even if thinkers are aware of their critical tendency and curb it discreetly in their working hours and social contacts, they (particularly TJs) will feel that at home they are entitled to blow off steam, forcibly, picturesquely, and with the TJ's characteristic exaggeration for the sake of emphasis. Among the targets of their casual criticisms may be the feeling type's friends, relatives, religion, politics, opinions on any subject, or merely something just told with an intent to amuse the thinker; and in this exaggerated form, the criticisms will not be true. The feeling partner will often be tempted to defend something or somebody against this undue severity. The temptation should be stoutly resisted.

For the sake of family peace, it is important for the feeling partner to learn the art of dealing with this 'conversational criticism,' which does not point out something that really should be corrected, but merely expresses the thinker's negative views ('I don't see how you can stand a featherbrain like Jones!'). The feeling partner needs to grant the thinker the luxury of expressing negative views without reprisals.

The feeling partner should not argue in defence of Jones, but will not wish to seem to concur. A relaxed laugh at the thinker's comment acknowledges the right of thinking to hold any opinion it pleases; a cheerfully casual comment such as 'Jones has good points, too' reserves the same right to the feeling partner's own feeling, and the tone of voice dismisses the subject.

Someday the thinking partner may criticise so bluntly that it seems to take the very ground from under the feeling partner's feet. There are at least two possibilities other than that the feeling partner's world has come to an end. One is that the remark is a failure in communication; the thinking partner did not mean it the way it sounded, and does not feel the way the feeling partner would have to feel to say a thing like that. The other and more likely possibility is that it was not the thinker who said it. It was only the thinker's shadow.

In any marriage, a type difference may at times produce an outright conflict between opposite points of view. When this happens, the partners have a choice. One or both can assume that it is wrong of the other to be different – and be righteously indignant, which diminishes the partner. They can assume that it is wrong of themselves to be different – and be depressed, which is self-diminishing. Or they can acknowledge that each is justifiably and interestingly different from the other – and be amused. Their amusement may be warm or detached, wry or tender, according to their types, but it will help in working out the situation and keeping intact each partner's dignity and the precious fabric of their marriage.

Despite the fact that half of the population is introverted, we are led to believe that seeking company is in itself a 'good thing' and seeking solitude a 'bad thing'. It's about time we challenged this – or at least it's time we introverts did. The late eminent British psychiatrist Anthony Storr wrote a remarkable book first published in 1988 as *The School of Genius*, later titled *Solitude*. From the back cover of the book:

> Storr challenges the widely held view that success in personal relationships is the only key to happiness. He argues persuasively that we pay far too little attention to some of the other great satisfactions of life – work and creativity. In a series of skilful biographical sketches, among them Beethoven, Henry James, Goya, Wittgenstein, Kipling and Beatrix Potter, he demonstrates how many of the creative geniuses of our civilisation have been solitary, by temperament or circumstance, and how the capacity to be alone is, even for those who are not creative, a sign of maturity.

From the introduction:

> It is not only men and women of genius who may find their chief value in the impersonal rather than in the personal. I shall argue that interests, whether in writing history, breeding carrier pigeons, speculating in stocks and shares, designing aircraft, playing the piano, or gardening, play a greater part in the economy of human happiness than modern psychoanalysts and their followers allow. The great creators exemplify my thesis most aptly because their works remain as evidence. That mysterious being, the ordinary man or woman, leaves little behind to indicate the breadth and depth of interests which may, during a lifetime, have been major preoccupations. The rich may accumulate great collections of the works of others. Enthusiastic gardeners can be notably creative and leave evidence of their passion which lasts for years, if not for as long as a book or a painting. But nothing remains of a passion for windmills or cricket.
>
> Yet we must all have known people whose lives were actually made worthwhile by such interests, whether or not their human relationships were satisfactory. The burden of value with which we are at present loading interpersonal relationships is too heavy for those fragile craft to carry. Our expectation that satisfying intimate relationships should, ideally, provide happiness and that, if they do not, there must be something wrong with those relationships, seems to be exaggerated.
>
> Love and friendship are, of course, an important part of what makes life worthwhile. But they are not the only source of happiness. Moreover, human beings change and develop as life goes on. In old age, human relationships often become less important. Perhaps this is a beneficent arrangement of Nature, designed to ensure that the inevitable parting with loved ones will be less distressing. In any case, there is always an element of uncertainty in interpersonal relationships which should preclude them

from being idealised as an absolute or seen as constituting the only path toward personal fulfilment. *It may be our idealisation of interpersonal relationships in the West that causes marriage, supposedly the most intimate tie, to be so unstable* [Author's emphasis]. If we did not look to marriage as the principal source of happiness, fewer marriages would end in tears.

I shall argue that human beings are directed by Nature toward the impersonal as well as toward the personal, and that this feature of the human condition is a valuable and important part of our adaptation. We share with other animals the prime biological necessity of reproducing ourselves; of ensuring that our genes survive, though we do not. But the long span of human life which extends beyond the main reproductive period also has significance. It is then that the impersonal comes to assume a greater importance for the average person, although seeds of such interests have been present from the earliest years.

The great creators, as we shall see, may in some instances have been deflected from human relationships toward their own field of endeavour by adverse circumstances which made it difficult for them to achieve intimacy with others. But this is a matter of emphasis rather than substitution. It does not imply, as some psychoanalysts assume, that creative endeavour is invariably an alternative to human relationships. One might argue that people who have no abiding interests other than their spouses and families are as limited intellectually as those who have neither spouse nor children may be emotionally.

Many ordinary interests, and the majority of creative pursuits involving real originality, continue without involving relationships. It seems to me that what goes on in the human being when he is by himself is as important as what happens in his interactions with other people. Something like one third of our total lifespan is, in any case, spent in the isolation of sleep. Two opposing drives operate throughout life: the drive for companionship, love, and everything else which brings us close to our fellow men; and the drive toward being independent, separate, and autonomous. If we were to listen only to the psychoanalytic 'object-relation' theorists, we should be driven to conclude that none of us have validity as isolated individuals. From their standpoint, it appears that we possess value only in so far as we fulfil some useful function vis-à-vis other people, in our roles, for example, as spouse, parent, or neighbour. It follows that the justification for the individual's existence is the existence of others.

Yet some of the people who have contributed most to the enrichment of human experience have contributed little to the welfare of human beings in particular. It can be argued that some of the great thinkers were self-centred, alienated, or 'narcissistic'; more preoccupied with what went on in their own minds than with the welfare of other people. The same is true of many writers, composers, and painters. The creative person is constantly seeking to discover himself, to remodel his own identity, and to find meaning in the universe through what he creates. He finds this a valuable integrating process which, like meditation or prayer, has little to do with other people, but which has its own separate validity. His most significant moments are those in which he attains some new insight, or makes some new discovery; and these moments are chiefly, if not invariably, those in which he is alone.

Although major talent is rare, creative people remain human beings with the same needs and wishes as the rest of us. Because they leave behind records of their thoughts and feelings in their works, they exemplify, in striking fashion, aspects of human striving which are common to us all but which, in the case of ordinary people, escape notice. Perhaps the need of the creative person for solitude, and his preoccupation with internal processes of integration, can reveal something about the needs of the less gifted, more ordinary human being which is, at the time of writing, neglected.

From the chapter, 'The Significance of Human Relationships':

The current emphasis upon intimate interpersonal relationships as the touchstone of health and happiness is a comparatively recent phenomenon. Earlier generations would not have rated human relationships so highly; believing, perhaps, that the daily round, the common task, should furnish all we need to ask; or, alternatively, being too preoccupied with merely keeping alive and earning a living to have much time to devote to the subtleties of personal relations. Some observers, like Ernest Gellner, suggest that our present preoccupation with, and anxiety about, human relationships has replaced former anxieties about the unpredictability and precariousness of the natural world. He argues that, in modern affluent societies, most of us are protected from disease, poverty, hunger, and natural catastrophes to an extent undreamed of by previous generations. But modern industrial societies are unstable and lacking in structure. Increased mobility has undermined the pillars of society. Because we have more choice as to where we live, what society we should join, and what we should make of our lives, our relations with the other people who constitute our environment are no longer defined by age-old rules and have therefore become matters of increasing concern and anxiety. As Gellner puts it, 'Our environment is now made up basically of relationships with others.'

Gellner goes on to affirm that the realm of personal relations has become 'the area of our most pressing concern'. Our anxieties in this field are compounded by the decline of religious belief. Religion not only provided rules of conduct regarding personal relationships, but also offered a more predictable, stable alternative. Relationships with spouse, children, or neighbours might be difficult, unfulfilling, or unstable; but, so long as one continued to believe in Him, the same could not be said of one's relationship with God.

Although I am far from agreeing with everything which Gellner has to say in his book about psychoanalysis, I think he is right in alleging that psychoanalysis promises a form of salvation; and that this kind of salvation is to be attained by purging the individual of the emotional blocks or blind spots which prevent him from achieving fulfilling interpersonal relationships. Gellner is also right in thinking that psychoanalysis has exerted so widespread an influence that it has become the dominant idiom for the discussion of human personality and personal relationships even by those who do not subscribe to all its doctrines.

From the chapter, 'The Capacity to Be Alone':

Modern psychotherapists, including myself, have taken as their criterion of emotional maturity the capacity of the individual to make mature relationships on equal terms. With few exceptions, psychotherapists have omitted to consider the fact that the capacity to be alone is also an aspect of emotional maturity.

One such exception is the psychoanalyst, Donald Winnicott. In 1958, Winnicott published a paper on 'The Capacity to Be Alone' which has become a psychoanalytic classic. Winnicott wrote:

It is probably true to say that in psychoanalytical literature more has been written on the *fear* of being alone or the *wish* to be alone than on the *ability* to be alone; also a considerable amount of work has been done on the withdrawn state, a defensive organisation implying an expectation of persecution. It would seem to me that a discussion on the positive aspects of the capacity to be alone is overdue.

Marriage must be particularly difficult for people who are *loners*. All too often the term is used in a pejorative manner. Which brings us on to a gem of a book, Anneli Rufus's *Party of One (The Loners' Manifesto)* (2003). From the back cover:

Isaac Newton, Michelangelo . . . they and countless others belong to a subculture that will never hold hands, a group whose voices will never form a chorus. They are loners – and they have at least one thing in common: They keep to themselves. And they like it that way.

Self-reliant, each loner swims alone through a social world – a world of teams, troops and groups – that scorns and misunderstands those who stand apart. Everywhere from newspapers to playgrounds, loners are accused of being crazy, cold, stuck-up, standoffish, selfish, sad, bad, secretive and lonely – and, of course, serial killers. Loners, however, know better than anyone how to entertain themselves – and how to contemplate and to create. They have a knack for imagination, concentration, inner discipline and invention – a talent for not being bored.

Too often, loners buy into society's messages and strive to change, making themselves miserable in the process by hiding their true nature – and hiding *from* it. In *Party of One*, Anneli Rufus delivers a long-overdue argument in praise of loners. Assembling evidence from diverse areas of culture, Rufus recognises loners as a vital force in world civilisation rather than damaged goods who need to be 'fixed'. A compelling, morally urgent tour de force, *Party of* One rebuts the prevailing notion that aloneness is indistinguishable from loneliness, and that the only experiences that matter are shared ones.

Rufus has some interesting points to make on her own marriage, and has advice on suitable partners for those loners who want one:

I'm married. To a loner. That makes two of us. Returning to the math-class metaphor, you might argue that *loner + loner = nonloners*, that being together obviates our loner status, cancels out our claim. Arguing back, I would say, 'Look at us' – well, don't, we're in our pyjamas, but I swear we're still loners, now as before. One of the public's biggest misconceptions is that loners care nothing for love: that we do not, cannot. Yet what drove Emily Dickinson's fieriest poems? Marie Curie, half of one of science's most famous and devoted couples, was a loner. . .

My loner husband and I live in a house masked by green hedges from nonexistent passersby on a lane so obscure that it has no sidewalks, in a district remote from the flutter of life in town, the route from there to here a maze of switchbacks on heart-attack grades. People who have spent decades in our town have never heard of our street. We know no one will ever just drop in. We knew that when we found the place, hidden in plain view as if under an enchantment. That was one of its major attractions. The realtor suggested cutting down the hedge. We caught each other's eyes and smirked. . .

As writers, pursuing a solitary profession, we hole up silently in different corners of the house. Mean as it feels to admit, each of us secretly applauds when the other goes out on errands, leaving the whole house empty save one, though neither of us wants those errands to last long. On holidays it is just us. Weekends, just us. To extraverts, this might all seem so inhospitable, so isolationist. But we have gone to great lengths to make our lives this way, on purpose.

In meeting him, I was lucky. I was not looking. (Lucky!) We hit it off right away, and one of the likenesses we recognised in one another at once was that we were loners. When two loners meet in a potentially romantic situation, the relief surges like a tidal wave. We are so much more likely to meet nonloners. And say we bond with one, say attraction or intellect or a shared interest in *Sailor Moon* overcomes this fundamental difference. . .

Loners who want partners are better off with loners. But if meeting strangers is difficult for loners, loners are also the most difficult strangers in the world to meet. Summon every dram of nerve and try a singles bar, a baseball game, a dance class – nonloners, nonloners everywhere. Scan the personal ads, and you will find phalanxes of nonloners for whom reaching out is the natural impulse. At parties, spy the loner lurking in the kitchen pretending to look for ice or napkins, or hovering by the door eager to leave. The loner at the party tries to appear occupied, peering with sham absorption at the liquid in her wineglass or the Erté poster next to his solitary post in a stiff chair no one else wants in the corner farthest from the sound system. Then again, sometimes it is he who mans the system, changing CDs and adjusting the volume with such busy efficiency that nobody would think to interrupt him. When the dancing starts, she freezes. Not a single tendon betrays the fact that she hears a beat. Not one thumb lifts. As couples rise and swirl and pound the floor, she vanishes. One way or another, she does.

Loners, if you can catch them, are well worth the trouble. Not dulled by excess human contact, not blasé or focused on your crotch while jabbering about themselves, loners are curious, vigilant, full of surprises. They do not cling. Separate wherever they go, awake or asleep, they shimmer with the iridescence of hidden things seldom seen.

On to genetics and the impact our genetic heritage might have on the likelihood of ourselves divorcing. I have a personal interest in this matter because my maternal grandmother left my grandfather when my mother was only five years old, in Canada in 1933; my mother and father separated when I was about eight years old; and I left my first wife and children when our youngest child was seven. Could there possibly be a genetic component to individuals' propensity to leave their spouses?

Which brings us to the paper *Genetic Influence on Risk of Divorce* written by Matt McGue and David Lykken of the Department of Psychology at the University of Minnesota, and published in *Psychological Science*, the Journal of the American Psychological Society, in 1992. I'm not a psychologist so I'll reproduce elements of the paper as presented, and keep my own views to a minimum. You might like to have a large dictionary to hand for this section. And a mug of strong coffee. But it's worth working through, for it has important implications for marriage and divorce:

If current rates persist, more than a third of all US children will experience the breakup of their parents' marriages (Bumpass, 1984). The impact of this disturbing demographic trend on offspring functioning is not fully known, but is likely to be complex and diverse. While it is clear that parental divorce is associated with significant psychological disturbance in some children, others appear to be largely unaffected (Emery, 1988).

Furthermore, recent longitudinal surveys in both the United States and Great Britain indicate that the adjustment difficulties seen with the children of divorced parents predate the time of parental separation (Block, Block, & Gjerde, 1986; Cherlin et al, 1991), suggesting that parental conflict rather than separation per se may be the critical variable influencing offspring adjustment.

An alternative explanation, which receives some empirical support in the present report, is that parental divorce and offspring adjustment difficulties share, in part, a genetic diathesis. That is, genetic risk factors that contribute to liability for divorce in the parents may also contribute to psychological maladjustment in their children.

Although much is known about divorces correlates, relatively little is known about its causes. Significant secular changes in divorce rates substantiate the importance of concomitant cultural changes in, for example, judicial practices (Weitzman, 1981) and female employment (Cherlin, 1981). Nonetheless, it remains difficult to forecast accurately within a given cohort which marriages will or will not end in dissolution.

While a previous divorce (Martin & Bumpass, 1989), an early age at marriage (Norton & Glick, 1979), premarital pregnancy (Billy, Lansdale, & McLaughlin, 1986), and unstable employment (Kelly, 1982) are all related to divorce risk, the vast majority of marriages ending in divorce carry none of these known risk factors.

Perhaps the most robust predictor of divorce risk is family background. Pope and Mueller (1979) summarised results from five large epidemiological surveys and reported that approximately 10% more of the marriages of respondents with divorced parents ended in divorce than the marriages of respondents without divorced parents. Although this association has been consistently replicated (eg Glenn & Kramer, 1987), the magnitude of the familial effect has been characterised as 'modest' (Kulka & Weingarten, 1979).

These previous family studies of divorce have considered the family background of only one of the principals. As we show here, the risk of marital dissolution is a function of the aggregate risk brought to the marriage by both spouses; when family background of both spouses is considered, the importance of familial factors no longer appears modest.

In the present study, divorce status was obtained on a sample of 722 monozygotic (identical) and 794 same-sex dizygotic (non-identical) twins, their parents, and their spouses' parents. Results strongly implicate a genetic influence on divorce risk. . .

We found a significant relation between parental divorce and offspring divorce. Indeed, the increase from 19% to 29% in rate of divorce among children of divorced parents falls well within the range reported by Pope and Mueller in four large samples of Caucasian Americans . . . The odds of divorce increase nearly sixfold if one has an identical twin who is divorced, but less than twofold if one has a parent or non-identical twin who is divorced, suggesting that divorce risk is strongly associated with genetic factors. . .

Our finding no evidence for shared environmental effects, although seemingly remarkable, is, nonetheless, commonplace in the behavioral genetics literature (Plomin & Daniels, 1987). . .

Our data implicate the importance of genetic factors in the prediction of divorce risk; the data do not, however, specify the mechanism that generates this association. Although it is clear that no single factor could account for the etiology of something as heterogeneous as divorce, we hypothesise that the genetic influence on divorce risk is mediated largely by inherited personality characteristics.

A couple is more likely to maintain a long-term relationship if both members hold strong traditional moral convictions than if they do not [Author's emphasis]; they are more likely to remain married if their union is a source of pleasure than if it is a source of distress.

There is much evidence relating personal values and individual capacity for happiness to risk of divorce. Thus, divorce is more likely among individuals who drop out of school (eg college dropouts) as compared with individuals who complete their educational commitments (eg high school graduates who do not pursue college degrees; Norton & Moorman, 1987); among individuals with an unstable pattern of employment as compared with those who are stably employed (Kelly, 1982); among individuals who marry before the age of 20 years as compared with individuals who wait until they attain the societally prescribed age of majority (Norton & Moorman, 1987); among individuals who have experienced an out-of-wedlock pregnancy as compared with those who have not (Billy et al, 1986); among individuals who are rated highly neurotic as compared with those who derive much pleasure from their lives (Kelly & Conley, 1987); and, finally, among those who are seen as impulsive as compared with those who are behaviorally controlled (Kelly & Conley, 1987). We predict that twins' concordance and discordance for divorce will be accounted for largely by similarity and difference in key personality factors. We are presently collecting the data necessary to test this prediction.

Finally, our findings have broad implications for understanding the effects of parental divorce on offspring functioning. Undoubtedly, some children with divorced parents suffer significant emotional, social and economic hardships not suffered by other children.

Our results suggest further that children whose parents divorce differ genetically from children whose parents do not divorce. Some children of divorced parents experience significant academic difficulties and externalising behavioral disorders, while others appear to be largely unaffected (Barber & Eckles, 1992), heterogeneity which we suspect may be due to genotype-environment interaction. That is, childhood adjustment difficulties may occur only with those offspring who both inherit a strong genetic diathesis (as reflected by dense family history) and are exposed to significant environmental provocation (eg parental conflict, limited economic resources). . .

So it is likely that 'key personality factors' govern individuals' propensity to divorce. But these factors are largely genetically determined and therefore would not have changed in the recent historical past. Is it reasonable to assert that we are now seeing something approaching the 'natural' rate of divorce in the developed world, at least among people not deterred from divorcing by cultural, financial, religious, and other considerations? I believe so. And it follows, I believe, that the lower divorce rate in previous times stemmed more from a lack of opportunity to divorce – in particular due to women's financial dependency on men before the modern era – rather than any higher degree of contentment in marriage. Tellingly, most divorce proceedings in the modern era are initiated by women.

The reality is that many children today in the developed world are not brought up within stable, loving families. Many are brought up within an environment of parents who are hostile to one another, but who remain together for financial or cultural or religious considerations, possibly with a vague feeling that they're at least doing something noble, 'staying together for the sake of the kids'. I have a strong suspicion that the 'kids card' is often played by the partner least willing to separate, in an effort to pile guilt on the other partner and thereby prevent him or her from leaving the family.

Because I'm an introvert I'm especially aware of how introversion can cause problems in marriage and indeed other relationships. But are there characteristics of *extraverts* that might cause problems in marriage? It's time to introduce you to an acquaintance, Paul Carrington, who first provided me with at least one answer to the question. Paul is the most extraverted person I've ever met. He's very well-known in my adopted home town of Bedford, England, as a 'larger than life' character, and he frequently plays the guitar and sings in public houses and clubs in the area. He always reminds me of the British comedian Al Murray's creation 'The Pub Landlord', and he also makes money as a self-employed chauffeur.

I've come to know Paul fairly well over the past few years. His colourful life story, along with those of seven other well-known guitarists who live in or near Bedford, is related in my book *Guitar Gods in Beds. (Bedfordshire: a Heavenly County)*. In the book he's titled 'Thunderin' Paul Carrington'.

After the failure of my second marriage in June 2007 I was in need of some rest, and Paul agreed to accompany me on a month-long holiday in France in August 2007. We enjoyed ourselves so much that we had another month-long holiday in France in July 2008. My book *Two Men in a Car (A Businessman, a Chauffeur, and Their Holidays in France)* relates the politically incorrect stories of the two holidays.

Over the holidays Paul and I discussed relationships in general, and marriage in particular, at some length. He himself had married three times (to Yugoslavian, Italian, and Ugandan women) and he was candid about his infidelities in most of his relationships with women, including his first two marriages. (One of his anecdotes about infidelity is to be found in *Guitar Gods in Beds*. It concerns a young Polish girl who visited his house when his wife was away on a short holiday. Unknown to Paul, the girl stole his wife's brand new shoes and left her own damaged shoes for his wife to find, by way of replacement.) Paul is very clear that marriage isn't a natural institution for most men and one of his typically robust sayings is, 'It's only adultery if you get caught!'

I strongly suspected that extraverts were *intrinsically* more likely to be adulterous than introverts. An internet search on the subject brought up the research abstract of an interesting paper written by an American researcher in the mid 1990s. The following is an extract:

Many studies have been conducted on how personality affects personal preferences or behaviors. Previous research has indicated that extraverts demonstrate a greater tendency toward promiscuity, a high rate of change in sexual partners and a high rate of sexual encounters. While studies regarding attitudes about sexual infidelity in dating and marital relationships have found that infidelity is more acceptable to men than women, infidelity in committed dating relationships is significantly more acceptable than marital infidelity.

The current research project was interested in whether a certain personality type or category was predictive of a person's tendency to be unfaithful. Specifically, this study is interested in determining if one, or more, personality type(s) was related to infidelity. Infidelity was defined as participation in behaviors determined unfaithful while involved in a monogamous relationship (ie a relationship based on the assumption of exclusive involvement). In today's society, infidelity can have detrimental effects ranging from mild/severe psychological implications to death. The people participating in unfaithful behaviors put not only themselves at risk, but also the people with whom they are involved.

482 subjects accessed a personal web page containing the experiment. There were 345 males and 137 females, so roughly 71% of the participants were males. 90% of subjects involved in this experiment had some level of college experience. Each subject took two surveys. . .

Completed surveys resulted in individual personality categories and fidelity rating of either faithful or unfaithful for each participant.

It was predicted that one, or more, personality type categories would be indicative of either faithful or unfaithful tendencies. Extraversion was the personality type category predicted to indicate a tendency toward infidelity.

The personality type was obtained by calculating the number of responses in each category. For example, a total of 10 questions were presented for the extraverted or introverted category. Each question contained one extraversion response and one introversion response. A subject obtaining an extraverted personality type would have to choose at least 6 of 10 extraversion responses. The fidelity score was obtained by determining if the subject had been unfaithful according to the answers chosen on the list of behaviors, as well as the responses chosen for the time factors. The list of behaviors (someone asked you for a date and you accepted, you asked someone out on a date, sexual intercourse, kissing, petting (breast or genital fondling, oral sex) were rated on a scale of 1 to 5. One being rated as faithful and five as unfaithful . . . Extraversion was the only category of personality to result in significant findings.

A final thought on introversion, from introverted Alan J (42), a businessman. I've never known a person read so many books on so many topics, both fiction and non-fiction, over so many years. When he takes his wife and teenage daughters to a shopping centre, he sits happily in Waterstone's and reads books for an hour or two, while they go shopping. I asked him why he thought introverts like himself are often avid book readers. He replied, 'Because books are more interesting than people. No damned small talk from them. To be perfectly honest, there are very few people's company that I prefer to my own.'

5

LOVE, LUST, SEX, FANTASY,
GENDER RANCOUR, ROMANTIC FICTION

Oh, life is a glorious cycle of song,
A medley of extemporanea;
And love is a thing that can never go wrong;
And I am Marie of Roumania.

(Dorothy Parker, *Comment*)

This chapter covers:

-   The evolution and psychology of love
-   Love as a solution to 'the commitment problem'
-   How men and women deceive each other
-   The commonality of adultery
-   Romantic love as 'a necessary madness'
-   Men and women's different fantasies
-   Gender rancour
-   Sexual arousal in men and women
-   Pornography, satisfying men's fantasies
-   The myth of the intensely erotic, mutually enjoyable, guilt-free, emotionally open, lifelong monogamous pair-bond
-   Romantic fiction, satisfying women's fantasies
-   How Adam Perry persuaded 3,000 women to sleep with him in ten years
-   Criminalising men who wish to pay for sex in the United Kingdom
-   The English Collective of Prostitutes' briefing paper on the Police and Crime Bill (2009)

Yale University Press published a fascinating book in 2006, *The New Psychology of Love*. Its declared aim is to 'present the full range of psychological theories on love – biological, taxonomical, implicit, cultural – updated with the latest research in the field'.

The book has more than a dozen expert contributors. The extract below is from a chapter titled 'The Evolution of Love', written by David Buss, a professor of psychology at the University of Texas (Austin):

LOVE AS A COMMITMENT DEVICE

If love is a universal human emotion, why did evolution install it in the human brain to begin with? Keys to the mystery come from three unique departures of humans from their most recent primate ancestors: (1) the evolution of long-term mating, (2) the concealment of female ovulation, and (3) the heavy investment by men in their children. Chimpanzees, our closest primate relatives, mate primarily when the female enters oestrus. Her bright red genital swellings and olfactory scents send males into a sexual frenzy. Outside of oestrus, males are largely indifferent to females. Among humans, ovulation is concealed or cryptic, at least for the most part. Although there might be subtle physical changes in women – a slight glowing of the skin or an almost imperceptible increase in her sexual desire – there is no solid evidence that men can actually detect when women ovulate.

The concealment of ovulation coincided with several other critical changes. Men and women started having sex throughout the menstrual cycle, not just around ovulation. Men and women engaged in long-term pair-bonded mating over the expanse of years or decades. And men, unlike their chimpanzee cousins, began investing heavily in offspring. Meat from the hunt went to provision the children, not just the mate and kin.

It requires taking a step back to realize how extraordinary these changes are. Some females began allocating their entire reproductive careers to a single male, rather than to whomever happened to be the reigning alpha male when they happened to be ovulating. Males began to guard their partners against rival males who might be tempted to lure their mates. Surplus resources that in many species go to the female as a specific inducement to copulation now were channelled to the wife and children. Indeed, males now had added incentive to acquire surplus resources, mostly in the form of hunted meat. Long-term mating, in short, involved the allocation of reproductively relevant resources to a single mate over a virtually unprecedented span of time. . .

The evolution of long-term mating required installing in the human psychological architecture a set of circuits designed to ensure a reasonable reproductive payoff to allocating all of one's resources to a single partner. It required some means for determining that one particular mate, above all other potential mates, would be there through thick and thin, through sickness and health. It required a solution to the problem of commitment.

My own initial outline of an evolutionary theory of love accords with that of the evolutionary economist Robert Frank: that the emotion we call love is, in part, an evolved solution to the problem of commitment. If a partner chooses you for rational reasons, he or she might leave you for the same rational reasons: finding someone slightly more desirable on all of the 'rational' criteria. This creates a commitment problem: How can you be sure that a person will stay with you? If your partner is blinded by an uncontrollable love that cannot be helped and cannot be chosen, a love for only you and no other, then commitment will not waver when you are in sickness rather than in health, when you are poorer rather than richer.

Love overrides rationality. It is the emotion that ensures that you will not leave when someone more desirable comes along. Love, in short, may be a solution to the commitment problem, providing a signal to the partner of strong long-term intent and resolve.

The causal arrow almost certainly also runs in reverse. Love may be the psychological reward we experience when the problem of commitment is successfully being solved. It is a mind/body opium that signals that the adaptive problems of mate selection, sexual congress, devotion, and loyalty have been met with triumph. The scientific explanation is that evolution has installed in the human brain reward mechanisms that keep us performing activities that lead to successful reproduction. The downside is that the drug sometimes wears off. Nothing in life comes with a guarantee. And after the drug wears off, we may leave a relationship that has outlasted its warrant, and fall in love with someone new. Commitment does not necessarily mean commitment for life. Love is both a solution to the commitment problem and an intoxicating reward for successfully solving it. . .

SNAKES IN THE GARDEN OF LOVE
Unfortunately that is not the happy end to the evolutionary love story. There are snakes in the garden, troubles in emotional paradise. One sort of trouble comes from the dual strategies in the human menu of mating. Once the desire for love exists, it can be exploited and manipulated ruthlessly. Men deceive women about the depth of their loving feelings, for example, to gain short-term sexual access. As Ovid noted, 'love is . . . a sexual behavior sport in which duplicity is used in order that a man might win his way into a woman's heart and subsequently into her boudoir.' Women, in turn, have evolved defences against being sexually exploited by imposing a longer courtship process before consenting to sex, attempting to detect deception, and evolving superior ability to decode nonverbal signals.

Women, too, engage in deception, but of a different sort. Whereas men are more likely to feign love in order to get sex, women are more likely to use sex as a means of getting love. One strategy is the 'bait and switch' tactic, whereby a woman might offer what appears to be 'costless sex' in the context of short-term mating, and then intercalate herself into a man's mind, transforming the relationship into one of long-term love. Just as women have evolved defences against false declarations of love at the hands of men, so it is reasonable to assume that men have evolved defences against being lured into long-term love when it is against their fitness interests to do so. The arms race of deception and detection of deception, of strategies and counterstrategies, continues with no end in sight. Because the reproductive interests of a man and a woman are rarely perfectly aligned, evolution has favoured strategies in each sex that can be carried out only at the expense of the other sex. . .

Another problem is that what comes up often comes down. People fall out of love as crashingly as they fall in love. We cannot predict with certainty who will fall out of love, but recent studies provide some critical clues. Just as the fulfilment of desire looms large when falling in love, violations of desire portend conflict and dissolution. A man who was chosen in part for his kindness and drive may be rejected when he turns cruel or lazy. A woman chosen in part for her youth and beauty may lose out when a newer model beckons her partner. An initially considerate partner may turn condescending. And a couple's infertility after repeated episodes of sex prompts each to seek a more fruitful union elsewhere.

The most crushing blow to long-term love comes from the harsh metric of the mating market. A mated couple initially equivalent on overall desirability may experience a widening gap over time. Consider an entry-level professional couple. If the woman's career skyrockets and the man gets fired, it puts a strain on both because their market values now differ. Sudden increases in status open up new mating opportunities. A '9' who was previously out of reach now becomes available (for the woman). In the evolutionary jungle of mating, we may admire a woman who stands by her loser husband. But few of those who did are our ancestors. Modern humans descended from those who traded up when the increment was sufficient to outweigh the manifold costs people experience as a consequence of breaking up.

From the same book, in a chapter titled 'The Drive to Love', by Helen Fisher:

Only 3% of mammals pair up to rear their young. *Homo sapiens* is among them. Today some 90% of women and men marry by age 50 in all but a few countries, and cross-cultural data confirm that humans primarily practice social monogamy, forming a socially recognised pair-bond with a single mate at a time. Although polygyny is permitted in 84% of human societies, in the vast majority of these cultures only about 10% of men actually maintain two or more wives simultaneously. Moreover, because polygyny in humans is regularly associated with rank and wealth, Daly and Wilson propose that monogamy was even more prevalent in prehorticultural, unstratified societies. . .

Humans are also adulterous. The National Opinion Research Centre in Chicago reports that approximately 23% of men and 15% of women cheat at some point during marriage. Other studies indicate that from 30%–50% of married men and women philander. Scholars may never establish the true frequency of adultery in either sex, due to reporting bias. Nevertheless, studies of American adultery from the 1920s through the 1990s report its occurrence. Extra-pair copulations occur frequently in every other society for which data are available, as well as in many other socially monogamous species. . .

Human divorce and remarriage, as well, and biological (as well as cultural) forces may be involved. Data on 58 human societies, taken from the *Demographic Yearbook of the United Nations* between 1947 and 1989, indicate a worldwide divorce peak during and around the fourth year of marriage. Because four years is the characteristic duration of birth spacing in hunting/gathering societies, and because many other socially monogamous avian and mammalian species form pair-bonds that last only long enough to rear the young through infancy, I have hypothesised that this human cross-cultural divorce peak represents the remains of a specific ancestral hominid reproductive strategy to remain together at least long enough to raise a single child through infancy.

The British clinical psychologist Frank Tallis, in his remarkable 2004 book *Love Sick*, convincingly explains that romantic love is 'a necessary madness designed to keep us together just long enough to guarantee the survival of the species', echoing David Buss's point. The reader is left in no doubt about the transient nature of romantic love, and its lack of fitness for sustaining long-term relationships. Tallis considers 'companionate love' more suited to the task. Examining historical artistic works, he writes:

> Even a superficial examination of artistic works on the theme of love will reveal a striking duality. Love is rarely described as a wholly pleasant experience. It is an amalgam of seemingly incompatible and ungovernable mood states. When in love, individuals describe odd combinations of pleasure and pain, rapture and grief, ecstasy and disappointment. Love seems to provide a shuttle service between only two destinations: heaven and hell. . . For as long as people have been writing about love, they have also been describing it as an illness. Indeed, the illness or sickness metaphor is one of the most consistent features of love poetry and love songs throughout the ages. There are many answers to the question 'What is love?' but 'A kind of illness' is one that appears (and reappears) with remarkable frequency. . .
>
> As we shall see, the illness metaphor is remarkably illuminating. If we are guided by its subtle logic, we will be able to answer questions such as: Why do men fall in love more than women? Why do women tend to become more addicted to love than men? Why do all lovers see their partners – at least for a time – as beautiful (irrespective of how they really look)? Why is heartbreak so painful? And why does wild, passionate love rarely last?

Tallis points out that *Homo sapiens* is the only living species with the intelligence to 'transcend' its instincts, as manifested for example in its use of contraception (whether through natural or artificial means). So a mechanism had to evolve to ensure the future of the species:

> New arrivals do tend to have a detrimental effect on the quality of the mother and the father's relationship. Research shows that marital satisfaction plummets after the birth of a first child. Subsequent children

reduce marital satisfaction even further. Sometimes there is an enormous discrepancy between what our genes make us do, and what actually makes us happy. . .

The conflict between intellect and evolutionary objectives does not arise in animals for obvious reasons: animals simply follow their instincts. When it comes to sexual reproduction, they are simply automata – and, to a very large extent, so are we. However, the very fact that we can self-reflect, and rebel, has perhaps necessitated the evolution of a safety mechanism – an emotional swamping of the mental apparatus to ensure that fundamental evolutionary objectives are met. We call this safety mechanism 'love'.

Another British clinical psychologist, Oliver James, had some interesting points to make on 'Sex and attraction as causes of gender rancour' in his 1998 bestseller, *Britain on the Couch: Treating a Low Serotonin Society.*

Worldwide, there appear to be substantial and consistent differences between the sexes as to what attracts them, what they fantasise about sexually, and what they want in bed. Let it be said at the outset that men will probably tend to be more enthusiastic about these findings than women, that most of the research on which they are based was done by men, and that some women may even find them insulting and offensive.

Despite these disclaimers, there is not much doubt that what you are about to read is true of the average man and woman all over the world today.

COMPARED WITH WOMEN, MEN . . .

- Value physical attractiveness higher than women whether it be for marriage, a date or casual sex
- Prefer partners who are younger than them and marry younger partners
- Care less about the social status and wealth of partners if they are physically attractive or actually prefer lower status and wealth in partners
- Place a higher premium on sexual intercourse
- Are keener on the idea of casual sex, more indiscriminate when considering it, think more often about sex, are more unfaithful and have more partners in practice
- Fantasise about a greater variety of partners, masturbate more, are more explicit about sexual acts during fantasies, picturing precise features of partners' anatomies, such as genitalia, and are more likely to base their fantasies on real people and situations
- Fantasise more about 'doing things to', rather than 'having things done to'
- Are more jealous of sexual infidelity

COMPARED WITH MEN, WOMEN . . .

- Place a higher value on the wealth and status of potential mates – even if they are themselves of high status and wealth
- Prefer and marry partners who are older than them
- Are more influenced by negative information about a potential mate
- Place less emphasis on sexual intercourse as a goal, are more faithful and have fewer partners overall
- Fantasise less about sex, are less sexually explicit in the fantasies, focus more on the build-up than the climax, focus more on the emotions and settings of the fantasies, are more likely to ascribe the partners a profession and personality and are more likely to base the fantasy on their imagination than on real people or situations
- Are more jealous of emotional rather than sexual infidelity

When I began to research this chapter, I was amazed at how abundant and robust is the evidence for these assertions, cross-nationally and historically. Despite several decades of intense debate and pressure for equality, apart from in a few respects, what women and men want sexually does not appear to have changed very much. The cliché that 'men use love to get sex and women use sex to get love' still has more than a little truth to it (as we shall see, it seems that you could equally substitute 'status, power and wealth' for the word 'love'). Why are men and women still so different? Will the differences remain, say, 50 years from now? Above all, has the durability of these differences affected gender rancour and, therefore, rates of depression and serotonin levels since 1950?

That these differences have endured has led some sociobiologists to go so far as to claim victory in the gender debate: 'despite decades of feminism, genes will out'. As we shall see, this is premature. There is still a long way to go before we know for sure what, if any, psychological differences in this area have been inherited. There are still good grounds for supposing that they could be largely a matter of conditioning, and evidence regarding the first two questions is inconclusive. But in the meantime, I do believe that the durability of these differences, coupled with recent social trends, is causing a good deal of gender rancour and adding significantly to our unhappiness.

The heart of the matter is that they cause considerable role strain for both genders in the sexual realm. The media still exploit these differences in films, magazines, advertisements, popular songs and books. Put crudely, the women are portrayed as wanting rich, powerful men, the men as wanting 'babes', and the products sell because these narratives play to audiences' real preferences to a surprising degree.

Yet alongside this commercial exploitation of our desires (whether natural or nurtured), there is also another pressure from the media which is telling us that it should not be so and offering a new way. Men are under considerable pressure to value women as people and as equals, and women to become independent and thrusting. Both sexes are being pulled in two directions and this increases aggression and depression. For, if it is true that most men still basically want to have sex with young, pretty women, think about sex more, want it as often as possible and still tend to be focused on intercourse as the goal, then these desires will clash with the contrasting desires of women listed above and with the prevailing ideology that men 'should' value women as human beings.

Most men want the old traditional femininity in women and are upset by the New Woman. Some men react angrily when their predilections are criticised or rejected by women and in the media; others conceal their 'true' predilections behind a carapace of New Man attitudes and feel dissatisfied; others still feel guilty or even 'unnatural' when they find themselves fantasising about what they really want.

Meanwhile, if most women still basically want a 'good catch' – a relatively well-to-do, high-status, older man – who will make a solid breadwinner and father, and if they are less focused on sex in general and intercourse in particular, these desires will also conflict with the desires of men listed above and the prevailing ideology that the New Woman should be an independent equal with the sexual appetites of the New Woman in *Cosmopolitan* magazine articles. In some cases this leads to a self-contradictory position in which a woman may be cursing 'the lack of real men who are not just wimps' in one breath and complaining of the overbearing arrogance or intransigence of men in the next.

Some women are furious when men exhibit classically male desires; others pretend to be New Women in front of their girl friends but act Old Woman with men; and others still act New Woman all the time and guiltily nurse Old Woman fantasies. Yet again, both sexes end up losers.

Steven Pinker, a Canadian-American psychology professor, has much of interest to say about the topic of sexual arousal in *How the Mind Works*, published in 1997, including:

> An awakening of male sexual desire by a new partner is known as the Coolidge effect, after a famous anecdote. One day President Calvin Coolidge and his wife were visiting a government farm and were taken on separate tours. When Mrs Coolidge was shown the chicken pens she asked whether the rooster copulated more than once a day. 'Dozens of times,' replied the guide. 'Please tell that to the president,' Mrs Coolidge requested. When the president was shown the pens and told about the rooster, he asked, 'Same hen every time?' 'Oh, no, Mr President, a different one each time.' The president said, 'Tell that to Mrs Coolidge.'
>
> Many male mammals are indefatigable when a new willing female is available after each copulation. They cannot be fooled by the experimenter cloaking a previous partner or masking her scent. This shows, incidentally, that male sexual desire is not exactly 'undiscriminating.' Males may not care what *kind of* female they mate with, but they are hypersensitive to *which* female they mate with. . .
>
> Men do not have the sexual stamina of roosters, but they show a kind of Coolidge effect in their desire over longer periods. In many cultures,

including our own, men report that their sexual ardour for their wives wanes in the first years of marriage. It is the concept of the individual person, not her appearance or other qualities, that triggers the decline; the taste for new partners is not just an example of variety being the spice of life, as in getting bored with strawberry and wanting to try chocolate ripple . . .

The male of the human species is aroused by the sight of a nude woman, not only in the flesh but in movies, photographs, drawings, postcards, dolls . . . He takes pleasure in this mistaken identity, supporting a worldwide pornography industry which in the United States alone grosses ten billion dollars a year, almost as much as spectator sports and the movies combined. . .

Pornography is similar the world over and was much the same a century ago as it is today. It depicts in graphic physical detail a succession of anonymous nude females eager for casual, impersonal sex.

It would make no sense for a woman to be easily aroused by the sight of a nude male. A fertile woman never has a shortage of willing sexual partners, and in that buyer's market she can seek the best husband available, the best genes, or other returns on her sexual favours. If she could be aroused by the sight of a naked man, men could induce her to have sex by exposing themselves and her bargaining position would be compromised.

The reactions of the sexes to nudity are quite different: men see nude women as a kind of invitation, women see nude men as a kind of threat. Women do not seek the sight of naked male strangers or enactments of anonymous sex, and there is virtually no female market for pornography. (*Playgirl*, the supposed counterexample, is clearly for gay men. It has no ads for any product a woman would buy, and when a woman has a subscription as a gag gift she finds herself on mailing lists for gay male pornography and sex toys.). . .

The desire for sexual variety is an unusual adaptation, for it is insatiable. Most commodities of fitness show diminishing returns or an optimal level. People do not seek mass quantities of air, food, and water, and they want to be not too hot and not too cold but just right. But the more women a man has sex with, the more offspring he leaves; too much is never enough. That gives men a limitless appetite for casual sex partners (and perhaps for the commodities that in ancestral environments would have led to multiple partners, such as power and wealth). Everyday life offers most men few opportunities to plumb the bottom of the desire, but occasionally a man is rich, famous, handsome, and amoral enough to try. Georges Simenon and Hugh Hefner claimed to have had thousands of partners; the late 7'1" basketball player 'Wilt' Chamberlain estimated that he had 20,000. [Author's note: Does this explain the nickname 'Wilt'?] Say we liberally adjust for braggadocio and assume that Chamberlain inflated his estimate by a factor of, say, ten. That would still mean that 1,999 sex partners were not enough.

Pinker on gender differences and 'the battle of the sexes':

Sometimes, of course, it does work. A man and a woman can fall in love, and the key ingredient is an expression of commitment. A man and a woman need each other's DNA and hence can enjoy sex. A man and a woman have a common interest in their children, and their enduring love has evolved to protect that interest. And a husband and wife can be each other's best friends, and can enjoy the lifelong dependability and trust that underlies the logic of friendship. These emotions are rooted in the fact that if a man and woman are monogamous, together for life, and not nepotistic toward their own families, their genetic interests are identical.

Unfortunately, that is a big 'if.' Even the happiest couples can fight like cats and dogs, and today 50% of marriages in the United States end in divorce . . . Conflict between men and women, sometimes deadly, is universal, and it suggests that sex is not a bonding force in human affairs but a divisive one. Once again, that banality must be stated because the conventional wisdom denies it. One of the utopian ideals of the 1960s, reiterated ever since by sex gurus like Dr Ruth, is the intensely erotic, mutually enjoyable, guilt-free, emotionally open, lifelong monogamous pair-bond. The alternative from the counterculture was the intensely erotic, mutually enjoyable, guilt-free, emotionally open, round-robin orgy. Both were attributed to our hominid ancestors, to earlier stages of civilisation, or to primitive tribes still out there somewhere. Both are as mythical as the Garden of Eden.

The battle between the sexes is not just a skirmish in the war between unrelated individuals but is fought in a different theatre, for reasons first explained by Donald Symons. 'With respect to human sexuality,' he wrote, 'there is a female human nature and a male human nature, and these natures are extraordinarily different . . . Men and women differ in their sexual natures because throughout the immensely long hunting and gathering phase of human evolutionary history the sexual desires and dispositions that were adaptive for either sex were for the other tickets to reproductive oblivion.'

Pinker on partner numbers over the course of human history:

In evolutionary terms, a man who has a short-term liaison (with a woman other than his long-term partner) is betting that his illegitimate child will survive without his help or is counting on a cuckolded husband to bring it up as his own. For the man who can afford it, a surer way to maximise progeny is to seek several wives and invest all their children. Men should want many wives, not just many sex partners. And in fact, men in power have allowed polygyny (the practise of having more than one wife) in more than 80% of human cultures. Jews practiced it until Christian times and outlawed it only in the tenth century. Mormons encouraged it until it was outlawed by the U.S. government in the late nineteenth century and even today there are thought to be tens of thousands of clandestine polygynous marriages in Utah and other western states. Whenever polygyny is allowed, men seek additional wives and the means to attract them. Wealthy and prestigious men have more than one wife; ne'er-do-wells have none. Typically a man who has been married for some time seeks a younger wife. The senior wife remains his confidante and partner and runs the household; the junior one becomes his sexual interest. . .

Oddly enough, in a freer society polygyny is not necessarily bad for women. On financial and ultimately on evolutionary grounds, a woman may prefer to share a wealthy husband than to have the undivided attention of a pauper, and may even prefer it on emotional grounds. Laura Betzig summed up the reason: Would you rather be the third wife of John F Kennedy or the first wife of Bozo the Clown? Co-wives often get along, sharing expertise and child-care duties, though jealousies among the subfamilies often erupt, much as in stepfamilies but with more factions and adult players. If marriage were genuinely a free market, then in a polygamous society men's greater demand for a limited supply of partners and their inflexible sexual jealousy would give the advantage to women. Laws enforcing monogamy would work to women's disadvantage. . .

Legal monogamy historically has been an agreement between more and less powerful men, not between men and women. Its aim is not so much to exploit the customers in the romance industry (women) as to minimise the costs of competition among the producers (men). Under polygyny, men vie for extraordinary Darwinian stakes – many wives versus none – and the competition is literally cutthroat. Many homicides and most tribal wars are directly or indirectly about competition for women. Leaders have outlawed polygyny when they needed less powerful men as allies and when they needed their subjects to fight an enemy instead of fighting one another. Early Christianity appealed to poor men partly because the promise of monogamy kept them in the marriage game, and in societies since, egalitarianism and monogamy go together as naturally as despotism and polygyny.

While there may be virtually no female market for pornography, there's a *huge* female market for romantic fiction. Simon Andreae, in his 1998 book *The Secrets of Love and Lust*, provides some insights into the phenomenon of romantic fiction:

Two factors are key to mate selection by females. Good looks (which roughly translate as 'good genes'), and the capacity to acquire status and resources. But, looked at from an evolutionary point of view, there should be a third essential component to female desire. To discover what it is, we must travel to the town of Don Mills, Ontario, for this is the headquarters of Harlequin Enterprises, the world's most successful publisher of the product through which female fantasy finds its widest and most profitable expression: romantic fiction.

Driven by purely commercial imperatives, the company has a clear remit to appeal to the largest possible number of consumers, and there is a constant feedback mechanism. The signal something's really hit the button is that it sells.

Harlequin was founded in Winnipeg by printing executive Richard Bonnycastle to meet the growing demand for paperback books in post-war Canada. At first, they published a wide range of genres, including Westerns, thrillers, craft books and classics, featuring such authors as Agatha Christie, Jean Plaidy, James Hadley Chase and Somerset Maugham. But also included in the list were a number of romances originally published by the British company Mills & Boon. It was Mary Bonnycastle, wife of the founder, who first noticed the popularity of what she called those 'nice little books with happy endings', and suggested that Harlequin should concentrate on selling them.

Fifty years later the company is in buoyant mood. It acquired Mills & Boon in the early 1970s, snapped up its major competitor, Silhouette, in 1984, and now has a 20% share of the total global market in popular fiction, selling over two hundred million books a year to over fifty million readers in more than a hundred countries around the world. The books themselves come in several styles, from the 'gentle, tender love stories' of Harlequin Romance to the 'provocative, sensuous, passionate stories' of the Temptation series. Yet despite their surface variety, each is informed by the same editorial principle. The heroes are universally handsome, adventurous, and accompanied by what Harlequin editors call 'the guarantee of satisfaction'. This guarantee, though usually hidden at the outset, stipulates that the hero will ultimately fall in love with the heroine and show every sign of being prepared to live with her in a state of lifelong happiness, providing her and their children with the benefit of his long-term and exclusive care. In the more traditional imprints, a trip to the altar will almost certainly take place. In the racier novels, children are sometimes already on the way.

Rita Clay Estrada's *The Stormchaser*, a recent best-seller from the Temptation series, gives us the entire recipe in spades. In many ways, the story is startlingly modern. The characters live in a world where unhappy childhoods, failed marriages, long working days and personal insecurity abound. They work on personal computers, eat junk food, and have clearly recognisable flaws (the hero drinks beer from a can, the heroine worries about her stretchmarks). Yet the innovations only throw the eternal essentials into sharper relief.

Cane Mitchell, the handsome 30-something hero, follows in the wake of natural disasters, working as an insurance adjuster. Investigating a claim, he meets Bernadette Conrad, a widow with an 18-year-old son of her own, whose house has been destroyed in an earthquake. Their instant mutual attraction is frustrated by differences in class and career, but most of all by Cane's reluctance to consider a serious relationship after the break-up of his marriage and a string of short-term girlfriends.

Nevertheless, they kiss and make love soon after they meet and, for a blissful interlude, they move into temporary accommodation together. Unfortunately, given their conflicting goals, it cannot last. Bernadette wants a lasting and deeply-rooted commitment that Cane is unwilling to give; they break up in a welter of tears and confusion. But there is a further, complicating factor. Unbeknown to Cane, Bernadette is pregnant with his child, conceived accidentally. Facing up to the future, she decides to go it alone and have the baby regardless. He, meanwhile, suffers agonies of separation and regret – and finally dares to attempt a reconciliation. Over the final pages, the denouement plays itself out in three distinct stages. First, Cane announces that he is deeply in love with Bernadette:

> Cane stood and faced her, letting the blanket drop to the concrete. His expression was heartbreakingly filled with love. 'No. I know what I want, and it's right here in front of me. Forever.'

After this, an oblique marriage proposal heralds his intention to look after her permanently:

> 'And do you want a formal wedding or can we elope?'

> Her solemn expression turned into a broad grin. 'A formal wedding, a big one.'

> 'Damn,' he muttered. 'I had a feeling you'd say that.'

Finally, Cane is faced with the first test of his promised permanent care, a child to look after as well as a wife.

> Taking a deep breath, she moved her hands down to her abdomen, cradling the slight roundness there. 'Hurricane Mitchell, if you run from me now, know that you'll be running from two of us. There will be no third chance for either one. We either commit to be together and raise this child with all the love and caring we all deserve, or we call it off now, while I can still function without you.'

'Hurricane' rises to the task, and the natural disasters he has spent his life chasing die away to be replaced by the solid stability of parenthood.

This type of happy ending, in which the man promises his long-term and exclusive care, is the third major dimension of female desire, and one which, from an evolutionary point of view, makes perfect sense. An attraction to handsome men can make women more likely to produce genetically healthy children; an attraction to rich men can make them more likely to furnish those children with a good start; but an attraction to men who will stick around, be faithful, and dedicate themselves to protecting and nourishing their families over the long term is in many ways the most useful attraction pattern of all.

Perhaps it's no coincidence that one of the best-selling photographic images of the 1980s showed a semi-nude male model, Adam Perry, cradling a tiny baby. Pictures of Adam alone sold steadily, but once he was shown devoting himself to a child, his career rocketed. Unfortunately, as in so many sexual battlefields, his image on paper didn't match his behaviour in real life. Perry was recently reported to have profited from the image in more than monetary terms: it had enabled him to seduce many of the 3,000 women he claims to have slept with over the last ten years. . .

Peggy La Cerra, in a parallel study to the one in which women were shown to prefer men in high-status clothes to men in low-status clothes, has now shown that men who are photographed smiling at babies consistently receive higher attractiveness ratings from women than men who are photographed either ignoring babies or on their own. Female desire really did seem to be zeroing in on men who could deliver the guarantee of satisfaction: lasting, loving commitment to their partners and their children. The ideal of the New Man is not an invention of the sentimental late 20th century; it's the rediscovery of a primal female fantasy.

Unfortunately, real-life Harlequin heroes and rich, handsome superdads are very thin on the ground, and for good reasons. Bearing in mind that inside every man is a polygynist waiting to get out, the call for extra-pair sex has rarely gone unanswered, especially by the rich and powerful. From the early despots, through today's pop stars, playboys and politicians to the chisel-jawed likes of Adam Perry, powerful, resource-laden and exceptionally handsome men have consistently had more sexual partners than the rest – simply because they can.

A man's desire to view pornographic material or have sex with a woman other than his wife is as 'natural' as a woman's desire to read romantic fiction. No man would suggest that women should no longer read romantic fiction on any grounds, even if it gives women unrealistic expectations of their partners.

Needless to say men are not extended the same courtesy, hence the efforts of some women to ban pornography and prostitution. The advent of the internet means that women in free societies have lost the battle against pornography, which has only increased their determination to ban prostitution. Their genuine motivation is to stop men having sex outside of long-term monogamous relationships, but this cannot be admitted. So they either resort to religious objections – increasingly ineffective in secular societies – or the politically correct argument that prostitutes are victims. Ideally drug-addled and controlled by male pimps, for good measure: all prostitutes, everywhere, at all times. There is no room for nuanced arguments in the world of the politically correct, as we shall see in a later chapter on the subject of political correctness.

A report in *The Daily Telegraph* of 14 May 2009:

Nurses vote for legalisation of small brothels
Brothels containing up to four prostitutes should be legalised to reduce rates of sexually transmitted diseases and protect women from violence, according to members of the Royal College of Nursing.

The 'stigma' which surrounds prostitutes means that many are afraid to visit doctors or hospitals and are left vulnerable to attack, delegates at the Royal College's annual congress in Harrogate heard yesterday.

A motion that up to four prostitutes should be allowed to work together legally, which would make it easier to get free condoms and screening for diseases, was passed at the conference.

Perfect common sense, which we would expect from nurses, whilst not expecting it from politicians. And so it is that at the time of writing the indomitable Rt Hon Harriet Harman QC MP is attempting to steer the proposed Police and Crime Bill (2009) through Parliament. The supposed driving force behind the section on prostitution was that many or even most prostitutes were being trafficked from other countries, for the personal gain of pimps and organised gangs. The bill would have made it an offence for a client (invariably a man, whether seeking a female or male prostitute) to pay for sexual services, and if caught doing so he would face a hefty fine and a criminal record. You'll be astonished to learn – or possibly not – that there was no mention of criminalising men in this way in Labour's 2005 election manifesto. To make matters worse, the offence would be a 'strict liability offence', committed regardless of whether the client 'is, or ought to be, aware that any of the [sex worker's] activities are controlled for gain'.

In response the English Collective of Prostitutes – a London-based body – developed a commendable briefing paper, which they sent to members of Parliament and the press. It successfully challenged much of the thinking behind the bill and helped lead to a number of amendments. I have reproduced below the full paper, with the kind permission of the Collective. It occupies the remainder of this chapter:

We urge you to oppose Clauses 13, 15, 16, 18, 20, & 25. The measures target anyone involved in prostitution whether or not there is force or coercion. They would drive prostitution further underground and sex workers into even more danger.

CLAUSE 13: 'Paying for sexual services of a prostitute controlled for gain.'

1. Any sex worker who receives help may be considered 'controlled for gain'. The Bill defines it as 'an activity which is controlled by (a person who is not the sex worker or client) in the expectation of gain' – no force or coercion needs to be proved. A co-worker, receptionist (usually referred to as a maid), partner, even a taxi driver may be considered to be 'controlling for gain'.

2. Safer premises will be targeted. In December, police raided premises in Soho threatening receptionists with being charged with 'controlling prostitution for gain'. Research shows that it is 10 times safer to work indoors than on the street. Receptionists are sex workers' first line of defence against violent attacks and exploitation. If they are prosecuted women will be left to work alone. Who will such criminalisation benefit?

3. Clients face a hefty fine and a criminal record. Paying for sexual services will be a strict liability offence, committed regardless of whether the client 'is, or ought to be, aware that any of the (sex worker's) activities are controlled for gain'.

4. Trafficking figures are flawed. Trafficking has been used as the main justification for these proposals. But the UK charge of trafficking for prostitution, unlike trafficking for any other industry, does not require force or coercion. This enables every woman with a foreign accent to be falsely labelled a victim of trafficking! The widely used claim that '80% of women working in the sex industry in the UK have been trafficked' was recently discredited on a BBC Radio programme: even if 80% of women working in brothels, saunas and massage parlours are not British, 'foreign does not mean forced'. In response to questions by John McDonnell MP, the Home Office has disowned these figures. And its latest estimate that 4,000 women are trafficked into the UK a year cannot be verified as the Home Office claims they come from an 'internal Home Office document'.

CLAUSE 15: Soliciting is persistent 'if it takes place twice over a period of three months'.

1. Such soliciting would more appropriately be described as occasional. To call it persistent shows an intention to criminalise. It makes a mockery of the abolition of the term common prostitute (Clause 15 (2) (a)) as it will bring no reduction in the number of women arrested.

2. Criminal records prevent women from getting out of prostitution. Women end up institutionalised as they cannot get other jobs, even when they are qualified for them.

3. Criminalisation breaks up families. Mothers end up in jail separated from their children, with disastrous consequences first of all for the children.

CLAUSE 16: Compulsory 'rehabilitation' under threat of imprisonment.

This was thrown out of the Criminal Justice and Immigration Bill a year ago. Why bring it back? Anyone arrested for loitering or soliciting would have to attend three meetings with a supervisor approved by the court. It is not an alternative to a fine as failure to comply may result in a summons back to court and 72 hours in jail. Women could end up on a treadmill of broken supervision meetings, court orders and imprisonment. Imprisoning women goes against recommendations of the widely respected Corston report (March 2007).

CLAUSE 18: Soliciting 'another for the purpose of obtaining sexual services'.

The only safeguard against false arrest would be removed. Kerb-crawling is an offence if it is 'persistent'. Removing the requirement to prove 'persistence, annoyance or nuisance' would increase police powers to arrest anyone on suspicion alone. Victims of institutionalised police racism and other prejudice are likely to be targeted. With a conviction rate for reported rape at a shameful 6%, why isn't rape being prioritised over prostitution?

CLAUSE 20: Extending closure orders to brothels.

1. This charge is modelled on 'crack house closures' which has been condemned by Release as 'insidious', based on 'tenuous evidence in which hearsay evidence is admissible'. Like ASBOs, Closure Orders are part of civil proceedings, but breach of an order is a criminal offence carrying a six month prison sentence. Release found that 'the court will never refuse a police application for a Closure Order'. They have witnessed 'numerous cases where vulnerable people become displaced, eventually homeless and face the threat of criminal charges'.

2. Most brothels are small self-help ventures. The word brothel conjures up images of big exploitative establishments, yet by law two prostitute women sharing premises to work constitute a brothel. Many women prefer to work in small self-run brothels because they offer greater safety, companionship and lower running expenses. Working indoors is 10 times safer than working on the street. Even Fiona McTaggert admits that. In January 2005, as Home Office Minister, she announced that two women should be able to work together from premises. Why has this been dropped in favour of punitive measures that drive women out of premises?

CLAUSE 25: Lap-dancing to be reclassified as 'sex encounter establishments'.

This would increase the cost of licensing and the stigma. Lap-dancers have described working collectively with other women with good safety systems, and earning more than they would in other jobs. Is this what the government finds objectionable? (See statement below.)

Proceeds of Crime – Profiteering from raids and the prosecution of sex workers. Since the Proceeds of Crime Act, raids have become profitable: the police keep 25% of any assets confiscated both at the time and from subsequent prosecutions; the Crown Prosecution Service keeps another 25%; and the Inland Revenue the rest. It is common for police to seize any money found on premises they raid. Even if no one is charged, the money is rarely returned as police take advantage of sex workers' reluctance to go public. Women who have worked for years to put money aside lose not only their livelihood but their home, car, life savings, jewellery, etc. This theft by law enforcement is the worst form of pimping. We believe it is a main reason why anti-prostitution raids are now high up on the police and government agenda.

Forcing prostitution further underground endangers lives. The proposals claim to offer protection and safety, and 'support those involved in prostitution to develop routes out'. They do not. As the economic recession hits, more women, especially mothers, are likely to resort to prostitution to support their families. If prostitution is forced further underground women will be exposed to greater dangers and be less able to come forward to get help. In Scotland, since clients were criminalised in October 2007, the number of assaults on sex workers has soared. Attacks reported to one project have almost doubled from 66 in 2006 to 126 last year, including eight reported rapes and 55 violent assaults.

English Collective of Prostitutes co-ordinates The Safety First Coalition which includes anti-poverty campaigners, church people & residents from Ipswich & elsewhere, the Royal College of Nursing, the National Association of Probation Officers, members of the medical & legal professions, prison reformers, sex worker & drugs rehabilitation projects.

Statements from women working in various areas of the sex industry

Cindy – working from premises:

> I started working because I couldn't live off benefits. Doing this work I wasn't having to worry every day how I was going to pay my bills.
> A woman like me who works for herself, whether on the streets or in premises, classes her situation as a business not a burden. A lot

of women have repeat clients and build up a rapport and a trust. Not only do the women provide company and maybe sexual favours but they become a counsellor and even a friend!! Criminalising clients would scare these men away. We would be pushed further underground forcing us to take more risks by having to find ways of contacting clients secretly. Women will be left on their own because you don't want to expose yourself by working with others.

Prosecuting a man would mean that the women's job would come to light. The media coverage would affect her family in many ways as it did with mine. Years later this is still a major strain on me. I had to move home and change my children's school as I didn't want what I did to provide for my children to tarnish them. And people judge you long term. It is even worse if you get prosecuted and end up with a criminal record. What chance then do you have to get out of prostitution?

Michaela – convicted as a 'trafficker':

I've been a victim of sexual abuse and domestic violence and believe every woman should be protected. I come from a poor rural area of Brazil. At age 12, I was forced to work as a domestic servant to help support my family. I was repeatedly sexually assaulted by two sons in the family.

I came to Britain to marry, after many years the relationship broke down, and I became a sex worker to get an independent life for me and my children. The wellbeing of people around me has been the focus of my life. That is why I opened a place to work indoors where it's safer. I saved to open a 'health club' in Manchester. I had all the health and safety checks by the council, and a receptionist to make sure women who worked there would be safe. I had a few women who came from Brazil and other countries. All were over 25 years, had been working in prostitution and were in no way forced. But because I am a woman of colour, and from another country, I was targeted.

I was arrested in October 2005 and convicted of trafficking. I pleaded guilty because the police threatened to charge my 18-year-old daughter if I didn't, and because my solicitor and barrister strongly recommended it. They told me that because the trafficking law does not require proof of force or coercion, only evidence that you helped someone from another country come into the UK who then works in the sex industry, then I was guilty.

The judge agreed I had treated the women 'kindly'. He accepted 'none of the women was coerced by you into acting as a prostitute . . . none was actually deceived as to the nature of the work they would be required to undertake . . . each had previously worked as a prostitute . . . You treated them in a kindly and hospitable way, inviting them to your home and social occasions.' The police often frequented the premises and went out socially with women working there. The judge used this against me saying that it 'undermined the public's confidence in the police' as if I should be punished for the police's behaviour. I was convicted because the police and CPS wanted to look like they had cracked a big criminal case – to get promotions and build careers.

For this, I was put in prison for nearly three years and separated from my children, the youngest was only six at the time. Children at that age need their mother's protection. I was terribly distressed, and my children were deeply affected. Their behaviour changed, and they are still recovering from that separation. My ex-partner tried to deny me the right to see my youngest, and has tried to get custody. I was also prosecuted under the Proceeds of Crime Act. We lost everything – our home, savings, even personal gifts and belongings – which I'd worked so hard for. I'm 45, a single mother with two children to support, having to start again with nothing. Me, my family and friends were vilified by sensational and false reporting in the local press before trial.

Any friends who tried to help me were either charged or threatened with charges by the police. My address was put in the local paper, and my daughter had to move home and could not attend college. Now the Home Office wanted to deport me. Legal Action for Women found me a good lawyer to try and stop the deportation. My British citizenship was revoked, yet I'd never committed a crime.

All I did was run a flat where women were able to work safely – why is that a criminal offence? Did I deserve to spend three years in prison for that, and to have my life and my family's life ruined?

Chloe – working as a lapdancer:

I've worked all around the country. I do three minute dances which cost the guys £10. I pay towards the cost of the venue, security and the DJ; after that, whatever I earn is my own. We work as a collective and prioritise safety. We have a good support network of door and bar staff. Someone always knows where I am. I take a lot of responsibility for the new girls as I've been around a long time.

I can earn £250 for four hours. Worse case, I walk out with £50 and that's still more than I would earn in a day job at £5 an hour. Nine out of ten women turn to prostitution or lap dancing because there's not enough money to survive. I work with students, mothers and all kinds of other women. Recently my mum couldn't afford a pair of school shoes for my brother and sister. When I worked a day job I couldn't help her, but now I can. If the government is offended by the work we do, then give us the financial means to get out of the industry.

There is no pressure to have sex with men, only opportunities. I could go to a nightclub and have ten times more of an opportunity to sleep with a man than I do in my workplace. In any case, if I want to have sex with a man, and if he wants to pay me, then so what? If I had kids and sleeping with a man for money meant my children could have food in their mouths, I would do it. And tell me one woman that wouldn't.

I haven't met any women who were forced to work in clubs. Some women from other countries come here for salvation and help because it is terrible for them back home.

They say we are degrading ourselves. Actually, no. The issue is what kind of protection we get from the police and courts. My friend was raped in a supermarket car park. Some one very close to me was abused as a child. The cases got thrown out of court.

If you bring in more regulations and criminalise the sex industry, you make it harder for women to work. Girls can't insist on good working conditions or their rights. The industry will go underground and it will be much worse.

Another woman complains:

> If the re-branding goes through, the stigma will increase and some women will be forced out of work or underground into the hands of pimps. Until two years ago, clubs were individually licensed with owners required to get health, safety and criminal record checks. Relaxing the licensing laws was a New Labour ploy to raise revenue. Why not demand a return to the previous system?
>
> Renaming clubs as sex encounter establishments is completely inaccurate and will set things back decades. You might as well re-brand night clubs as drugs and alcohol encounter establishments. What about sex scandals and immoral behaviour in parliament? If women want to get on their soapboxes they should find a better target than other women's livelihoods.

From an off-street sex worker:

> I don't live a *Belle de Jour*-type existence, but nor am I the trafficked, drug-addled, pimped victim . . . I am a single mother with two young children aged four and six. Prior to doing this job – and it is a job – I was employed as a PA in a large, city-based firm. My job was a typical 9-to-5 one – which, as everyone who has ever worked in such a job will know, means 7:30am to 6:30pm by the time you take into consideration travelling and (unpaid) overtime. I was dropping my children off at breakfast club at 8am and collecting them at 6pm, by which time we would all be completely knackered. The children go to bed at 7:30pm, meaning we were left with precisely 90 minutes to prepare and eat our evening meal, have baths, get ready for bed and read bedtime stories.
>
> It was like we were living in a whirlwind. I felt I never saw my kids – let's face it, I didn't (much) – there was certainly never much time for playing or talking or simply just sitting cuddling on the sofa.

The guilt was getting to me. I was unhappy. I hoped they weren't, but I was never sure. . . By the time my monthly pay packet came around, I would have literally just a few pounds in the bank. . . My children are fantastic human beings and I wanted to spend more time in their company without us suffering financially, it was as simple as that. I wanted a job which would allow me to work flexible hours to fit around the children's schooling, fewer hours, but without taking the drop in wages which a part-time office job would have led to.

Escorting seemed like the natural solution. I say 'natural' because it felt natural to me. I am well aware that this is not a job everybody could do. But as a sexually-aware and sexually-experienced woman in her mid-30s, the thought of having sex with strangers did not terrify me. I remember thinking that I might even enjoy it (and that has proved to be the case).

I work from a flat on which I pay the mortgage – I do not have any landlord to worry about. I charge £150 per hour and I get enough enquiries to enable me to choose my own working hours. In a typical day I drop my children off at school at 9am, return home, shower and get changed into my alter-ego, Lara (we never use our own names). I then might have an hour's appointment at 11am and another at 1pm, leaving me with a break of an hour in between to shower and refresh myself. I then fetch myself a late lunch and am at the school again to collect my children at 3:30pm. It works. I never see more than two clients a day; most days I see only one; on other days none at all. Yet in just three hours' work I can earn the same as I used to earn in a week working at the office.

My clients are on the whole middle-aged businessmen. I have never been treated with anything less than respect by any one of them. I have not been physically or sexually abused by any of them. Of course I have my security systems in place should anything go wrong, but so far nothing has. My children have their mother now, and not just on a part-time basis. I have time with them to enjoy their childhoods, without any of us suffering financially. I am not making big bucks – but I am earning a little more money to boot.

Criminalisation of men would only serve to drive the industry further underground, leaving the women who are victims of trafficking even more vulnerable. Making criminals of all men who pay for sex would result in myself and thousands of other women who choose to work in this industry becoming unemployed, and thus instead of contributing to the state (through our taxes) we would be taking from the state in the form of income support, housing benefit and so on. This is how we make a living; it's an industry that prevents many, many women and their children from living on the breadline. If you are going to take our livelihoods from us, the consequences will be devastating.

6

READINESS FOR MARRIAGE, COMPATIBILITY, MARITAL DISHARMONY, DEPRESSION AND PERSISTENCE, PREDICTING OUTCOMES

For the first time since sudden love had thrown them into each other's arms, she had found herself beginning to wonder if her Blair was quite the godlike superman she had supposed. There even flashed through her mind a sinister speculation as to whether, when you came right down to it, he wasn't something of a pill.

(PG Wodehouse, *Hot Water*)

[Author's note: the above reflections are not attributable to Cherie Blair, wife of the former British Prime Minister, Tony Blair. Sorry.]

This chapter covers:

- Premarital assessment of individual aptitude for marriage, and mutual compatibility
- Couples' abilities to resolve conflicts
- Unrealistic expectations about what a 'good marriage' is and isn't
- The links between depression and relationship difficulties
- Two theories about the causes of marital disharmony
- The link between persistence and depression
- A theory on why America has the highest rate of depression in the world
- Human changeability
- The formula that tells you (with 94% accuracy) whether you will get divorced
- The possible impact of a boarding school education on marriage

We start with the key topics of individual aptitude for marriage and mutual compatibility with a partner, and Jeffry Larson's excellent *Should We Stay Together? A Scientifically Proven Method for Evaluating Your Relationship and Improving its Chances for Long-Term Success* (2000). Larson writes:

The book was written for single individuals and (unmarried) couples interested in improving their chances of being happily married . . . but it can also be helpful to married couples who are wondering what went wrong or whether to make a fresh start – together or separately. . . This book will help you with key insights and decision points:

- Understand your personal assets and liabilities as a potential spouse. I call this your *marriage aptitude*.
- Evaluate your relationship's assets and liabilities.
- Evaluate the contexts of your relationship eg parental and friends' approval.
- Set goals for personal and couple development so you are better prepared for marriage.
- Decide who to marry and when to marry.
- Find high-quality resources to help you prepare for marriage.

The book is well-researched, insightful, and full of well-designed questionnaires. Larson is a lifelong member of the Church of Jesus Christ of Latter-day Saints (LDS or Mormon Church). He relates his personal story about ending his studies at New York University because of the shortage of female students of the same religion, and attending Brigham Young University in Utah, where 98% of the 34,000 students are Mormon. The key elements of the story are related in chapter eight of this book. Suffice it at this point to say that Larson considers religious compatibility between marriage partners to be important. There's a lot of evidence around to suggest he's right.

An excerpt from the book's second chapter should give a flavour of the content:

After reviewing the premarital prediction literature and conducting our research, we found that the two dozen or so specific premarital predictors could be logically categorized into a triangular model of three major factors ('The Marriage Triangle'):

- your individual and relationship *contexts*
- your *individual traits* including your personality, attitudes, and skills
- your *couple traits* including couple communication, couple history, similarities and so on

Larson then invites the reader to complete the following questionnaire:

	Strongly Disagree	Disagree	Undecided	Agree	Strongly Agree
1. My father was happy in his marriage.	1	2	3	4	5
2. All things considered, my childhood years were happy.	1	2	3	4	5
3. My mother showed physical affection to me by appropriate hugging and/or kissing.	1	2	3	4	5
4. I feel I am a person of worth.	1	2	3	4	5
5. I avoid getting irritated or mad.	1	2	3	4	5
6. I am an outgoing person.	1	2	3	4	5
7. We understand each other's feelings.	1	2	3	4	5
8. We sit down and just talk things over.	1	2	3	4	5
9. When we are in an argument, we recognise when we are overwhelmed and than make a deliberate effort to calm ourselves down.	1	2	3	4	5

[Author's note: Isn't point six basically the same as 'I am an extravert', thereby implying that introversion is a potential problem in marriage?]

1. To score these items, sum your responses to items 1–3 and write your answer here: ____
2. Sum your responses to items 4–6 and write your answer here: ____
3. Sum your responses to items 7–9 and write your answer here: ____

Items 1–3 measure your perceptions of the characteristics in your individual context – your father's marital satisfaction, the level of affection in your family of origin, and your parent–child relationship satisfaction. Your score may range from 3 (lowest) to 15 (highest). This score is a rough indicator of your overall satisfaction with your family-of-origin experiences.

Items 4–6 are measures of your individual traits including self-esteem, anger management, and extraversion. Again, scores may range from 3 to 15 and reflect your perception of your mental health.

Items 7–9 are measures of your perceived couple traits, more specifically, communication and problem-solving skills. Scores range from 3 to 15 and reflect the overall quality of your couple communication skills.

A total score below 9 on one of these tests suggests a potential problem in that area of the Marriage Triangle. For example, a total score of 7 on items 7–9 indicates poor couple communication or conflict resolution skills. A score of 11 or more indicates good couple communication or conflict resolution skills. In which area – contexts, individual traits, or couple traits –

did you score the highest? The lowest? Why? These questions and scoring guidelines are generalizations because to assess each factor in the triangle comprehensively requires answering more questions from each area in the triangle.

I completed the questionnaire as I imagined I would have before my second marriage, and it became starkly clear that the marriage was never likely to have been a successful one, for reasons overwhelmingly connected with myself rather than with my wife.

We come to the complex issue of conflict resolution in marriage. Once again we draw on John Gottman's *Why Marriages Succeed or Fail: And How You Can Make Yours Last* (2007). Gottman studied over 2,000 marriages over two decades. Early in the book he outlines the following:

> If there is one lesson I have learnt from my years of research it is that *a lasting marriage results from a couple's ability to resolve the conflicts that are inevitable in any relationship*. Many couples tend to equate a low level of conflict with happiness and believe the claim 'we never fight' is a sign of marital health. But I believe we grow in our relationships by reconciling our differences. That's how we become more loving people and truly experience the fruits of marriage.
>
> But there's much more to know than how to fight well. Not all stable couples resolve conflicts in the same way. Nor do all couples mean the same thing by 'resolving' the conflict. In fact, I have found that there are three different styles of problem solving into which healthy marriages tend to settle. In a *validating marriage* couples compromise often and calmly work out their problems to mutual satisfaction as they arise. In a *conflict-avoiding marriage* couples agree to disagree, rarely confronting their differences head-on. And finally, in a *volatile marriage* conflicts erupt often, resulting in passionate disputes.
>
> Previously, many psychologists might have considered conflict-avoiding and volatile marriages to be pathological. But our current research suggests that all three styles are equally stable and bode equally well for the marriage's future.
>
> Of course, following one of these three styles won't guarantee a happy marriage. These adaptations work only to the degree that they allow you to achieve the right balance between positive and negative interactions with your spouse. Amazingly, we have found that it all comes down to a simple mathematical formula: no matter what style your marriage follows, you must have at least five times as many positive as negative moments together if your marriage is to be stable.

Gottman proceeds to outline the key components of the book:

I will map out for you the downward spiral that begins in couples who are unable to find the equilibrium of a stable type of marriage. . . I will show how strong differences between men and women in how they handle emotions can feed this process. Negativity builds, with increasingly damaging results. It begins as laughter and validation disappear, and criticism and pain well up. Your attempts to soothe one another's hurt feelings and get communication back on track seem useless. Partners become lost in hostile and negative thoughts and feelings, as their bodies react to the stress, making it harder to think rationally, to respond calmly. Soon, the destructive interactions I call 'The Four Horsemen of the Apocalypse' take over. They are criticism, contempt, defensiveness, and withdrawal. At this point, unless a couple makes changes, they are likely to find themselves sliding helplessly towards the end of their marriage.

The book helps the reader identify marital 'trouble spots' and outlines remedies.

Steven and Sue Simring, 'America's foremost husband-and-wife marriage counselling team', have some interesting things to say about marriage in their book *Making Marriage Work For Dummies* (2001). Chapter 1 is entitled 'A Candid Look at Marriage' and contains the following:

Most people are told at a very young age that someday they're going to get married and have children. That's the way people are taught to lead their lives, and it's constantly reinforced by movies, popular songs, and TV commercials. It's natural to assume that marriage is inevitable. But marriage isn't for everybody – even if people sometimes have to get married to figure that out.

Some men and women don't want the closeness or the commitment that comes with matrimony. These people should not get married – at least not until their mindset changes.

If your partner says that she doesn't want to get married at a particular point in time, don't ignore those words. Such feelings may or may not change later on. No matter how difficult this decision may be for you to accept, remember that this is a valid and very personal decision that must be respected. . .

Many of the ideas people have about marriage come from the images they see in movies and TV. Not surprisingly, these images give a distorted picture of marriage, because couples are usually depicted as completely harmonious or fighting like cats and dogs. We also get ideas about marriage from other biased sources, including our families, friends, and communities. Despite good intentions, this kind of advice may lead you to very unrealistic expectations about marriage.

Because you're so often bombarded with these warped images of marriage, it pays to spend some time to deprogram your notions about what a good marriage is and isn't. Take a few minutes to answer each of the following eleven questions with a 'yes' or 'no':

- Do you believe that there is only one person in the world for you?
- Do you believe that true soulmates never have major differences?
- Do you believe that partners in a good marriage rarely argue?
- Do you believe that husbands and wives must each have specific roles in a marriage?
- Do you believe that happily married couples should do everything together?
- Do you believe that your partner's strengths can make up for your shortcomings?
- Do you believe that your strengths can make up for your partner's shortcomings?
- Do you believe you can choose to ignore either of your families of origin, and it will not affect your marriage?
- Do you believe that people can resolve their differences without much effort as long as they are in love?
- Do you believe you can make your husband or wife change bad habits after you marry?
- Do you believe two people who love each other will automatically grow closer over time?

A 'yes' answer to any of the above questions indicates that you may be harbouring unrealistic expectations that are bound to lead to feelings of disappointment about the state of your marriage. Instead of allowing those feelings to get you down, we urge you to take advantage of the mythbusters we offer in the following section.

We return to the book written by the British clinical psychologist Oliver James, *Britain on the Couch: Treating a Low Serotonin Society* (1998). One illuminating section concerns depression, 'gender rancour', and divorce:

DEPRESSION AND GENDER RANCOUR
There are sound scientific, as well as anecdotal, grounds for supposing that the increases in depression and aggression since 1950 have resulted in a rancorous disharmony between the sexes. That there is so much more recorded violent crime is a self-evident indication that aggression has increased. The role of increased depression is a less commonsensical indicator of increased rancour.

DEPRESSED   PEOPLE   MAKE   DEPRESSING,   HOSTILE PARTNERS
Until the publication of Myrna Weissman's classic 1974 account (co-authored with Eugene Paykel) of *The Depressed Woman*, it was widely assumed that depressed people were passive and withdrawn (it should be stressed that most of Weissman's findings probably apply to depressed men as well). Their aggression was turned against themselves, as was evident in the savage negativity they displayed towards themselves

mentally, and at its most extreme, in the physical attacks they made against their bodies, not just in suicide attempts, but in such self-destructive illnesses as the eating disorders bulimia and anorexia nervosa, both of which are more common among the depressed.

The assumption was that outwardly directed hostility must be reduced since it is all turned against the self. However, this view had to be modified after Weissman's careful comparison of 40 depressed women with 40 nondepressed ones. It showed that depressed women are anything but unaggressive in intimate relationships. They displayed 'significantly more overt interpersonal hostility in most relationships, and the intensity of these feelings ranged from resentment, general irritability, through arguments of increasing intensity, to physical encounters.'

The brunt of this hostility was borne by their children, with whom they had twice as much friction as their spouses. However, they were also significantly more hostile to their spouses than to their extended family members, friends and professional colleagues: 'Marital relationships become an arena for the depression and are characterised by friction, poor communication, dependency and diminished sexual satisfaction. The depressed woman feels a lack of affection towards her husband together with guilt and resentment. Communication is poor and hostility overt.'

That this marked viciousness was confined to intimates explained why researchers had not noticed the pattern before. Not being intimates, the researchers doing the studies did not evoke it: 'The depressed patient's behaviour at interview is a poor sample of her actual behaviour outside. In the initial psychiatric interview she is cooperative, compliant and not hostile.'

Given that depressives are like this, the finding that depressives create unhappiness in their intimates is no surprise. Partners of depressives are themselves more likely to be depressed, to get ill, to abuse alcohol and to commit both suicide and homicide. The relationship suffers. Compared with couples where neither party is depressed, in couples with one depressive, the depressed one is more likely to be domineering and overbearingly insistent in solving disputes. The couple are likely to use destructive methods for doing so, to feel miserable about their relationship, be secretive and uncommunicative and provide little support to each other.

This miserable list could double up as a fair definition of the word 'rancour'. Given that there has been a large increase in the number of such depressed adults, it is almost certain that there has been a concomitant increase in the number of disharmonious couples and therefore, in the amount of gender rancour.

DOES DEPRESSION CAUSE DIVORCE, OR VICE VERSA?

An important effect of such increased rancour may be on the divorce rate – itself an important cause of the increase in depression since 1950. One study of 56 married depressives followed over a two-year period found they were nine times more likely to have divorced than the general population. Not only do couples with a depressive member show more disharmony, they are more at risk of divorce. This is not surprising if depression is such a powerful cause of gender rancour. At the same time, as noted above, other studies show that marital disharmony and divorce are a cause as well as an effect of depression. Disentangling them is not done easily and there are two very different theories.

The first, which became extremely fashionable during the 1960s and 1970s and remains dominant today, is the 'marital compatibility' view. Troubled marriages are seen as the product of ineffectual communication patterns resulting from personal incompatibility. John Gottman, for example, asked over 100 newly-wed couples to pick a perennial bone of contention between them and videotaped the ensuing discussion. How they dealt with the problem predicted whether they were still together four years later. In this view, successful marriage is a case of finding the right person for you and making sure that destructive patterns of problem-solving do not develop – unsuccessful marriages cause depression.

That this perspective became so popular during a period (after 1960) when millions of dissatisfied husbands and wives were asking themselves if they were with the right partner may be no coincidence. The perspective is also supported by considerable evidence and there is little doubt that unhappy marriages can cause previously stable and well-adjusted individuals to develop depression and other problems. However, this view has become so dominant that the alternative has been almost totally forgotten: that emotional problems, often dating back to childhood, in one or both of the partners could cause the marital problems. In this view, there are people whose personalities would have put them at high risk of divorce whoever they had married.

As one author bluntly put it back in 1935, 'One would hardly expect a man and a woman, both highly neurotic, to achieve a very high order of marital happiness.' In order to test this theory properly a study would ideally have followed a large sample from childhood to late adulthood. Only then would it be clear how much any emotional problems during marriage preceded the union. No studies have gone as far back as that, but there are no fewer than seven which tested the personalities of couples before they married and followed up what happened to them subsequently. In all of these, 'neuroticism' (in these studies, 'neuroticism' includes mild or more severe depression as part of its definition) and lack of 'impulse control' (in the male partner) predicted subsequent disharmony and divorce compared with people without these traits before marriage.

There are also several other studies suggesting that males with poor impulse control are more likely to have marital problems (it may be recalled that low impulse control correlates strongly with low levels of serotonin). To this can be added a British study which found that high neuroticism among girls at age 16 predicted subsequent increased risk of divorce. . .

To some, the idea that depressed, neurotic and impulsive people are more at risk of divorce might seem to be plain old-fashioned common sense. But so deep rooted is our reluctance to 'stigmatise' individuals that we dare not suggest that one individual has got a problem. Rather, we blame it on The Relationship. Others might also feel that it may be true but best left unsaid since it seems very negative. Yet many marriages might be greatly helped by this understanding. Where one individual is clearly suffering from depression, rather than encouraging both to agonise over their compatibility, it can be extremely helpful for the disturbed person to seek treatment for their individual angst. It is particularly so with depressives, who (as Weissman's and subsequent studies prove) are especially liable to be paranoid and to blame everything on their intimates and then to launch a barrage of hostility and aggression towards them. The 'personal incompatibility' model is very convenient for such people but they may find the same problems recurring with subsequent partners – divorcees are more likely to divorce if they remarry than first-time unions.

This is not to say that incompatibility never happens or that there are not men and women who treat each other intolerably badly and for whom divorce is the only sane response. Both statements are true, and incompatibility and poor communication skills remain well-established causes of divorce. It is simply that the emphasis on relationship rather than individual pathology has been so all-consuming in recent years that it is important to redress the balance in explaining divorce.

RELATING THE INDIVIDUAL TRAIT PERSPECTIVE TO THE RISE IN DEPRESSION, RANCOUR AND DIVORCE SINCE 1950

The Individual Trait approach helps a great deal in explaining this rise.

Firstly, given that there has been a large increase in depression since 1950 and given that we know depressives are hostile and aggressive partners and that they have higher rates of divorce, it could be that the increase in depressed people has partly directly caused the increase in divorce.

Secondly, we saw in the last chapter that the divorce increase is also due to a significant extent to changes in values, especially to changing sex roles, increased individualism and increased expectations of relationships as a source of gratification. It seems highly probable that the new freedoms and accompanying values will not have affected everyone in the same way.

Neurotic and impulsive people may always have had a greater risk of unhappy marriages but in the past have been protected by social pressures from expressing them in ultimately self-destructive attacks on their marriages. Furthermore, such people may have been made even more neurotic and impulsive by the excitement and overheated expectations of the prevailing *zeitgeist*. This might have caused their marriages to become even unhappier and increased the likelihood of divorce in an era when it was fashionable to believe the relationship was to blame and there was a better partner somewhere out there just waiting to meet you.

Thus, the rise in depression, the increase in gender rancour and the ascending divorce rate may have all impacted on each other to create a firestorm of rage and despair.

James's 'Individual Trait' commentary may help explain the phenomenon of people who marry many times, always seeking 'the one'. Maybe they genuinely don't see that they themselves are the problem, and that 'the one' probably doesn't exist. All too often when relationships fail we tell people to seek a new intimate relationship – 'there are plenty more fish in the sea' – but might it not be kinder to tell some of them (such as myself) that they could simply be unsuited to intimate long-term relationships? I think so. The truth might hurt. But surely it will hurt less than an unhappy marriage, divorce, family breakdown, and the rest of the sorry mess that results from unsuitable people marrying.

People who struggle to make a success of marriage in the long term are sometimes accused of lacking persistence. Persistence is generally viewed as a desirable human quality. So I was intrigued to read an article on the evolutionary origin of depression in *The Economist* of 27 July 2009:

> Clinical depression is a serious ailment, but almost everyone gets mildly depressed from time to time. Randolph Nesse, a psychologist and researcher in evolutionary medicine at the University of Michigan, likens the relationship between mild and clinical depression to the one between normal and chronic pain. He sees both pain and low mood as warning mechanisms and thinks that, just as understanding chronic pain means first understanding normal pain, so understanding clinical depression means understanding mild depression.
>
> Dr Nesse's hypothesis is that, as pain stops you doing damaging physical things, so low mood stops you doing damaging mental ones – in particular, pursuing unreachable goals. Pursuing such goals is a waste of energy and resources. Therefore, he argues, there is likely to be an evolved mechanism that identifies certain goals as unattainable and inhibits their pursuit – and he believes that low mood is at least part of that mechanism.
>
> It is a neat hypothesis, but is it true? A study published in this month's issue of the *Journal of Personality and Social Psychology* suggests it might be. Carsten Wrosch from Concordia University in Montreal and Gregory Miller of the University of British Columbia studied depression in teenage girls. They measured the 'goal adjustment capacities' of 97 girls aged 15–19 over the course of 19 months. They asked the participants questions about their ability to disengage from unattainable goals and to re-engage with new goals. They also asked about a range of symptoms associated with depression, and tracked how these changed over the course of the study.
>
> Their conclusion was that those who experienced mild depressive symptoms could, indeed, disengage more easily from unreachable goals. That supports Dr Nesse's hypothesis. But the new study also found a remarkable corollary: those women who could disengage from the

unattainable proved less likely to suffer more serious depression in the long run.

Mild depressive symptoms can therefore be seen as a natural part of dealing with failure in young adulthood. They set in when a goal is identified as unreachable and lead to a decline in motivation. In this period of low motivation, energy is saved and new goals can be found. If this mechanism does not function properly, though, severe depression can be the consequence.

The importance of giving up inappropriate goals has already been demonstrated by Dr Wrosch. Two years ago he and his colleagues published a study in which they showed that those teenagers who were better at doing so had a lower concentration of c-reactive protein, a substance made in response to inflammation and associated with an elevated risk of diabetes and cardiovascular disease. Dr Wrosch thus concludes that it is healthy to give up overly ambitious goals. Persistence, though necessary for success and considered a virtue by many, can also have a negative impact on health.

Dr Nesse believes that persistence is a reason for the exceptional level of clinical depression in America – the country that has the highest depression rate in the world. 'Persistence is part of the American way of life,' he says. 'People here are often driven to pursue overly ambitious goals, which then can lead to depression.' He admits that this is still an unproven hypothesis, but it is one worth considering. Depression may turn out to be an inevitable price of living in a dynamic society.

The premise of many 'self-help' books on personal relationships and marriage is that if you change yourself and/or your behaviour, your relationships or marriage will improve. But what if changing yourself and/or your behaviour is considerably more difficult than many of those books would have you believe? We return to Martin Seligman's *What You Can Change . . . and What You Can't* (2007):

> Two worldviews are in collision. On the one hand, this is the age of psychotherapy and the age of self-improvement. Millions are struggling to change: We diet, we jog, we meditate. We adopt new modes of thought to counteract our depressions. We practice relaxation to curtail stress. We exercise to expand our memory and to quadruple our reading speed. We adopt draconian regimes to give up smoking. We raise our little boys and girls to androgyny. We come out of the closet or we try to become heterosexual. We seek to lose our taste for alcohol. We seek more meaning in life. We try to extend our life span.
>
> Sometimes it works. But distressingly often, self-improvement and psychotherapy fail. The cost is enormous. We think we are worthless. We feel guilty and ashamed. We believe we have no willpower and that we are failures. We give up trying to change.

Trudy, like tens of millions of Americans, is desperate because she believes, quite incorrectly, that she is a failure. She finds herself even worse off after ten years of trying everything to lose weight.

Trudy weighed 175 pounds when she graduated from Brown a decade ago. Four times since, she has slimmed to under 125lbs: Weight Watchers, Nutri-System, six months under the care of a private behavior therapist, and, last year, a diet product. With each regime the weight came off quickly, if not painlessly. Each time the fat returned, faster and more of it. Trudy now weighs 195 and has given up.

In its faith that we can change anything, the self-improvement movement expects Trudy to succeed in her fight against fat, even though she is such an obvious loser in the weight game. On the other hand, there is a view that expects Trudy to fail. For this is not only the age of self-improvement and therapy, this is the age of biological psychiatry. . .

The brain systems underlying sex, hearing, memory, left-handedness, and sadness are now known. Psychoactive drugs – external agents – quiet our fears, relieve our blues, bring us bliss, dampen our mania, and dissolve our delusions more effectively than we can on our own. Our very personality – our intelligence and musical talent, even our religiousness, our conscience (or its absence), our politics, and our exuberance – turns out to be more the product of our genes than almost anyone would have believed a decade ago. Identical twins reared apart are uncannily similar in all these traits, almost as similar as they are for height and weight. The underlying message of the age of biological psychiatry is that our biology frequently makes changing, in spite of all our efforts, impossible.

But the view that all is genetic and biochemical and therefore cannot change is also very often wrong. Many individuals surpass their IQs, fail to 'respond' to drugs, make sweeping changes in their lives, live on when their cancer is 'terminal,' or defy the hormones and brain circuitry that 'dictate' lust or femininity or memory loss.

Clay is one of many who ignored the conventional wisdom that his problem was 'biological' and found just the right psychotherapy, which worked quickly and permanently.

Out of the blue, about once a week, Clay, a software designer, was having panic attacks. His heart started to pound, he couldn't catch his breath, and he was sure he was going to die. After about an hour of terror, the panic subsided. Clay underwent four years of psychoanalysis, which gave him insight into his childhood feelings of abandonment but didn't lessen the panic attacks. Then he was on high doses of Xanax (alprazolam, a tranquilizer) for a year; during that time he only panicked once a month, but he was so sleepy most of the time that he lost his two biggest accounts.

So Clay stopped taking Xanax and the panic returned with unabated fury. Two years ago, he had ten sessions of cognitive therapy for panic disorder. He corrected his mistaken belief that the symptoms of anxiety (e.g. heart racing, shortness of breath) are catastrophic: symptoms of an impending heart attack. Since then he hasn't had a single attack.

As the ideologies of biological psychiatry and self-improvement collide, a resolution is apparent. There are some things about ourselves that can be changed, others that cannot, and some that can be changed only with extreme difficulty.

What can we succeed in changing about ourselves? What can we not? A great deal is now known about change. Much of this knowledge exists only in the technical literature, and it has often been obfuscated by vested commercial, therapeutic, and, not the least, political interests. The behaviourists long ago told the world that everything can be changed – intelligence, sexuality, mood, masculinity or femininity. The psychoanalysts still claim that with enough insight, all your personality traits can be 'worked through.' The Marxist left, the 'politically correct,' and the self-help industry added their voices to this convenient chorus. In contrast, the pharmaceutical companies, the biologists mapping the human genome, and the extreme right wing tell us that our character is fixed, that we are prisoners of our genes and the chemicals bathing our brains, that short of powerful drugs, genetic engineering, or brain surgery, nothing basic can change: certainly not mood, or intelligence, or sexuality, or masculinity. These are all ideologically driven falsehoods.

Here are some facts about what you can change:

- Panic can be easily unlearned, but cannot be cured by medication.
- The sexual 'dysfunctions' – frigidity, impotence, premature ejaculation – are easily unlearned.
- Our moods, which can wreak havoc with our physical health, are readily controlled.
- Depression can be cured by straightforward changes in conscious thinking or helped by medication, but it cannot be cured by insight into childhood.
- Optimism is a learned skill. Once learned, it increases achievement at work and improves physical health.
- Dieting, in the long run, almost never works.
- Kids do not become androgynous easily.
- No treatment is known to improve on the natural course of recovery from alcoholism.
- Homosexuality does not become heterosexuality.
- Reliving childhood trauma does not undo adult personality problems.

To deal with what we cannot change, the first step, all too often evaded, is to know what about ourselves will not yield. But that is not the end of the matter; there are usually ways of coping. Much of successful living consists of learning to make the best of a bad situation. My purpose here, in part, is not only to point out what will not easily change but to impart the skills for coping with what you cannot change.

This book is the first accurate and factual guide to what you can change and what you cannot change. I am going to argue that so many loudly trumpeted claims about self-improvement, psychotherapy, medication, and genetics are not to be believed, that some things about you will not change no matter how much you try, but that other things will change easily. . .

In the domain of human personality, what are the facts? That, of course, is what this book is about. I want to provide an understanding of what you can and what you can't change about yourself so that you can concentrate your limited time and energy on what is possible. So much time has been wasted. So much needless frustration has been endured. So much of therapy, so much of child rearing, so much of self-improving, and even some of the great social movements in our century have come to nothing because they tried to change the unchangeable. Too often we have wrongly thought we were weak-willed failures, when the changes we wanted to make in ourselves were just not possible. But all this effort was necessary: Because there have been so many failures, we are now able to see the boundaries of the unchangeable; this in turn allows us to see clearly for the first time the boundaries of what is changeable.

The knowledge of the difference between what we can change and what we must accept in ourselves is the beginning of real change. With this knowledge, we can use our precious time to make the many rewarding changes that are possible. We can live with less self-reproach and less remorse. We can live with greater confidence. This knowledge is a new understanding of who we are and where we are going.

From chapter two, 'Booters and Bootstrappers: The Age of Self-Improvement and Psychotherapy':

What Americans believe people can change is – in historical perspective – truly astonishing. We are told from childhood that we can improve ourselves in almost every way. This is what our schools are supposed to help us accomplish. Our children are not just to be filled up with facts but taught to read, to be good citizens, to be lovingly sexual, to exercise, to have high self-esteem, to enjoy literature, to be tolerant of people who are different, to play baseball, to sing on key, to be competitive as well as cooperative, to lead and to follow, to have good health habits, to be ambitious, to use condoms, to obey the law.

The reality may fall short, but that is the mission of American schools. Improving is absolutely central to American ideology. It is tantamount in importance to freedom in our national identity; indeed, advancement is probably the end for which Americans believe freedom is the means.

Every boy and, at last, every girl might be president of the United States – with enough work and ambition. The reality may fall short, but that is the ideal that Americans profess. This is more than empty rhetoric. There is an enormous, and profitable, self-improvement industry that plays to your desire to achieve.

Here's a crazy idea. What if we stopped trying to change ourselves to suit the institution of marriage, and changed the institution to suit *us*? We shall return to this matter in the final chapter.

The journalist Caroline Gammell reported the following in *The Daily Telegraph* of 26 March 2009, under the title 'The formula that tells whether you will get divorced':

A professor and his team have perfected a model whereby they can calculate whether the relationship will succeed. In a study of 700 couples, Professor James Murray, a maths expert at Oxford University, predicted the divorce rate with 94% accuracy.

His calculations were based on the simplest of things, a 15-minute conversation between a couple. They were asked to sit opposite each other in a room on their own and asked to talk about a contentious issue, such as money, sex, or relations with the in-laws. Each couple was told to talk about the same topic – one with which they have been at loggerheads for some time – for the whole 15 minutes.

Prof Murray and his colleagues recorded the conversation and awarded the husband and wife positive or negative points depending on what was said. The points range from plus four to minus four:

RELATIONSHIP ARITHMETICS
First decide on a topic of conversation which is a consistent source of trouble between you, then lock yourselves away and record the interaction on video.

Then watch it back and give yourselves the following points every time you demonstrate these responses:

Affection	+4
Humour	+4
Joy	+4
Agreeing	+4
Interest	+2
Anger	- 1
Domineering	- 1
Sadness	- 1
Whining	- 1
Stonewalling	- 2
Defensiveness	- 2
Belligerence	- 2
Disgust	- 3
Contempt	- 4

Chart your score as positive or negative. Repeat periodically and a trend will emerge. A negative trend indicates a worsening relationship, and a positive trend an improving relationship.

The partner who showed affection, humour or happiness as they talked was given the maximum points, while those who displayed contempt or belligerence received the minimum.

Prof Murray, a Fellow of the Royal Society, said contempt was deemed more destructive than disgust, sadness or anger. He said the scores of the wife and the husband were fed into the mathematical model and plotted onto a graph. The point at which the two lines meet illustrated the marriage's chances of success or failure.

'I am still absolutely amazed that human emotions can be put into a mathematical model and that a prediction can be made,' he said. 'What astonished me was that a discussion, sometimes highly charged and emotional, could so easily and usefully be encapsulated in what is actually a simple model of a couple's interaction. It is not so much of an equation, it is trying to assess and quantify how a couple interact by giving them a scoring system. We take those figures and plot them on to a graph. If either the husband or the wife is consistently negative then they are going to get a divorce.'

Prof Murray said married couples could be divided into five groups – two of which were stable, two which were not and another category in between. 'Marriages can be classified into only five general types, some of which are stable and others not,' he said. 'Depending on the group, some couples might as well get divorced right away.'

The first identifiable category is the 'validating' couple who are calm, intimate, who like to back each other up and share a companionable relationship. They prefer shared experience instead of individuality.

The second group are the 'avoiders' couple who do their best to eschew confrontation and conflict. They only respond positively to their partner.

Prof Murray said: 'The most stable relationships are those which take a more old-fashioned view and see marriage as mainly about companionship.'

The 'volatile' couple, who are romantic and passionate but have heated arguments, are a mix of stable and unstable, but generally tend to be more unhappy than not.

The 'hostile' category is when one partner does not want to talk about an issue and the other agrees, so there is no communication.

The final 'hostile-detached' couple is where one is fiery and wanting to argue, while the other one is just not interested in discussing the issue.

Prof Murray, who is giving a lecture on the subject tonight at the Royal Society in London, said the original forecast of who would get divorced in his study of 700 couples was (initially) 100% correct. But, he added: 'What (later) reduced the accuracy of our predictions (to 94%) was those couples who we thought would stay married and unhappy, actually ended up getting divorced.'

On to a subject which will be of interest to anyone educated in a boarding school, and anyone married or related to them. We come to Nick Duffell's *The Making of Them (The British Attitude to Children and the Boarding School System)*. The material in the remainder of this chapter is drawn from the book. Duffell himself attended 'a top public school' and later graduated from Oxford University. From the introduction:

> This book explores why the British choose to send their children away to boarding school, what may happen to these children, and what sort of adults they may subsequently become. It offers some suggestions why sending young children away to board is a particularly British habit, and what may have caused their remarkable attitude to children.
>
> The book proposes that children who board are compelled to 'survive' psychologically – sometimes to their great cost. It argues that in order to cope with their loss of family and to adapt to their school environment, children unconsciously construct a 'Strategic Survival Personality', and that such a personality structure invariably becomes counter-productive in adult life. The book also offers suggestions for reversing the effects of 'boarding school survival' by means of the development of self-awareness and through psychotherapeutic help.

In chapter one Duffell relates the thinking that led to him developing the first Boarding School Survivors workshop in October 1990 (they still run to this day). He then goes on to explain how his thinking developed in the times that followed:

> Some things seemed very straightforward. The more I spoke to and listened to those who had been sent away to school as small children, the more I became certain that we were mainly dealing with issues of loss and denial. Through being sent away they might lose the very fundaments of life: trust and innocence, the sense of belonging, a sense of it being all right to be a child and to have a childhood. Then they would have to cope with these losses. Suppression of their emotional life and denial of the problem would be their main coping mechanisms.
>
> I started to think that this denial must operate on a massive scale, since for years the power base in Britain has been largely in the hands of boarding-school men. Even in John Major's new look 'one-nation' Conservative government of 1993, 16 of the 20 men in the cabinet had been to public school, 12 as boarders. The emblem of the English ruling class has traditionally been the old school tie. The public schools were still operating as hot-houses to cultivate new stock. Any attempt to question their desirability would not only seem to threaten the business of these private enterprises, but might also appear a threat to the 'fabric of British life.'

This must have been the reason why our Boarding School Survivors workshops were attracting such enormous interest from the media. We had hit upon a raw nerve. Psychologically, this nerve must be somewhere very close to the core of the British national personality. Its exposure was a subject of fascination, while to successful ex-boarders, I speculated, it would remind them of a secret door to a basement of fear, protected by a solid lock, forged in self-protection, and never to be re-opened.

The more I went into it, the more I began to suspect that the phenomenon of boarding schools and the shame, fear, denial and fascination about them was linked to some fundamental mindset in the British psyche. I began to deduce from this the existence of an underlying attitude towards children, which had long persisted in this country and was quite inexplicable to most foreigners.

This was an attitude which implied that it was really not OK to be a child at all. Children were inconvenient – they were 'un-made' and in the way until they became civilised adults. It was an attitude which permitted very small children, sometimes from the age of four, but more often from seven or eight, being sent away from their families and raised in institutions which turned them into premature adults. The aim was that their families might feel certain of being identified with the right social class, and satisfied that they had done the best for their child. Whether the child might be adversely affected by this was immaterial compared to the enormous social advantage that this education conferred. The issue could be rationalised away in a culture that regards children as a mistake. This attitude, I reckoned, was part of our unconscious heritage. In other words, people are generally quite unaware that they might hold a mindset of children as incompetent, 'un-made', and in the way.

The success of this set up depended, I reasoned, on the children buying into the game, and keeping quiet. Their silence needed to be enforced internally as well as externally. Of the two, the internal enforcement was much the more powerful and seemed to operate in two main ways. First, by the mixture of shame for letting their parents down and fear of losing more of their love (if they had already been sent away what might happen if they proved ungrateful?). And secondly, by the need to adapt and survive in the school.

This surviving and keeping quiet was so successful in the majority of cases that 'old boys', even if they had suffered themselves, would not neglect to send their own children away when they were of 'school age'. I guessed that this was because they still feared bringing shame upon themselves and provoking their parents' disapproval, by implicitly challenging the decision made a generation earlier. Furthermore, they had survived and been 'made' into adults. The 'un-made' child was now their own son or daughter, and these children were now ready to be 'made'. If these parents were to admit that they themselves had suffered at school their own success at secretly surviving their ordeal might be called into question. Thus the system continued in a perfect cycle. It seemed unbreakable. Thinking about this took my breath away.

In chapter four Duffell quotes and comments on the boarding school survivors' own words, including 'one of the most common statements, unequivocally expressed by one writer':

> My own experiences of boarding school have left me with lifelong problems in forming and sustaining relationships due to an inability to express or even acknowledge my emotions.

Duffell continues:

> Some people write saying that they are desperate for help, but unable to come forward because of their shame, or because of their difficulty in trusting others – particularly counsellors or 'shrinks'. Often wives write in hoping that someone will be able to 'fix' their husbands. I was warned by one woman that her husband would never attend a workshop:
>
> > He ran away twice, and I put his dependence on alcohol as the result of his unhappy schooling . . . (including) corporal punishment, a daily occurrence.
> >
> > Another wife, sounding angry and desperate, wanted to know whether I counselled 'women and children whose emotional health is at risk from these men.' Her husband had attended boarding schools from the age of 6 to 18, and was 'A workaholic and unable to support his family in any emotional or committed way.'
>
> Marriage is of course a difficult undertaking for anyone and takes two partners to make it work, so we must listen to such stories with some alertness. But we should also remember that boarding school is a poor training for marriage. Most survivors leave school with less knowledge about the opposite sex than if they had gone to the local comprehensive. So it is not surprising that we receive many such letters from partners of emotionally retentive survivors eager that someone might persuade their spouses to look at their unresolved issues.

Details on *The Making of Them*, and the Boarding School Survivors workshop, can be found on www.boardingschoolsurvivors.co.uk.

7

POLITICAL CORRECTNESS

I suppose true sexual equality will come when a general called Anthea is found having an unwise lunch with a young, unreliable model from Spain.

(John Mortimer, *The Spectator*, 26 March 1994)

This chapter covers:

- Why political correctness particularly antagonises those of a right-of-centre political persuasion
- The antipathy of political correctness towards Western values
- Political correctness is cultural Marxism
- Political correctness as the solution to patriarchal hegemony
- The 'unacceptable' gender pay differential
- The 'acceptable' differential between the retirement ages of men and women
- Discrimination, now one of the most unforgivable sins
- How political correctness undermines marriage
- A triumph of British common sense – how to reduce the number of divorces
- Harriet Harman's suspicion of ageism on *Strictly Come Dancing*

Political correctness antagonises those of a right-of-centre political persuasion (such as myself) more than it does those of a left-of-centre persuasion. I can thank the author of one splendid book for helping me understand why this is the case. The author is Anthony Browne, the book the snappily-titled *The Retreat of Reason: Political Correctness and the Corruption of Public Debate in Modern Britain* (2006). It was published by Civitas, The Institute for the Study of Civil Society. From chapter one, 'What is Political Correctness?':

> The phrase 'political correctness' conjures up images of left-wing councils banning black bin-bags, nativity scenes being banned by the Red Cross and handicapped people being called 'otherwise-abled'. Some of these cases, such as renaming firemen as firefighters, merely reflect a changing

reality. Others are just the most overt symptoms of political correctness, and easily ridiculed: he's not dead, he's metabolically challenged.

But political correctness is more than a joke or updating of historic language usage. It is a system of beliefs and pattern of thoughts that permeates many aspects of modern life, holding a vice-like grip over public debate, deciding what can be debated and what the terms of debate are, and which government policies are acceptable and which aren't. It has grown in influence over the last few decades to the extent that it has now become one of the most dominant features of public discourse, not just in Britain, but across the Western – and particularly the Anglophone – world.

PC is also surprisingly unexamined as a phenomenon, the subject of few academic treatises and few books, at least outside the US. Criticism of it has rarely graduated from ridicule to analysis. Part of the problem is that there is no standard definition of political correctness. Peter Coleman, a former Australian government minister from the Liberal Party, wrote:

> Political Correctness is a heresy of liberalism. It emerges where liberalism and leftism intersect. What began as a liberal assault on injustice has come to denote, not for the first time, a new form of injustice.

He said that it was liberalism that has been taken over by dogmatism, that it is 'intolerant', 'self-righteous' and 'quasi-religious'. The Politically Correct are more intolerant of dissent than traditional liberals or even conservatives. Liberals of earlier generations accepted unorthodoxy as normal. Indeed the right to differ was a datum of classical liberalism. The Politically Correct do not give that right a high priority. It distresses their programmed minds. Those who do not conform should be ignored, silenced or vilified. There is a kind of soft totalitarianism about Political Correctness.

The US conservative commentator Paul Weyrich, the President of the Free Congress Foundation, is also exercised by the intolerance of political correctness, although his main concern is its antipathy to Western values:

> The United States is very close to becoming a state totally dominated by an alien ideology, an ideology bitterly hostile to Western culture. Even now, for the first time in their lives, people have to be afraid of what they say. This has never been true in the history of our country. Yet today, if you say the 'wrong thing', you suddenly have legal problems, political problems, you might even lose your job or be expelled from college. Certain topics are forbidden. You can't approach the truth about a lot of different subjects. If you do, you are immediately branded as 'racist', 'sexist', 'homophobic', 'insensitive', or 'judgmental.'

The US commentator William Lind, director of the Center for Cultural Conservatism, is among those who have described PC as 'cultural Marxism', declaring that it is 'Marxism translated from economic into cultural terms'. [Author's note: Marxism. Does *this* explain why political correctness makes us see red?] He wrote:

> The cultural Marxism of Political Correctness, like economic Marxism, has a single factor explanation of history. Economic Marxism says that all of history is determined by ownership of means of production. Cultural Marxism, or Political Correctness, says that all history is determined by power, by which groups defined in terms of race, sex, etc, have power over which other groups. Nothing else matters.

The *New York Times'* culture correspondent, Richard Bernstein, who came out against multiculturalism in his book *The Dictatorship of Virtue*, was also concerned about how PC tried to overturn the dominant culture and power structures. In a landmark 1990 article which sparked debate about PC in the US, he wrote:

> Central to pc-ness, which has its roots in 1960s radicalism, is the view that Western society has for centuries been dominated by what is often called 'the white male power structure' or 'Patriarchal hegemony.' A related belief is that everybody but white heterosexual males has suffered some form of repression and been denied a cultural voice.

Across much of Britain's public discourse, a reliance on reason has been replaced with a reliance on the emotional appeal of an argument. Parallel to the once-trusted world of empiricism and deductive reasoning, an often overwhelmingly powerful emotional landscape has been created, rewarding people with feelings of virtue for some beliefs, or punishing with feelings of guilt for others. It is a belief system that echoes religion in providing ready, emotionally satisfying answers for a world too complex to understand fully, and providing a gratifying sense of righteousness absent in our otherwise secular society. . .

Because the politically correct believe they are not just on the side of right, but of virtue, it follows that those they are opposed to are not just wrong, but malign. In the PC mind, the pursuit of virtue entitles them to curtail the malign views of those they disagree with. Rather than say, 'I would like to hear your side', the politically correct insist: 'you can't say that'.

Believing that their opponents are not just wrong but bad, the politically correct feel free to resort to personal attacks on them. If there is no explicit bad motive, then the PC can accuse their opponents of a sinister ulterior motive – the unanswerable accusations of 'isms'. It is this self-righteous sense of virtue that makes the PC believe they are justified in suppressing freedom of speech. Political correctness is the dictatorship of virtue. . .

But what is the point of political correctness? Why are some things politically correct, and others not? At its most fundamental, political correctness seeks to redistribute power from the powerful to the powerless. At its most crude, it opposes power for the sake of opposing power, making no moral distinction between whether the power is malign or benign, or whether the powerful exercise their power in a way that can be rationally and reasonably justified. . .

America, as the world's most powerful country, can never do any good, even though it is the world's most powerful liberal democracy, the largest donor of overseas aid, and it defeated both Nazism and Communism.

The West, as the world's most powerful cultural and economic group, can safely be blamed for all the world's ills, even though it is largely responsible for the worldwide spread of prosperity, democracy and scientific advance.

Multinational corporations are condemned as the oppressors of the world's poor, rather than seen as engines of global economic growth with vast job-creating investments in the world's poorest countries, pushing up wages and transferring knowledge.

Conversely, political correctness automatically supports the weak and vulnerable, classifying them as nearly untouchable victims, irrespective of whether they merit such support or not. . .

In the battle between emotion and reason, emotion wins most of the time for most people: the heart trumps the head because it is more difficult to live with bad feelings than bad logic. Few are the souls tortured by bad reasoning; many are those tortured by guilt. However overwhelming the evidence, people believe what they want to believe, and find it very difficult to believe what they don't want to.

The easiest way to overcome the dissonance between what you want to believe and the evidence is not to change what you believe, but to shut out the evidence and silence those who try to highlight it. . .

People tend to believe that which makes them feel virtuous, not that which makes them feel bad. Most people have a profound need to believe they are on the side of virtue, and can do that by espousing beliefs publicly acknowledged as virtuous. Nothing makes multimillionaire Hollywood actors who live in Beverly Hills feel better about themselves than campaigning against world poverty by demanding more aid from the West (rather than holding African leaders responsible for the plight of their people by demanding better governance).

From the chapter 'How Political Correctness Affects Policies':

One of the rallying cries of the politically correct is the 'unacceptable' gender pay gap between men and women: women's full-time hourly pay is on average just 80% of that of men. Unions and the Equal Opportunities Commission regularly launch campaigns on the issue, insisting it shows just how prevalent sex discrimination still is in the workplace. Few ask whether the gender pay gap may be due to other factors, because that would be to appear to justify the pay gap and thus sex discrimination.

It is clear that, other factors being the same, equal pay for equal work is not just fundamentally fair and just, but also an essential basis for an efficient economy taking optimal advantage of the skills of all workers. If women are paid less for equal work than men just because of their gender, then that is irrational, prejudicial and unjust.

But even in a workforce with a total absence of sex discrimination, there could still be a gender pay gap. The presumption that any pay gap is only explicable by sex discrimination is a presumption that men and women are identical in all their lifestyle choices and legal rights, when they are not.

Men's legal retirement age is five years later than women's, encouraging them to work longer careers, which uplifts their average earnings. Women get far more extensive parental leave than men, encouraging career breaks and limiting their lifetime work experience, thus depressing their average wages. On average, each week, men work nearly twice as many hours in paid employment as women, building up considerably more experience in their careers, which in a meritocracy would be reflected in greater pay. In addition, surveys suggest that women opt for more socially rewarding or emotionally fulfilling jobs, while men put a higher priority on high wages at whatever cost.

The danger is that if the only accepted explanation for income differentials is discrimination, then a range of policies will be adopted that may either be counterproductive, or actually introduce discrimination. Policies that specifically favour women at the expense of men are not only unfair, but by undermining meritocracy they undermine the efficiency of the labour market.

From the chapter 'The Trouble with Discrimination':

Once upon a time, 'discrimination' – which is so central to much of political correctness it is worth special consideration – was seen as a positive attribute, which enabled people to discriminate between good and bad. People of discernment actually tried to educate themselves to become 'discriminating', a by-word for having good judgement.

Now 'discrimination' – an ill-defined, catch-all term – has become one of the most unforgivable sins, something that no respectable person would seek to justify under any circumstances. Anything that is portrayed as 'discriminatory' in any way is automatically deemed intolerable.

The fight against discrimination is one of the foundation stones of political correctness, underpinning and motivating much of it. Shami Chakrabarti, on becoming director of the left-wing pressure group Liberty, declared she believed in 'zero tolerance of any form of discrimination'. The European Charter of Fundamental Rights promises to outlaw all discrimination, turning politically correct sloganeering into Europe-wide law upheld by a court in Luxembourg:

> Any discrimination based on any ground such as sex, race, colour, ethnic or social origin, genetic features, language, religion or belief, political or any other opinion, membership of a national minority, property, birth, disability, age or sexual orientation shall be prohibited.

There are noble intentions behind these declarations that few civilised people would disagree with, and making these declarations rewards the declarers by making them feel virtuous (as one government lawyer said to me). The fight against discrimination has righted many hideous wrongs, such as denial of services to ethnic minorities and women's disenfranchisement. But having won the most obvious and justifiable battles, the intentions are often rendered meaningless by the flawed, often hypocritical and usually intolerant thinking behind them. . .

There are widespread double standards on various forms of discrimination. In general, discrimination – even irrational, prejudicial discrimination – is either tolerated or promoted so long as it is against the powerful, while discrimination against those deemed vulnerable is deemed indefensible. 'Gender profiling' by police forces that targets men is perfectly acceptable, while 'racial profiling' which targets blacks is not.

Those who wage war on 'all forms of discrimination' often promote so-called 'positive discrimination', which is nonetheless discrimination which should thus supposedly be worthy of 'zero tolerance'.

The difference in retirement age between men and women is irrational prejudicial discrimination, the continuation of which (at least until 2020) is only explicable because it is men (otherwise perceived to be privileged) who are discriminated against. It is inconceivable that if it were women who were discriminated against that it would not have ended by now, even though it would be slightly more justifiable because women actually live longer.

There are no longer any male-only colleges in Oxford and Cambridge, having come under great pressure to change. But women-only colleges, which are just as blatantly sexist, continue to justify their existence on the grounds that they benefit women – despite the fact that women greatly outperform men at all levels of the education system, up to and including the attainment of first-class university degrees.

I contend that men are become increasingly frustrated by the yawning gap between how some women in the developed world continue to portray themselves – as *still* disadvantaged – and the reality they see all around them in their working and personal lives. And I suggest that this frustration leads to increasing animosity among men towards women, which manifests itself in two ways: firstly, in men's increasing reluctance to enter the institution of marriage while it remains so disadvantageous to them, particularly in financial terms upon divorce; and secondly, as another contributor to gender rancour, which helps drive up the divorce rate.

Steve Moxon's insightful 2008 book *The Woman Racket* is 'a serious scientific investigation into one of the key myths of our age – that women arc oppressed by the patriarchal traditions of Western societies'. Drawing on the latest developments in evolutionary psychology, Moxon convincingly demonstrates that the opposite is true. He shows how men – or at least the majority of low-status males – have always been the victims of deep-rooted prejudice, and have been manipulated by women, because women have always been the 'limiting factor' in reproduction. That is, they have power over men because they control which men can, and which cannot, have children. Moxon explains why the idea that men exercise 'power' over women is nonsense, biologically speaking. He shows that domestic violence – even of the most violent nature – is more often committed by women against men than vice versa. And he overturns numerous other gender-related myths. It hardly needs saying, but Harriet Harman makes a number of appearances in the book.

From *The Daily Telegraph* of 13 February 2009, an article by Nick Allen entitled 'Marriage at lowest rate ever recorded':

> The number of marriages is at its lowest level since records began nearly 150 years ago, as an increasing number of people choose to live out of wedlock. High-profile divorce cases, the rising cost of weddings, and the failure of the Government to support the institution of marriage are among the factors blamed. It is now likely that official figures will show married couples to be in a minority by next year.
>
> Latest figures from the Office for National Statistics for the year 2007 in England and Wales showed that 21.6 out of every 1,000 men got married, down from 23 the previous year. The rate for women was 19.7 per 1,000, down from 20.7 in 2006.
>
> The levels were the lowest since records began in 1862. There were 231,450 marriages in 2007, a fall of 3.3% in a year, and the lowest total since 1885, when the population was little more than half its present level.
>
> The figures predate the current financial crisis, which is likely to have exacerbated the downward trend as couples put off their weddings because of the cost. Average costs have more than doubled over the past decade to more than £21,000.
>
> The Government has been accused of reinforcing the breakdown of marriage by introducing changes to the tax and benefits system that left married couples up to £5,000 a year worse off than people who stay single. The Conservative Party has promised to provide incentives for married couples and shift the tax burden away from families. Publicity surrounding divorce cases and large payments for wives are also thought to have encouraged people to avoid the altar.
>
> Civil ceremonies accounted for 67% of all marriages, while religious ceremonies fell 4.5% to 77,490. The average age of people getting married for the first time was 31.9 for men and 29.8 for women, a slight increase

on the previous year. In 1862, when marriage rates were first calculated, 58.7 men per 1,000 and 50 women got married. Even during the Second World War, the marriage rate for women never dropped below 40 per 1,000.

A triumph of British common sense. How do you reduce the number of divorces? By reducing the number of marriages. Marvellous.

I couldn't resist ending this chapter with another newspaper article involving the indefatigable Harriet Harman. The article was written by Anita Singh for *The Daily Telegraph* of 17 July 2009 and entitled ' "Ageist" BBC must reinstate Arlene, says Harman':

> Arlene Phillips, the *Strictly Come Dancing* judge who was dropped from the show in favour of a younger star, was the victim of age discrimination, according to Harriet Harman. In a surprising government intervention [Author's note: Hardly 'surprising' given that the intervention involves Harriet Harman; the woman has the stamina of ten ordinary mortals] Labour's deputy leader and the Equalities Minister described the BBC's decision to replace Phillips as 'absolutely shocking' and called for her to be reinstated.
>
> The veteran choreographer, 66, has been replaced by Alesha Dixon, 30, a pop star who won the ballroom competition in 2007. The male judges, who range in age from 44 to 65, and the show's 81-year-old host, Bruce Forsyth, have been retained, while the ballet dancer, Darcey Bussell, 40, will also join the show.
>
> Miss Harman told the Commons yesterday, 'It's shocking that Arlene Phillips is not going to be a judge on *Strictly Come Dancing*. As Equalities Minister I am suspicious that there is age discrimination there. So I'd like to take the opportunity of saying to the BBC: if it is not too late, we want Arlene Phillips in the next edition of *Strictly Come Dancing*.'

Harriet Harman. The gift that just keeps on giving.

8

RELIGION

I've a definite sense of spirituality. I want Brooklyn to be christened, but don't know into what religion yet.

(David Beckham, *Daily Mail*, 5 September 2002)

This chapter covers:

- Traditionally-minded people, religion and marriage
- *Marriage is Ministry, not Misery*
- The importance of religious compatibility in marriage
- Religious convictions and predicted impact on marital happiness
- The attractiveness of the concept of personal Gods
- 'Cultural Christians' including Richard Dawkins
- The 2006 poll which showed that 'Britain is basically a humanist country'
- The poor vigour of Christianity in the United Kingdom compared with Christianity in the United States
- Different religions' teachings on marriage and divorce

It has long been clear to me that many people with religious convictions – and particularly those with *very* strong convictions – differ from those of us who don't have them. They share many of the characteristics of traditionally minded, irreligious people. They're respecters of authority – they rarely get speeding notices, or fines for illegal parking – and they happily take on board 'received wisdom' from clerics and others.

For an insight into a traditional Christian viewpoint on gender roles in marriage, we turn to *Marriage is Ministry, not Misery (A Wife's Handbook)* by Donna A Gantt. From the back cover:

> Donna A Grant is a native of Dallas, Texas. She has been married 32 years to Paul E Gantt. Donna has been a teacher of women for over 20 years. She uses God's Word as the only foundation for building lives and a healthy marriage designed by God. Donna is an anointed speaker imparting Biblical truths, as well as her own marital experiences, with transparency of the struggles she faced in her marriage. Donna is much sought after as a speaker across the country.

This book is for the wife who has said, 'I will NOT be SUBMISSIVE, I will NOT be a DOORMAT.' You will come face-to-face with God and your very own attitude on submission, respecting your husband's leadership, the home, God's design for marriage and more. God will open your heart to receive His principles with JOY. God will ask you specific questions only you can answer. We as wives have contributed to the MISERY of our marriages also. Therefore, when we STOP pointing fingers at our husbands and become obedient to God's Word and function in our specific roles, then we'll stop being MISERABLE in our marriages.

Onto the chapter 'The Divine Origin of Marriage':

God is a Master Artist. Greater than Picasso or DaVinci could ever have been. God created a masterpiece that these two artists could never create with a brush. God wanted a perfect picture of marriage that only He could paint. God, the Master Artist, had more colours and tools to play with.

Viewing the Master at work, as He paints the picture of a sanctified marriage

With His paintbrush, God painted a picture of a man, whom He called Adam.

Genesis 1:26 – 'And God said, Let us make man in our own image, after our likeness.'

With that same brush, He painted a picture of a woman, whose name was Eve.

From the chapter 'Lord, Show Me The Joy of Submission':

If you want to get to the heart of your husband [Author's note: My second wife said that the most effective way to do this was to plunge a sharp knife between the third and fourth ribs], then become the submissive wife you are called to be by God. There is much truth in the statement, 'Only what we do for Christ will last.'

The world has butchered the word submission, to the point that it's taboo. The world has said that you are a slave or doormat if you are submissive. Many Christian women have bought into the world's perception of submission. The women's lib movement has made fools of a lot of women. They think just because they have great careers, or make more money than their husbands do, they don't have to be submissive. They have the mindset of, 'I pay the cost to be the boss'. . .

God never intended for the wife to be a doormat or slave to her husband. God designed marriage with structure and organisation, just as He's done within all realms of His creations. You as a wife should never feel inferior to your husband, because submission is not about inferiority. It's about God's design for a chain of command for order. A wife is as equal to the husband as Jesus is equal to God, but with different functions.

Stay with me on this, I'm going to spend a great deal of time on the issue of submission. This is where I believe wives need the most healing.

Ephesians 5:22–24 says, 'Wives, submit to the husband as to the Lord. For the husband is the head of the wife as Christ is the head of the church, his body, of which he is Saviour. Now as the church submits to Christ, so also wives should submit to their husbands in everything.'

Although the perspective here is rooted in Christianity, broadly similar arguments would surely be made by adherents of a number of some other major faiths.

I referred in an earlier chapter to Jeffry Larson's *Should We Stay Together?* On the subject of religion, I was particularly interested in one passage from the book:

> *Importance of religion:* Many people consider their religious beliefs and practices to be their most important life values. Their religious beliefs define what life, marriage, and family mean. They provide meaning to life and a direction. They provide a set of behaviour standards (for example, forgiveness is good). Hence, similarity of religion or beliefs is very important to your future marital satisfaction. Many others have lost touch with religious values entirely, and conduct their lives according to more or less clearly formed ethical principles.

Larson's point is well made. He is professor and director of the marriage and family therapy graduate programmes at Brigham Young University. A quick look on Wikipedia informs us that the university, located in Provo, Utah, United States, is a private, coeducational research university owned by the Church of Jesus Christ of Latter-day Saints (LDS or Mormon Church). It is the oldest existing institution within the LDS Church educational system, is America's largest religious university, and has the second-largest private university enrollment in the United States. Approximately 98% of the 34,000 students at BYU are Mormon; two-thirds of its American students come from outside the state of Utah.

So Brigham Young University is very unlike the institutions which most students – from a variety of religious and non-religious backgrounds – would encounter in the United Kingdom and indeed elsewhere. Larson relates an interesting personal tale:

Some people feel pressurised to marry the most eligible person in their home town of 500 people! In such situations, the pool of eligible partners is necessarily very limited. So they marry someone who is not really a very good match for them, thinking, 'You're not much but you've got to be better than no one at all!'

Not true! Such thinking may work when selecting a car, home, or what to eat for dinner. But settling for second best in the most important relationship decision of your life is not wise. If the pool of eligible partners is small where you live, move to a larger city! . . . Don't take second best in marriage!

A personal example of this phenomenon may illustrate this idea. My freshman year at college was frustrating because the pool of eligible women was tiny. I wanted to date women who shared my religion, but at the university I attended (20,000 students) I found a total of five single women who I wanted to date who shared my religious values and who were about my age! Perhaps I didn't look long or closely enough to find the right girl; nevertheless, I was frustrated and discouraged. So at the end of the year, I transferred to another university in a different state where my pool of eligible women went up to approximately 2,000 single women with my same religious values, all about my age! I thought I had died and gone to heaven! As a result my exam scores suffered, due to all the extracurricular girl-related activities I was engaged in. I never regretted that decision. (I met my future wife at church there, by the way – but it took several enjoyable years of looking, first.)

Expanding on Larson's theme, how might differences in religious convictions be expected to play out in marriage? We shall see that commonality of religious convictions should lead to a stronger marriage, and differences can lead to difficulties. An acquaintance of the author, twice-divorced John N (56), says:

I have a deep personal interest in this subject because I was brought up a Roman Catholic, indeed I went to single-sex Roman Catholic schools between the ages of seven and sixteen. When I was in my mid-teens my faith simply disappeared, and I've never regretted that. I consider myself to be rational, and while I may have lost the hope of heaven, this has been more that compensated by the loss of the fear of hell.

Over the intervening 40 years my atheistic convictions have remained strong, to the point that for many years I have found it difficult being in the presence of religious people when they talk about their beliefs. My second wife was a devout Christian. She wanted me to join her at her church on Sundays, while I wanted to persuade her of the 'rightness' of my own convictions.

I regret to say that of the two of us, I was far more assertive on the issue of religious beliefs. On a very deep level I struggled with having a partner who believed things which were beyond the realm of rational discussion. I now recognise that the differences between our convictions inflicted considerable stress upon both of us. I realise that I would have found a partner of *any* religion difficult to live with. I felt I was just 'hard wired' to challenge her thinking. Why some people are 'hard wired' to think and act like this, while others appear hard-wired to be tolerant of others, I don't know. If people in the first group force themselves to *appear* tolerant, it would still put a great mental strain on them.

Table 8.1 represents my efforts at predicting how differences in religious convictions might play out in a marriage, where one or both partners do not have naturally tolerant dispositions, and *all else being equal.* And we should perhaps remember that research over many years has shown women in general are more likely than men to hold religious convictions.

Table 8.1 Predicted impact of religious convictions on marital happiness

Partner #1	Partner #2	Variance	Predicted impact on marital happiness
1. Strong believer in religion R, denomination D (a)	As partner	Nil	HIGHLY POSITIVE Beliefs likely to bind couple together and to deter divorce
2. Strong believer in religion R, denomination D	Moderate believer in religion R, denomination D	Low	MILDLY POSITIVE Beliefs likely to bind couple together and to deter divorce
3. Strong believer in religion R, denomination D	As partner but denomination D2 (b)	Low to moderate	VARIABLE Could have positive or negative implications
4. Strong believer in religion R	Moderate believer in religion R2 (c)	Moderate to high	NEGATIVE Beliefs likely to drive partners apart unless they show *genuine* tolerance of each other's faiths
5. Strong believer in religion R	Strong believer in religion R2	High	HIGHLY NEGATIVE As above but more likely to drive partners apart
6. Strong believer in religion R	Agnostic (d)	Moderate to high	NEGATIVE
7. Strong believer in religion R	Atheist (e)	High	HIGHLY NEGATIVE
8. Moderate believer in religion R, denomination D	As partner	Nil	POSITIVE
9. Moderate believer in religion R denomination D	As partner but denomination D2	Low to moderate	VARIABLE
10. Moderate believer in religion R	Agnostic	Moderate	MILDLY NEGATIVE
11. Moderate believer in religion R	Atheist	Moderate to high	NEGATIVE
12. Agnostic	Agnostic	Nil	POSITIVE But will not deter an unhappy couple from divorcing
13. Agnostic	Atheist	Low	VARIABLE But will not deter an unhappy couple from divorcing
14. Atheist	Atheist	Nil	POSITIVE But will not deter an unhappy couple from divorcing

(a) For example, R = Christianity, D = Roman Catholicism

(b) For example, D2 = Conservative Protestantism

(c) R2 = any religion other than R

(d) Definition of 'agnostic' (*Chambers*): 'a person who believes that we know nothing of things beyond material phenomena, that a Creator, creative cause and an unseen world are things unknown or unknowable; loosely, a sceptic'.

(e) Definition of 'atheist' (*Chambers*): 'one who disbelieves in the existence of a god'.

Many British people speak of having 'a personal God', sometimes whilst still calling themselves 'Christians'. Having interviewed a number of these people I've come to the conclusion that they're attracted to a number of aspects of Christianity, but they don't accept the literal truth of the Bible, nor will they follow any of the established denominations. To my mind they're 'cultural Christians', a grouping which can include atheists, as we shall see shortly.

Personal Gods are interesting. I didn't come across a single believer in a personal God who felt that the entity gave guidance on the institution of marriage, or indeed divorce. Personal Gods appeared content to let believers make up their own minds; a position in stark contrast with, say, God as depicted in Roman Catholicism. Perhaps this helps explain the appeal of personal Gods, at least in part?

The British scientist Professor Richard Dawkins is possibly the most widely-known and widely-respected atheist in the world. But he counts himself a 'cultural Christian', which is probably true of most Britons in the modern era. From the BBC news website in 2008:

Scientist Richard Dawkins, an atheist known worldwide for arguing against the existence of God, has described himself as a cultural Christian. He told the BBC's *Have Your Say* that he did not want to 'purge' the UK of its Christian heritage. The comments came after Tory MP Mark Pritchard accused 'politically correct' people of undermining Christmas. Professor Dawkins, author of *The God Delusion*, added that he liked 'singing carols along with everybody else'.

On *Have Your Say*, Mr Pritchard told Prof Dawkins there was an 'increasing feeling' that 'many of the main Christian festivals are being sidelined and marginalised, sometimes by stealth, sometimes openly'. This, he argued, would allow groups such as the British National Party to utilise

Christian imagery for their own ends. Prof Dawkins, who has frequently spoken out against creationism and religious fundamentalism, replied: 'I'm not one of those who wants to stop Christian traditions. This is historically a Christian country. I'm a cultural Christian in the same way many of my friends call themselves cultural Jews (or culturally members of other faiths) . . . So, yes, I like singing carols along with everybody else. I'm not one of those who wants to purge our society of our Christian history. If there's any threat of this nature, I think you will find it comes from rival religions and not from atheists.'

Dawkins is one of 13 vice presidents of the British Humanist Association (BHA). The following was posted on the website of the BHA (www.humanism.org.uk) on 24 November 2006:

In the 2001 census 7 out of 10 people ticked the 'Christian' box but, with church attendance now below 7% and under one in three marriages taking place in church, this figure was clearly more about cultural identity than religious belief. Today an Ipsos MORI poll has shown that 36% of people – equivalent to around 17 million adults – are in fact humanists in their basic outlook. They:

- feel scientific and other evidence provides the best way to understand the universe (rather than feeling that religious beliefs are needed for a 'complete understanding')
- believe that 'right and wrong' can be explained by human nature alone, and does not necessarily require religious teachings, and
- base their judgments of right and wrong on 'the effects on people and the consequences for society and the world'.

Humanism is a non-religious ethical outlook on life and these answers summarise its key beliefs. These are the key figures from the poll, along with analysis of the Ipsos MORI poll on how many people believe:

- Overall, faced with the choice, 62% said 'scientific and other evidence provides the best way to understand the universe' against 22% who felt 'religious beliefs are needed for a complete understanding of the universe'.
- Similarly, 62% chose 'Human nature by itself gives us an understanding of what is right and wrong', against 27% who said 'People need religious teachings in order to understand what is right and wrong'.
- In the last question, faced with three choices, 65% said that what is right and wrong 'depends on the effects on people and the consequences for society and the world'. The rest split almost equally between two profoundly un-humanist views: 15% said right and wrong were 'basically just a matter of personal preference' and 13%

said what was right and wrong was 'unchanging and should never be challenged'.
- 36% chose all three of the humanist answers, and another 30% chose two out of three. Only 13% chose none of them.
- 41% believe this is our only life.

Another question found that 41% endorsed the strong statement: 'This life is the only life we have and death is the end of our personal existence'. Fractionally more – 45% – preferred the broad view that 'when we die we go on and still exist in another way'. Of those choosing all three of the 'humanist' answers, 54% said this was our only life, against 38% who believed in some sort of continued existence. And of those seeing this as our only life, 79% chose two or all three of the 'humanist' answers to the other questions. (Interestingly, 22% of those who endorsed the need for religion in answers to other questions also said this was our only life.)

A spokesperson for the British Humanist Association said, 'Britain is basically a humanist country, and this poll shows it. We have always been aware that many people who do not identify themselves as humanists, and this includes quite a few people who do not know what humanism is, live their lives by what one might describe as humanist principles. People who join the Association often tell us that they have been humanists all their lives, or for the last 20 years or so, but didn't know it. It is very encouraging to find that 36% of the British population are not simply non-religious, but actually humanist in their outlook and their morality, and that very many others don't feel they need religion to understand the universe, or to guide their moral decisions.

Americans are considerably more likely than Britons – indeed, more likely than Europeans in general – to be actively religious. And far more likely to believe in the literal truth of the Bible, as expressed for example in a widespread refusal to accept the theory of evolution, surely a damning indictment of the American education system over the past century. And yet, contrary to our reasonable expectations, the divorce rate in the United States has long been at least as high as in most European countries where divorce is readily attainable. What might explain this? I turned to an American lady friend for her thoughts:

Two traits we Americans are known for – impatience and idealism – don't augur especially well when aiming for a lifelong union of happiness comprised of two flawed human beings. We tend to expect more from the institution of marriage than other cultures do, and so we become disillusioned more easily when reality doesn't meet our expectations. It is very difficult to form a strong, permanent union in a society that constantly stresses the importance of individual achievement and remaining separate but equal in almost every conceivable way. And for the introverts among us, it can be an even rougher road due to the ongoing need we have for frequent solitude.

Maybe we can also add the nature of Christianity in the United States. Commentators have pointed to the remarkable proliferation of Christian denominations in the United States, and they suggest that Americans can more readily find a denomination that suits their temperament and convictions than can Europeans. This is surely helpful for those seeking a less 'rigid' brand of Christianity than, say, Roman Catholicism. But the large number of Christian denominations in the United States may in itself lead to widespread rancour between partners of different denominations.

British Anglicans must look at the vigour of Christianity in the United States – and indeed much of the world – and weep. Fewer that 7% of British adults now attend weekly religious ceremonies, and the number appears to be in terminal decline.

On to an interesting book published in the United States in 2008, *The Role of Religion in Marriage and Family Counselling*, edited by Jill Onedera, a Catholic counsellor educator and assistant professor in the Department of Counselling and Student Affairs at Western Kentucky University. In the book adherents of different faiths outline their understanding of their religions' teachings about the following:

-       Definition of marriage
-       Dating and cohabitation
-       Roles within marriages and families
-       Childbearing, birth control, abortion, teenage pregnancy
-       Finances
-       Dissolving relationships, divorce, annulment
-       Managing family after separation and/or divorce
-       Death and dying
-       Homosexuality in couples and families

A number of the major religions – and indeed even the different Christian denominations – have remarkably different teachings on marriage, divorce, and related matters. The following excerpt from Onedera's book takes up the remainder of this chapter:

<u>Catholicism</u>
Marriages in the Catholic Church are seen as a permanent communion between two persons . . . marital indissolubility is the goal or norm under which the Catholic approach to marriage must operate, except by the death of one spouse.

The *Catechism of the Catholic Church* states that there may be 'some situations in which living together becomes impossible for a variety of reasons.' In such extraordinary cases, physical separations are allowed; however the couple still is considered married and is not allowed to contract a new union with another partner . . . [Divorce is] considered immoral and gravely sinful . . . The Catholic Church takes the position that there is no authority that can dissolve a marriage. However, the Church does not ignore the fact that some marriages fail. The annulment process is the Church's official declaration that what seemed to be a valid Christian marriage was in fact not one at all . . . if the marriage can be shown to be invalid, the individuals are allowed to enter into a true marriage in the future.

<u>Conservative Christians</u>
Conservative Christians, also known as conservative Protestants or as evangelicals, are those who maintain certain views on God, the Bible, the nature of salvation and the historic doctrines of the Christian faith . . . Conservative evangelicals are distinguished from other Christian groups by the special emphasis they place on retaining their faith in its purity. This includes an unusually high priority on the doctrine of God, the nature of Scripture as the authoritative and inspired word of God, and on salvation as God's work through Jesus Christ . . . Conservative Christians hold an array of positions about if and when divorce is an appropriate choice for a Christian couple. Christians recognise that the general voice of the Bible is pro-marriage, and conclude that divorce is usually not an acceptable option for a couple. However, most Christians also see that there are situations in which the Bible permits divorce as a response. What these situations are and when they apply is debated among conservative Christians.

Two biblical exceptions are generally acknowledged in conservative Christian thought. First, Jesus states, 'whoever divorces his wife, except for sexual immorality, and marries another, commits adultery' (Matt. 19:9). Jesus accepted sexual immorality as a reason divorce is permissible. Infidelity by a spouse is accepted by most as clear grounds for divorce, along with other forms of sexual immorality, assuming the offence is of a serious nature.

Christians accept desertion of one spouse by the other, especially if the deserting spouse is not a Christian, as a second possible biblical reason for divorce. 1 Corinthians 7:15 says, 'If the unbelieving partner separates, let it be so. In such cases the brother or sister is not enslaved.'

Liberal Protestant Christianity

The recurring themes (of liberal Protestantism) include the central authority of scripture, which includes critiquing scripture; being reformed, always being reformed, and the accompanying resistance to idolatory; openness to other sources of knowledge including the arts and sciences; sexuality as a good gift from God; absolute dependence on the grace of God for justification and salvation. Additional themes include faith and reason held in creative tension, not opposition (faith-based understanding); balance between individual agency and a sense of community – the self is always a self-in-relation; appreciation for diversity; contextual awareness; concern for those on the margins and commitment to social justice.

In line with these recurring theological themes and characteristics, no church doctrine or practice, no interpretation of scripture, no institution, and no established tradition is considered infallible. To claim such would be to commit idolatory. . .

Given all that is involved in marriage, divorce for Christians has complex legal, psychosocial, and theological ramifications . . . Protestant churches, and particularly the Presbyterian church have recognised divorce as legitimate, not only on grounds of adultery (which Jesus sanctioned, according to Matthew 19:9) or desertion (the old terms in the Westminster Confession of Faith) but also 'where a continuation of the legal union would endanger the physical, moral, or spiritual well-being of one or both of the partners or that of their children' (Book of Church Order 215:5).

Judaism

There are several forms of Judaism in North America, each interpreting and applying the Jewish tradition in its own distinctive way. Only 46% of American Jews belong to a synagogue. Of those 39% affiliate with a Reform synagogue, 33% with a Conservative one, 21% with an Orthodox one, 3% with a Reconstructionist one, and 4% with other types (*National Jewish Population Study, 2000–2001*) . . . Some Jews who have not joined a synagogue nevertheless see themselves as religiously Jewish and others ('secular Jews') identify with Jewish culture and values . . . but not Jewish religious beliefs. . .

From the biblical period to the early 20th century, marriages were arranged by parents, sometimes with the help of a matchmaker, known to many through *Fiddler on the Roof*. This mode of finding a spouse bespeaks the tradition's understanding of what to expect in marriage. Unlike contemporary American conceptions, marriage is not primarily for purposes of happiness and sex, although it certainly includes those. It is rather to care for each other, raise a family, and build lives together. As the couple in that musical sing after 25 years of marriage, articulating that they love each other 'doesn't change a thing, but it's nice to know.'

Jewish law defines a Jew as a person born to a Jewish woman or converted to Judaism . . . The importance of marriage, within the Jewish tradition, is not only for reasons of propagation and companionship, as important as they are; it is also to educate children in the Jewish tradition so it can continue across the generations . . . Until the last century, most Jewish marriages were arranged by the parents of the bride and groom. Both the man and the woman had to agree to marry each other, but, like the author's own grandparents, they may not have met until the day they were married. Among other things, this guaranteed that Jews would marry Jews, in accordance with Jewish norms from biblical times to our own. During most of the last two millennia Jews were kept from interfaith marriage not only by their own laws and customs but also by the laws and anti-Semitism of the people among whom they lived. . .

Although divorce is always sad, Judaism does not consider it a sin. In fact, the Torah itself provides some instructions about the form of a divorce (Deut. 24:1-3), and the Mishnah and Talmud include an entire section on divorce law. If the couple agrees to the divorce, they need not supply any justifications; incompatibility is enough. . .

Traditional Jewish law as practised in the Orthodox and Conservative Movements requires that the couple be divorced in Jewish law in addition to civil law; neither suffices without the other. Traditional Jewish law required the husband to give his wife a writ of divorce (a *get*); the wife cannot initiate the proceeding. In a small minority of cases, even when the couple has divorced in civil law, the husband refuses to give his wife a *get*. Unless the husband has good reason for this (eg the woman is not granting him access to their children in accordance with the civil court's decree), rabbis will first try to convince him to give his wife a *get*, then they will put pressure on him through his friends and employer. Finally, if necessary, Conservative rabbis will annul the marriage so that the woman can remarry.

Buddhism

Buddhism, according to the teachings of Lord Buddha, does not actually solemnise marriages. Marriage ceremonies are a civil ceremony in the Buddhist world. Rituals are not led by the clergy nor is the Buddha invoked to consecrate the union . . . Culturally courtship in the Buddhist world has many expressions. Generally courtship has parental supervision and the parents can even require an arranged marriage. The more traditional the family the more this is the case. Nowadays with the relaxation of traditional values many Buddhist families are open-minded and allow marriage to be based on mutual attraction and love.

There is one form of arranged marriage that we may not be familiar with in the West. This is the marriage of several brothers to one woman. I knew of a young Tibetan Buddhist man who was destined to marry the wife of his three older brothers. The reason for this arrangement was to ensure no division of the family estate. The logic was if all the brothers were to father their children through one woman then the land remained intact.

Buddhist marriage requirements and ceremonies vary greatly. An example of cultural variance is Thailand. All mature Thai men must by law spend three months in a monastery as a monk before they marry. This ensures they have an opportunity to know the monk's life of peace and contemplation. Buddhist monks and nuns are taught worldly life is mixed with suffering. The teachings state that if the mind is deluded then the causes of suffering exist. The monk's or nun's life is an alternative. Those with ordination are living a life free of attachment and are on a path to lead them to freedom from disturbing emotions and delusions. If the eligible young man finds religious life satisfying then he can remain in the monastery. Men who do not like monastic life and its discipline are free to return to lay life and marry.

Buddhism is pragmatic about the legalities of marriage and divorce. All the issues of separation and divorce are dealt with by the laws of the land or by responsible members of the community. Marriages in Buddhist countries are based on a marriage contract and this is either written by the families or preset by law. Thus all issues in a divorce are handled by the courts.

Hinduism
Hinduism, a term that was first used by West Asian Muslims to distinguish non-Muslim inhabitants of the subcontinent, is one of the oldest living religions in the world. Hinduism constitutes a wide range of philosophy and practices ranging from monotheism, polytheism, as well as henotheism (choosing one deity for special worship, while acknowledging the divinity of others), to animism and even agnosticism and atheism (Vanita, 2004). Marriage is one of the most important social institutions in India. It is not only a union of two individuals but also an alliance between two families and thus starting a new network of relationships. Marriage is considered to be a sacred duty . . . Hindu marriage is a sacrament and the ceremony is only complete after the performance of several sacred rites. It is a sacred and lifelong commitment. . .

In India, as in the majority of the world's cultures, marriages are arranged by family members, not by the bride and groom (Skolnick, 1987). In his theory of love and marriage across cultures, Goode (1959) argued that in cultures with traditions of strong kinship networks and strong family ties, romantic love is viewed as irrelevant or even disastrous to marriage. . .

For a Hindu, marriage is a way to continue the family and thus pay one's debts to the ancestors. Begetting a son, who will perform the social and religious rites as prescribed by the scriptures, is the primary goal of Hindu marriages. Orthodox Hindus believe that only the son can perform the rites and thus save the father from entering hell, called *putt* in Sanskrit. The son is therefore called a *putra*, who saves his father from *putt*. . .

Divorce in India is highly stigmatising and objectionable (Rao & Sekar, 2002) . . . Rao & Sekar also stated that education level of women is an important variable associated with divorce. Although not always, women with a higher level of education were more likely to end marital incompatibility by divorce.

9

THE LAW RELATING TO MARRIAGE AND DIVORCE IN ENGLAND AND WALES, ASSET DIVISION IN DIVORCE SETTLEMENTS

I don't think I'll get married again. I'll just find a woman I don't like and give her a house.

(Rod Stewart)

This chapter covers:

- A fine day for justice in England and Wales
- The law in England and Wales on post-divorce asset division
- How the law on asset division operates in practice
- Mediation and collaborative law
- Solicitors' fees for divorce
- Prenuptial and postnuptial agreements
- 'Why can't couples stick together any more?'
- 'We don't *have* to get married'
- Divorce as a positive outcome
- The lack of official guidance on prenuptial and postnuptial agreements
- 'Well-heeled women go for prenups to beat the gold-diggers'
- 'Don't get even, get Tooth!'
- 'Wonderfully frank advice for gold-diggers'
- Women still marry to improve their economic well-being
- John Cleese – 'The system is insane' and 'Feeding the beast'
- 'A rum do' – an ex-wife is awarded 105% of her ex-husband's fortune
- The Divorce Doctor

In future divorce may not be such an easy road to wealth in England and Wales. July 2 2009 was a fine day for justice as exercised by the courts of England and Wales, but a *very* bad day for one Frenchman. Stephen Adams filed the following report – 'Landmark victory for heiress in prenup case' – in the next day's *The Daily Telegraph*.

Prenuptial agreements were recognised in English law for the first time yesterday after a German heiress won a landmark legal battle with her former husband. Three Appeal Court judges ruled that the assets of Katrin Radmacher, a paper industry heiress said to be worth £100 million, should be protected from her French-born former husband because of the agreement they signed before their marriage. They said that in future, judges deciding the division of marriage assets should give 'due weight' to prenuptial contracts freely entered into.

In what one divorce solicitor described as a judgment 'hell-bent' on enshrining prenuptial contracts in law, the judges suggested the agreements could be an alternative to the 'stress, anxieties and expense' of divorce hearings.

Miss Radmacher, 39, had brought her case to the court to challenge an earlier High Court ruling that she should give £5.85 million to Nicolas Granatino, despite him having signed a contract promising not to make claims if they parted. That ruling had been made by Mrs Justice Baron, who said it would be 'manifestly unfair' to hold Mr Granatino to the prenuptial contract as such agreements had never been legally binding in this country.

Although the agreement was signed in Germany, the couple married in London in 1998, which was why the case was being heard in England. They lived together in Britain and New York before the marriage broke down in 2003 when Mr Granatino, 37, left his well-paid banking job to become a £30,000-a-year biotechnology researcher at Oxford University. They divorced in 2006.

In yesterday's ruling, Mr Granatino's settlement was cut to about £1million as a lump sum in lieu of inheritance, with a fund of £2.5million for a house which will be returned to Miss Radmacher when the youngest of their two daughters, who is six, reaches 22. His debts of about £700,000 are to be paid by the heiress, who had already agreed to this settlement.

But the ruling made clear that the money was being awarded for the children, which the prenuptial contract stated fell outside its remit. Lord Justice Thorpe, sitting with Lord Justice Rix and Lord Justice Wilson, said, 'In so far as the rule that such contracts are void survives, it seems to me to be increasingly unrealistic. It does not sufficiently recognise the rights of autonomous adults to govern their future financial relationship by agreement in an age where marriage is not generally regarded as a sacrament and divorce is a statistical commonplace.'

Lord Justice Thorpe stressed that 'a carefully fashioned contract should be available as an alternative to the stress, anxieties and expense of a submission to the width of the judicial discretion.'

The contracts are still not binding under English law, as there is no provision for them under Section 25 of the 1973 Matrimonial Causes Act. Lord Justice Rix called for Parliament to clarify the law, saying he could see 'great force' in the argument that they be treated as 'presumptively valid'.

David Lister, of solicitors Mishcon de Reya, said it was the most important ruling on the agreements to date. He added, 'They appear to be hell-bent on creating a judgment that says, 'Please take prenups more seriously.'

In an adjoining article Melissa Lesson, a partner at Mishcon de Reya, wrote:

Yesterday's Court of Appeal ruling is likely to result in a seismic shift in the way courts apply the law regarding prenuptial contracts. Although prenuptial agreements are, and always have been, enforceable, their enforceability is subject to the court's right to veto or amend their terms. Until now, it has been up to the party relying on the agreement to persuade the court to uphold it. In its latest decision, the Court of Appeal has recognised that the application of the law has become too capricious and uncertain.

Times have moved on and couples are sufficiently sophisticated to be entitled to enter into agreements that settle arrangements for their futures that cannot be ripped up by the courts. This will require Parliament to debate the adequate checks and balances that would need to be put into place to make prenuptial agreements bombproof. Additionally, couples need to be better educated about exactly what they are signing up to and what claims they are contracting out of when they enter a prenup.

In the meantime, the family courts are likely to follow the Court of Appeal's guidance and, in future, the legal burden will therefore start to fall on the person who wants to extricate themselves from the prenup rather than, as now, on the person who wants to uphold it.

I found it interesting that the Court of Appeal made the judgment they did in a case where a *wife* was potentially benefiting from a prenup agreement. Maybe to have done so to benefit a husband would have been more contentious. And the wife was trying to stop just 5% of her fortune going to her ex-husband, a man who had given up a highly-paid banking career to be with her, and with whom she had children. Incredible. Money really does flow in only one direction in divorce settlements, from men to women, with very rare exceptions.

Perhaps not surprisingly, given the sums of money at stake, Mr Granatino sought permission to appeal the verdict from the then recently-formed Supreme Court of the United Kingdom, which began its work on 1 October 2009. He was given permission to appeal. So the future validity of prenups in the United Kingdom is uncertain as I write this (December 2009).

For insights about the current law in England and Wales, as it relates to the division of assets upon divorce, I am indebted to an acquaintance, 'JS', who is head of family law at a law firm in the Midlands. The following is a transcript of our conversation (which predated the Appeal Court decision on prenups reported above):

JS   In England and Wales there is no 'scientific' method by which assets are divided. The only guidance we have is a checklist in the Matrimonial Causes Act 1973, Section 25. It's a list of eight issues the court must take into account. The relevant extract from the Act is as follows:

> Matters to which the Court is to have regard in deciding how to exercise its powers in relation to a party to the marriage: the Court shall in particular have regard to all the circumstances of the case, first consideration being given to the welfare while a minor of any child of the family who has not attained the age of eighteen. The court shall in particular have regard to the following matters:

- The income, earning capacity, property and other financial resources which each of the parties to the marriage has or is likely to have in the foreseeable future, including in the case of earning capacity any increase in that capacity which it would in the opinion of the Court be reasonable to expect a party to the marriage to take steps to acquire.

- The financial needs, obligations and responsibilities which each of the parties to the marriage has or is likely to have in the foreseeable future.

- The standard of living enjoyed by the family before the breakdown of the marriage.

- The age of each party to the marriage and the duration of the marriage.

- Any physical or mental disability of either of the parties to the marriage.

- The contributions which each of the parties has made or is likely in the foreseeable future to make to the welfare of the family, including any contribution by looking after the home or caring for the family.

- The conduct of each of the parties, if that conduct is such that it would in the opinion of the Court be inequitable to disregard it.

- In the case of proceedings for divorce or nullity of marriage, the value to each of the parties to the marriage of any benefit which, by reason of the dissolution or annulment of the marriage, that party would lose the chance of acquiring.

In the day-to-day cases that a provincial firm like this deals with, in effect you are taking your average case of a middle-class couple with 2.4 kids, and trying to re-house two people and their children out of one house. And therein lies the problem, really. Where there is less money, settlements deemed just and fair to both parties are more difficult to work out, because then you are more often than not resigned to concentrating on needs and resources.

Up until about 2000 or 2001 the law was very much in the man's favour, because the courts at that point were only looking at the wife's reasonable needs. The landmark case of White vs. White then came along and said that there should be a yardstick of equality. Equality, though, does not necessarily mean equal division. And since then, there has been a lot more said and, in terms of identifying matrimonial assets, even looking at compensating the wife for lost years in bringing up the children. White vs. White was very much about putting a stop to discrimination towards the wife, in having given up her career, and not looking at her reasonable needs. The courts acknowledged that there should not be discrimination between the breadwinner and the home maker.

MB Let's consider an example of a 40-year-old couple who divorce after being married for 20 years, and the wife has been a housewife for 20 years. They have two young children. Her earning capacity will be markedly less than her husband's, so would that be taken into account in the divorce settlement?

JS Yes, absolutely. That inequality might be addressed by an unequal division of capital in her favour or maintenance or both, and the court also has the power to split the husband's pension (assuming that his is the largest pension pot). What is 'fair' is a very subjective view. Very often the arguments we have in court are the wife saying that her reasonable capital housing needs are £50,000 more than what the husband thinks is reasonable: the style of house she wants, the better area, and it has to have maybe four bedrooms instead of three. And the husband is saying, 'Well, no, actually, you can go and live in shared ownership property, because where am I going to live? I still need to have the children overnight; that seems to be more fair to me.' I can understand men who get divorced concluding there is some form of 'the wife gets it all' scenario.

Even now with the large majority of couples who have children, particularly where there are two or more children, there is going to be an in-built inequality, because the husband has been the breadwinner. The wife has taken a break in her career; the husband's income, therefore, is going to be better, because his career is more developed, so his pension will be better etc. And things just snowball from there. Particularly if she has taken enough time off to affect her long-term earning capacity, she might never be able to recover that in terms of income and pension provision.

It's very difficult for a court to accept after the event that where the wife has taken time off, and not returned to work even when the children are 10, 13 or older and they don't need so much of their mother's support, that the husband hasn't accepted that position. Because he could have said within a year, 'Well, you're not prepared to return to work and I'm not doing this all on my own, so I want a divorce now.' Very often men don't do that; they wait another seven to ten years, and *then* they seek a divorce. By which time there is an element of acquiescence, I think. It is perhaps too late to expect the wife to retrain and the court will have to take that into account. I think part of it is circumstantial: men can't bear children therefore they are not going to be the ones interrupting their careers.

But going back to your original question, how do the courts work out division of assets? Section 25 is our starting point. The rationale is that there isn't any community of property law, and every case is considered on its own merits. Some couples might have kids, some don't, some might have disabilities etc. And there are also differences in ages. So as things have developed, we've got a tranche of case law that seeks to demonstrate how the Section 25 checklist should be interpreted.

MB   Okay. So if you come across a new case, your experience or your research will guide you towards similar settled cases, and thereby suggest how to approach the new case?

JS   Yes. Some of the high profile or big money cases come out with all sorts of principles. But to a provincial office like this one, which deals with couples where there is not a lot of money, the cases are not always a great deal of help. Again you're coming back to the main issues such as accommodation for the kids, which is usually going to be with the wife, therefore her needs are going to be greater.

There are a lot of general principles to be considered. The man shouldn't be left with all the pension, and the wife left with all the liquid assets. Inheritances should be dealt with separately, provided there's enough marital assets. The concept of financial compensation is quite a new one, but the Law Lords have used the term to describe reward for taking years off and not carrying on with a career.

MB   Looking down the Section 25 list of issues, there's one which seems to me utterly perverse, and in high profile cases the issue makes my blood boil. John Cleese's latest divorce is a good example. The issue is that the court should have regard to the standard of living enjoyed by the family before the breakdown of the marriage. Isn't this just an open invitation to gold-diggers to do their worst?

JS   It is. You do get some very perverse cases, such as Miller vs. Miller: a very short marriage, a big money case, and they were married something like three years. The wife got £5 million after the divorce. Being cynical, that's not a bad pay packet, is it? In the case of Parlour vs. Parlour, the footballer and his wife, the court recognised that the wife had effectively saved his career through helping him to continue playing football despite his alcoholism. The court said, 'Well, you haven't got enough capital, but he earns absolutely loads, so you're going to get a huge amount of maintenance every year. But you're expected to save it for a rainy day.' Standard of living, again on a day-to-day case, rarely comes into account, but it certainly does in the big money cases.

For many years the courts have rarely invited argument over the other spouse's conduct, so conduct rarely comes into play in the court's decision on asset distribution after divorce. The proceedings are not in public; courts don't want to unpick every year of a marriage and take it apart, which would only increases legal costs. Particularly where there are children, arguments about conduct would only increase the acrimony in proceedings and generally it's got to be really serious misconduct. I've had only two such cases in the last ten years. The conduct would also generally have had to cause a financial loss, such as gambling.

MB How often can couples manage to reach an amicable agreement over asset distribution? A number of male acquaintances who've divorced say that their previously reasonable wives become red-eyed grasping monsters when divorce loomed. They've often been egged on by female friends to 'bleed the bastard dry'. All reason seems to go out of them.

JS You're right, I'm afraid. Mediation and collaborative law is being pushed by the Ministry of Justice and the courts, probably to try to save costs. But in my experience they rarely work in the first six to eight months after separation.

One partner or the other is going to be licking his or her wounds quite a bit; they carry too much baggage to be able to think rationally about financial arrangements. I also think that there is a social issue there as well. I think middle- and upper-class people are more likely to engage with mediation than factory workers. Better educated people are going to think more rationally, and I think men are built to compartmentalise their emotions more effectively than women.

MB   You mentioned collaborative law. What's that?

JS   Collaborative law is very similar to mediation. Effectively, you sign up with your lawyer not to go to court during the process of negotiation. And if everything subsequently breaks down, and you *do* want to go to court, you have to go and get yourself a new lawyer. I've never done it myself. You have to be a trained mediator, which I'm not. In some cases, particularly where parties qualify for legal aid, we *have* to refer to mediation, unless there are exceptional circumstances. But the amount of early referrals that run successfully with mediation isn't large, probably under 30% of cases.

I think it's down to the emotions. Where a couple has been separated for a couple of years everything's cooled down a bit, and the prospects for successful mediation are better.

MB   What's been your experience in those cases that *do* go to mediation?

JS   I've had some cases where mediation has been very successful. They still have their own lawyers and they go to mediation with an independent mediator. They can come and see us if they have any issue over which they would like advice, or they may come to an agreement and we would then prepare the papers to record it. It can work, but I think it has to be for particular personality types.

MB   In the sorts of cases you deal with, are you able to tell me what your typical fees would be for a divorce?

JS   A divorce of itself would be £1,000. A financial agreement where you have an obligation to make sure that both parties know what each other has got and there is full and frank financial disclosure, anywhere between £2,500 to £3,500. A contested hearing, if they can't agree, I would have said you were closer to £10,000 for each party. I've had some cases where each party will pay £40,000 or £50,000. We then went to appeal, and the appeal was another £10,000.

The average value of a house in the UK is about £160,000 now. Rarely do people have mortgage-free houses, and if the only other major asset is a pension, £20,000 across the couple for a contested hearing is quite a big percentage of what is available to split between them.

MB Can we move on to prenuptial and postnuptial agreements? There was an interesting programme on the radio a month or two ago, where a lady divorce lawyer was unhappy about a divorce settlement in the courts. The couple had agreed a postnup, the wife had subsequently been unfaithful, and the husband sought a divorce as a result.

The court upheld the postnup, and a lady lawyer commenting on the case said she could understand the court's ruling on postnups, but she didn't think prenups should be binding, because a man could refuse to marry a woman unless she signed one. Her perspective was that it was quite acceptable for men to go into marriage facing the possibility of losing a great deal of money if the marriage didn't succeed for any reason. Incredible.

I personally think prenups should be obligatory under law, because people often get married with an unrealistic idea of the odds that the marriage will be long and happy. They are quite simply deluded. Are prenups, postnups, or even both enforceable under British law?

JS No, they're not legally enforceable, but the courts here now are taking quite a lot of influence from foreign countries including the United States.

MB What's causing that? What happens to make judges change their opinions over time?

JS   To some extent changes in the law reflect changes in the society we live in. At the present time the courts won't allow prenups to oust the jurisdiction of the court. But where both parties come to the table with full knowledge of each other's financial worth, they have received proper legal advice, and they're not asked to sign an agreement an unreasonably brief period before the wedding ceremony – which might then cause undue influence or pressure – then because they're adults these agreements should be seriously considered, because they've been entered into freely. A prenup in reality could say almost anything you wanted it to, as long as it appears to be fair.

A number of recent cases have guided the courts with respect to prenups and postnups, a good example being M vs. M (Prenuptial Agreement) in 2001, which will give you a flavour of the area:

BACKGROUND – The parties, both Canadians, entered into a prenuptial agreement very shortly before their marriage. The wife was pregnant, and anxious to get married; the husband, who had been very distressed by the breakdown of a previous marriage, was not prepared to marry again without a prenuptial agreement. The agreement signed by both parties provided that, in the event of marital breakdown, the husband would pay the wife £275,000. After five years of marriage the couple separated and the wife sought relief for herself and the five-year-old child of the marriage. She argued that she should not be bound by the agreement, having been pressurised into it at a time when she was very vulnerable, and that she was entitled to a lump sum of £1,300,000.

The wife's total net worth was about £300,000, including the value of a property occupied by her mother: the husband's net worth was about £7,500,000. By the date of the hearing, which followed a complex forum debate, the wife had incurred costs of £326,888 and the husband had incurred costs of £442,092.

HELD – awarding the wife a lump sum of £875,000, and an order for periodic payments for the child of £15,000 pa plus school fees and expenses – it did not matter whether the court treated the prenuptial agreement as a circumstance of the case or as an example of conduct which it would be inequitable to disregard; under either approach, while the court was not in any way bound by the terms of a prenuptial agreement, the court should look at it and decide in the particular circumstances what weight should, in justice, be attached to the agreement. This agreement did not dictate the wife's entitlement, but had been borne in mind as one of the more relevant circumstances of the case and had tended to guide the court to a more modest award than might have been made without it. It would have been as unjust to the husband to ignore the existence of the agreement and its terms as it would have been to the wife to hold her strictly to those terms. Other relevant factors in departing from equality were the comparative shortness of the marriage and the fact that her husband had created the family wealth.

Another interesting case is Crossley vs. Crossley (2008), which involved a 14-month marriage between individually wealthy people. Their prenup provided that they would each take only what they brought into the marriage. On that occasion the court put the wife in a position that she had to explain/argue why the prenup should not be upheld.

If you go back to the Section 25 list, the court will look at all the circumstances of the case, including the conduct of either party. Actually entering into a prenup could be conduct in itself. Whether it's the circumstances or whether it's the conduct, either way the court in certain circumstances should have regard to it. Which is fine, but I would have thought that if a marriage breaks down within the first couple of years and there's no children you're probably on quite safe grounds.

Things become more complex as the years roll by, kids come along, there's an inheritance or a mixture of the marital assets, someone might lose a leg, or become disabled, or whatever. You can't foresee all eventualities, so unless it's provided for in your prenup, the court could well come to its own conclusion.

MB   Okay. What about postnups?

JS   They're looked at in a similar fashion to prenups: contractual agreements with the same reasons for them being taken into account to some degree, or not.

MB   Do you see legislation coming that will *require* prenups to be drawn up?

JS   I don't think that they will be made obligatory but I think there's a lot more development that's going to happen with prenups. The courts are keen that no jurisdiction that is provided by statute is ousted. They ultimately want to keep a handle on it.

I've got mixed feelings, personally. I'm not married, I've never been married, and if I married someone with little or no money, I would probably insist on a prenup. Having worked very hard for the last 20 odd years, would I want my partner to take half of my wealth if we were to divorce? No, of course I wouldn't. But then you start looking at contributions in the Section 25 list, contributions are one thing and pre-acquired and post-acquired assets are another. That's why there are so many cases to consider. The court has so much discretion, it really can do anything it wants.

MB   I find the cultural and societal issues around this subject fascinating. Let's say you're engaged to a woman, then over breakfast you mention casually that you would like a prenup. I can imagine the crockery flying.

JS   One of this firm's partners who remarried has got a prenup. He remarried last year, and he agreed a prenup with his fiancée some months before he got married. I imagine he had to fortify himself with a large whisky before he raised the subject with her (laughs).

Why don't couples stick together any more? To some extent this is a by-product, I think, of the emancipation of women. If women didn't go to the pub or nightclubs or go out to work then they wouldn't have the opportunities, they wouldn't meet other men. Also, women are much more financially independent. They go out to work, have their own careers, and have their own money. Additionally, society is more relaxed about divorce; there is little or no stigma attached.

MB   For one of my other books, *Guitar Gods in Beds. (Bedfordshire: A Heavenly County)* I interviewed eight well-known guitarists in and around Bedford, and related their life stories. Some were talking about their parents back in the 1950s and 1960s, and I was struck by how often they reported their mothers being housewives, and happy and fulfilled. I often get the sense that with all the opportunities in the world open to them today, many young and middle-aged women are markedly less happy than their mothers and grandmothers.

JS   True. And I can remember my dad going to work and then coming home; he would almost never go to the pub to meet his mates. So there was no opportunity to mix with other women. Women didn't have their own money, but nowadays we can all live single lives: we don't *have* to get married.

MB   I think divorce can be seen as a positive outcome. People who are divorcing often see themselves as failures, but what is divorce, if not ceasing to be with the person that you no longer want to be with? At least for one of the partners, generally both I suspect, it's positive. Whereas those people who have been married 40 years and are miserable together, what sort of an achievement is that?

I'm going to be honest in the book, because society tells you that if you can't make your marriage work there's something wrong with you: you need to stick at it; you're at fault if you divorce. I disagree. Just look at the Republic of Ireland. When divorce first became possible, an enormous number of couples split up and divorced. Those weren't previously happy marriages, just because they hadn't divorced. Marriage is the cause of a huge amount of stress and misery for so many people in the modern era.

JS   I see that every day of the week with my work. Maybe that's why I'm not married myself!

MB   Thanks, Jane.

I was somewhat surprised that prenuptial and postnuptial agreements *might* be taken into account by divorce courts, and even accepted in their entirety. Not exactly common knowledge, and a number of friends and acquaintances were similarly surprised. Such agreements would more commonly protect the financial interests of the partner more likely to have the greater financial resources of the two partners upon entering the marriage, or to have earned more during the marriage. The husband.

We live in an age of advice being freely and speedily available through the internet. I think it not unreasonable that someone exploring official advice websites, and enquiring about prenuptial and postnuptial agreements, should know the reality about their *potential* validity. So I visited three major official and semi-official websites, and keyed 'prenuptial agreement', and also 'pre nuptial agreement' and 'pre-nuptial agreements' for good measure. The sites were:

www.direct.gov.uk: 'Directgov – the official government website for citizens. Easy access to the public services you use and the information you need, delivered by the UK government.'

www.adviceguide.org.uk: 'The website prepared and updated by the Citizens' Advice Bureau.'

www.advicenow.org.uk: 'Advicenow is an independent, not-for-profit website providing accurate, up-to-date information on rights and legal issues.'

From the last of these websites:

> Advicenow is a winner of the Plain English Web Award, for the clear language, design and organisation of the site. Our site has plenty of original material, and we also help people find relevant and helpful information from other organisations.
>
> Our information service brings together the best information on the law and rights from over 200 UK websites. We don't use a search engine, every link has been hand picked and summarised by our team of experienced advisers.
>
> Our Features pages contains a range of articles including topical issues and news items on changes in the law, quizzes, polls and more detailed information designed to increase knowledge and understanding of the law and rights.
>
> Advicenow is a project of Advice Services Alliance, the coordinating body for independent advice services in the UK. ASA members including adviceUK; Citizens Advice; DIAL UK; Law Centres; Shelter and Youth Access are our main partners along with other leading advice and information providers.
>
> Advicenow is currently funded by the Legal Services Commission, the Ministry Of Justice and the Esmee Fairbairn Foundation. We are grateful

for previous grants from the New Opportunities Fund, now the Big Lottery, and the Treasury's Invest to Save Budget.

It may not surprise you to learn that not one of the three websites had even one reference to prenuptial or indeed postnuptial agreements. A visitor to the sites might reasonably conclude that they would not be considered by a divorce court, especially if the person accepts the 'common knowledge' that they would not be. And thereby he – for it will usually be the prospective husband – stands to lose a great deal of money, and possibly his home, as a result of this lack of advice. Keeping men in the dark about their rights, in the context of marriage and divorce, is clearly a substantial and successful project.

I asked a number of female acquaintances how they'd feel if their fiancé raised the issue of signing a prenuptial agreement some months before their wedding day. The majority said they'd be outraged or at least annoyed – a typical comment being 'that would be like saying he thought I was a gold-digger' – while a minority said they wouldn't be happy, but would be willing to discuss the matter. Several of the latter women said they'd consider a fiancé raising the matter of a prenuptial agreement 'unromantic'.

From an article written by Matthew Moore, 'Well-heeled women go for prenups to beat the gold-diggers', in the 24 April 2009 edition of *The Daily Telegraph*:

> Wealthy women are increasingly acting to protect their fortunes from unscrupulous men by insisting that their partners sign prenuptial agreements, family lawyers have reported.
>
> Contracts stipulating how much money each party would receive if a marriage collapsed have traditionally been demanded by successful businessmen wary of 'gold-digging' wives. But growing numbers of women – many of whom received large payouts from previous divorce settlements – are now turning to the law to ensure that their future husbands are not entitled to half their riches.
>
> Vanessa Lloyd Platt of matrimonial law experts Lloyd Platt and Co said that the firm had received more 'pre-nup' requests from women than men in the past two months – representing a vast increase in female enquiries. 'There has been a surge of interest. With the recession hitting, there is an awareness among women that men are going to take their money unless they protect it,' she said.
>
> Although British courts do not consider prenuptial agreements to be legally binding, recent cases have established that judges will recognise fair

and reasonable contracts, providing there has not been a dramatic change in the finances of the couple. Solicitors at Pannone, a law firm based in Manchester, reported a doubling in the number of women taking out prenuptial agreements in the past year.

Fiona Wood, a partner with the firm, said her clients included professionals, entrepreneurs, women who had inherited family riches and individuals who acquired money and property through a divorce. 'Women are becoming more savvy when it comes to realising that it's not only men who may be targeted for their money,' she said. 'Many, particularly those who have been married before, have told us that they would very much like to find a partner but are cautious when it comes to what happens to their cash. They have read stories about other wealthy women who have lost substantial sums in divorces and have stressed their determination not to follow suit.'

So it's unromantic for a man to ask his fiancée to sign a prenuptial agreement, but not – one assumes – for a woman to ask her fiancé to sign one? What a double standard.

From *Money Week*, 20 March 2009, a profile of a London divorce lawyer in an article titled ' "Don't get even, get Tooth" – London's ruthless yet charming divorce lawyer':

Top divorce lawyer Raymond Tooth has such a ferocious reputation in court that he is known as Jaws. Renowned for landing ex-wives – including Sadie Frost and Cheryl Barrymore – huge settlements, he is a man in demand. 'Don't get even,' runs the motto, 'get Tooth.'

Tooth, 68, whose uncle by marriage Rex Harrison was married six times ('he didn't make a great success of it'), has a lifetime of experience – he has himself been through the divorce courts twice. But he seems to have broken even his own record for settlements, says the *Sunday Times*. It emerged last week that his client Ingrid Myerson, ex-wife of City fund manager Bryan Myerson, is now entitled to 105% of her husband's assets.

Myerson is appealing for the £11m settlement to be re-written after his fund, Principal Capital Holdings, suffered heavy losses. He claims he now needs to borrow £500,000 to honour the deal. If successful, the appeal could see a flood of similar claims. But first, Myerson's team has to defeat the doughty Tooth. As he told *The Times*: 'If a man's wealth is all in shares and they drop 50%, that's one thing. But if they rose in value, would a wife be able to go back for a larger share?'. . .

Many of his clients are high maintenance: one woman rang him 14 times in an evening and on the 15th call asked his advice on where she might dine. But Tooth, who has twice fallen in love with clients (he stresses after their divorces were finalised), is clearly accommodating. He never loses sight of the bottom line. Marrying a rich man is still a woman's most lucrative option, he told *The Sunday Times*. 'It's a lot more profitable than working, if you marry the right person'. . .

Tooth has a formidable record: he claims to have won 90% of his cases. So what is his advice to warring couples in the teeth of recession? 'Wives would be better now to wait, as the courts are being very wary about awards because of the problems of making payments,' he told *The Sunday Times*. 'This is the most important financial transaction you'll ever make,' he says. 'Hang on in there until times get better.' His advice to men is the opposite: 'Move on now while your star is low in the sky. You can escape with less.'

Timing is vital in divorce, says *The Times*, and never more so than now. 'The market is so volatile that you fix on a figure and by the time it reaches the point of being finalised, the market has changed,' says Kathryn Peat, a partner at Gordon Dadds. 'So you get husbands delaying until the 11th hour and some will be reluctant to settle at all.' Mediation may be the answer, but Tooth's not a fan. 'Clients don't want you to be reasonable. They want you to take a tough line. That's part of the therapy.'

Tooth has some 'wonderfully frank' advice for gold-diggers, says *The Sunday Times*. 'Look good, speak well, and go to the right places. Dinner parties, art galleries, charities. The best place to divorce is England or America, if you're the wife. France if you're the husband. The French are not very generous towards women.' But the rich shouldn't contemplate marriage without a prenuptial agreement. Ultimately, Tooth reckons, the marriage sacrament is a busted flush. 'Marriage is basically a money-based social transaction. In 25 years' time, there'll be renewable agreements.'

For all the talk of love and commitment uttered by people getting married, one fact remains constant and it's revealed by women saying they're looking for 'security' from marriage: women still marry to improve their economic well-being, among other reasons. Rich men may marry beautiful women of little means, and when they divorce the wife is often set up financially for life. Women are more calculating than men when it comes to their economic well-being. Rich women (with few exceptions) do not risk their fortunes by marrying men of little means, handsome or otherwise. The obvious consequence of women marrying to improve their economic well-being? Their future husbands will potentially *damage* their economic well-being by marrying them.

Michael Seamark filed the following story on the *Daily Mail* website on 30 October 2008:

> Given that he's on his third divorce, John Cleese is hardly speaking from a position of strength with his views on marriage. [Author's note: I beg to differ, but let's move on. The *Daily Mail* is aimed squarely at a female readership.] But the comedian yesterday proposed the idea that wedding licences should be regularly renewed – a little like dog licences (he was

speaking from Los Angeles). As for becoming parents, Cleese, a father of two, said couples should have to pass tests before being able to have a child.

Asked whether he would have liked to have spent the past 40 years with one woman, the 68-year-old replied: 'No. I think it should be like dog licences. I think you should have to renew marriage licences every five years, unless you have children. And I think before you have children you should have to go and pass various tests and get a licence to have a child. Because it's the most transformative and difficult thing of your life.'

The *Fawlty Towers* and *Monty Python* star also revealed that he must keep working to help fund the acrimonious and expensive divorce from his third wife, American-born psychotherapist Alyce Faye Eichelberger. 'People would think I'd have enough money, but I do have a very expensive, or comparatively expensive, divorce,' he said.

'When I divorced Barbara (Trentham, his second wife) in about 1988, that cost me £2.5 million. And now this divorce with Alyce Faye – I mean, I'm paying more than £1 million a year right now. And we never had children. When I got divorced from Connie (Booth, his first wife) . . . and when I got divorced from Barbara, I didn't need lawyers on either occasion, because I just sort of said: "Why don't I give you this?" And they said: "That's very fair, very generous. Thank you." End of story.'

Cleese's third wife is asking for a multi-million pound chunk of property as part of the divorce settlement after 16 years of marriage. 'I feel angry sometimes,' he told *The Times*. 'But my anger is not so much about sharing the property but having to go on working hard to provide alimony for someone who's already going to have at least $10 million worth of property, and who's getting £1 million this year. At some point you say, "Well, what did I do wrong? You know, I was the breadwinner." The system is insane.'

Despite his divorce, Cleese said: 'This is the happiest I have ever been and I feel that at 68 now I want as many years as I can get.' . . . He said he doesn't want a new partner at the moment. 'I don't want to have to start being unselfish again. The great thing about being on your own is you do what you damn well like.'

In the light of the severe economic recession around the world, the Cleese story took an interesting and heartening turn in subsequent months. Journalist Judith Woods wrote an article, 'The newly "broke" in search of cut-price divorces', for the 24 March 2009 edition of *The Daily Telegraph*:

News that John Cleese has successfully halved his £1.3 million annual divorce settlement has surely come as a relief to the *Monty Python* star, who had complained bitterly that at the age of 69 he would be required to continue working in order to pay maintenance to his third wife, a situation he unflinchingly described as 'feeding the beast'.

Cleese will still have to pay £650,000 a year to American psychotherapist Alyce Faye Eichelberger, 64, to whom he was married for 15 years, but the fact that a US judge agreed that the original amount was excessive in the current recession, after the value of the star's extensive property portfolio had dropped, is a hugely significant sign of the times.

On this side of the Atlantic, lawyers have already warned women that they face being forced to accept reduced payouts from high-earning men who are seeking to have their divorce terms revisited because of a rapid decline in their earning power.

The divorce courts – never happy places at the best of times – have become the setting for extraordinary scenes of financial wrangling, as former husbands battle to have settlements and maintenance payments slashed in line with shrinking bonuses.

'I recently had a two-hour meeting with a client who was sounding me out about the cost and likely outcome of his divorce – which house would his wife get, how big a lump sum would he have to hand over and so on,' says Tom Amlot, head of family law at the London firm Harbottle & Lewis. At the end of the discussion he stood up and didn't say a word, so I asked him whether he was going to stay or leave the marriage. He replied that he needed to study the figures in more detail and he was going to run it through his spreadsheet that evening and then make a decision.

'Even to a cynical lawyer like me it was genuinely shocking that someone would conduct their personal life via a spreadsheet.'

Businessmen who once shrugged off a six- or seven-figure settlement to their ex-wives are now claiming poverty. In recent days a number of high-profile cases have made headlines.

Fund manager Brian Myerson told the Court of Appeal that his £14 million post-divorce fortune had been wiped out and so he could no longer afford the £9.5 million he owed to Ingrid, his former wife. The couple, who were married in December 1982 and had a daughter and two sons, were divorced in February 2008. Myerson, 50, was ordered to pay his sculptress wife a lump sum of £7 million and £2.5 million over four years.

Mrs Myerson, 48, received 43% of the couple's assets – which were worth £25.8 million – including their £1.5 million South African home. Almost all of her husband's 57% was tied up in shares in his investment company – the value of which has plunged so dramatically that his £14.6 million fortune would now apparently be £500,000 in the red if he complied with the divorce order.

When the High Court in London was told that Myerson possessed minus 5% of the couple's assets while Mrs Myerson owned the equivalent of 105%, a titter broke out and Lord Justice Thorpe was prompted to remark, in fabulously *Rumpole Of The Bailey* fashion, that the situation was 'a rum do'.

Myerson is represented by London's leading divorce lawyer, Raymond Tooth, a man not exactly noted for his hearts and flowers approach to marriage guidance. 'Wives would be better now to wait, as the courts are being very wary about awards because of the problem of the ability to make payments,' he says, bluntly. 'Can you put up with it for two years?

Unless it's intolerable, I should hold on. It's the most important financial transaction you'll ever make: get it right.'. . .

It's hard to feel much sympathy when the jet-set complain of feeling fleeced, but Sandra Davis, head of family law at Mishcon de Reya, points out that when the super-rich sneeze, the rest of us will, eventually, catch cold. 'The City felt the pinch six months or so before the rest of the population. The increased trend in relationship breakdown that sector felt is now repeating itself across the rest of society,' says Davis. 'The average couple will also have found that the relative value of their assets has fallen in the same way as the high fliers.'

Davis predicts that estranged couples will take a hard look at their finances and wonder how they can maintain two households from a static or reducing income. The reason these cases have attracted such interest lies in the fact that the husbands are seeking to have lump sum payments, even if staggered, reduced. It's common for individuals to apply for changes to maintenance payments as a result of fluctuations in income, and there has been a huge rise in City workers doing just that. But the alteration of a capital settlement has enormous implications.

'It would be a dangerous precedent because it would mean that anyone would be able to reopen a settlement,' says divorce lawyer Vanessa Lloyd Platt. 'If a husband takes a gamble and decides to give his wife the liquid assets while he keeps the shares, because he reckons they will be worth more, should the wife really be penalised because he made the wrong choice?'

But it's not only husbands who are calculating which way the financial wind blows. Many shrewd wives are doing their sums. 'Some women are deciding to bale out as soon as they can, before their husbands lose their jobs, and they find their home is at risk,' says Lloyd-Platt. 'Other, very wealthy women are hanging fire because they are determined to wait until things improve economically rather than cutting loose when their joint assets are at their lowest.'

Sitting tight until the green shoots of recovery appear may be the only avenue open to an estranged couple, but it is not an easy co-existence, says Lesley Gordon, head of family law at leading Scottish firm Lindsays. 'Some may see it as a positive that couples are finding it more difficult to separate, but the reality is very different,' says Gordon. 'We are spending a significant amount of time dealing with desperately unhappy couples who really do not want to be together. It's an invisible, difficult and very human impact of the credit crunch.'

Marriage counsellor and personal coach Francine Kaye, known as the Divorce Doctor, also reports a growing number of relationships under unbearable strain. 'I have one couple living in a Chelsea townhouse that was worth £1.9 million and is now valued at £1 million and they can't sell it, so they are living there together, unhappily, with their four children,' says Kaye. 'They have allocated certain rooms to each other and have set times when each of them can use the kitchen. It's a horrible atmosphere, but they feel trapped.'

Kaye is running a workshop entitled 'Recession-proof Your Relationship' to give advice and support to couples doing their best to weather the financial downturn. 'Working at your marriage isn't such a bad thing, given the cost of the alternative,' she says. 'It doesn't matter if you live in a three-bed semi or a mansion, if you're mortgaged to the hilt then you're in the same predicament – if you divorce you'll end up with almost nothing.'

The Cleese divorce story was approaching a climax as I completed this book. Liz Hunt of *The Daily Telegraph* included the following article – 'Divorce laws are a recipe for injustice' – in her column of 19 August 2009:

In public, John Cleese betrays scant evidence of a sense of humour, His interviews reveal an introspective curmudgeonliness characteristic of those who have over-indulged in therapy. And I suspect that he is not always easy to live with, as the fact that he has three ex-wives may suggest.

Yet whatever his faults, Cleese is still the man who gave us *Monty Python*, Basil Fawlty and *A Fish Called Wanda*. He co-wrote (with his psychiatrist) a best-selling book called *Families and How to Survive Them*, and built a lucrative training film business from scratch. For this combination of talent and hard work, over a long career, he was richly rewarded. So the fact that he has to now share so many of these riches with one Alyce Faye Eichelberger is staggeringly unfair.

As *The Daily Telegraph* reported yesterday, the newly ex-Mrs Cleese – whose name has a certain Pythonesque quality – has waltzed away from her 16-year marriage with £8 million in cash and assets, plus another £600,000 a year for seven years. Apparently, this will help soften the blow of no longer being 'entertained by royalty and dignitaries in castles' as Cleese's consort. It also precludes a return to the council flat where, as a divorcee with two sons, she was living when they first met.

Alyce Faye, whose favourite film is *It's a Wonderful Life* (isn't it just), and who extols the virtue of giving to the less fortunate on her website, is now – according to Cleese's friends – wealthier than her former husband. Indeed, her settlement makes Heather Mills McCartney (as was) seem positively reasonable in her post-marital demands. She and Paul did at least have a child together, whereas there were no offspring from the Cleese / Alyce Faye union. Yet Cleese claims that if they were both to die today, her two children would benefit more from his money that his own two daughters.

Divorce is a dirty business: much flak has flown over the 19 months that it has taken to finalise this one. But the outcome is an indicator of outdated divorce laws that are unfairly loaded in favour of wives.

Yes, this settlement was reached in the Californian courts, a byword for legal lunacy. But London, the divorce capital of the world, is not far behind: there has been a succession of cases similar to the Cleeses'.

Nicholas Mostyn QC, known as 'Mr Payout' for the generous sums he has won for ex-wives, has some succinct advice: 'If you want to protect your money from the powers of the court, don't get married.'

According to lawyers, the turning point in Britain was the case of White vs. White in 2000. This landmark ruling stipulated that there should no longer be any legal bias 'in favour of the money-earner and against the home-maker and the child-carer'. The intention was just: to recognise and compensate those women who had subsumed their lives over many years to the needs of their husbands and children.

However, it also opened the floodgates to huge payouts for the less deserving. Too often, settlements are failing to reflect the brevity of a marriage, the absence of children, the rise of the serial divorcee, or the fact that a woman might have pursued her own lucrative career during the union. (Although not in Cleese's income bracket before their marriage, Alyce Faye did have a long and successful career as a psychotherapist. If anything, adding 'Cleese' to her name improved her professional fortunes – if not, why is she still using it on her website?)

To reflect these significant social changes, demand is growing for an overhaul of the laws governing divorce settlements, and for Parliament, rather than judges, to decide on it. Until then, many more women can hope to hit paydirt, and many more men will be left lamenting the fact they ever met them. Unless, of course, they turn it to their advantage: to help pay for the settlement, Cleese is developing a one-man show called 'My Alyce Faye Divorce Tour'. It is likely to be a sell-out.

I've heard women say that 'it serves men right' when marriages fail and well-off men have to make large settlements – possibly both property and money – to their ex-wives. But what's the other side of this coin? Many men are presumably staying with their wives only because the alternative is financial ruin, or at least a drastic reduction in their quality of life. Are their wives proud that only this reality keeps the couple together?

As a man, I'd be ashamed to remain with my partner solely for financial reasons. Many men would be the same, and surely most. But too many women want not only the opportunity of a highly paid career and a comfortable life with a well-off husband, but also the expectation of a large proportion of their ex-husband's wealth in the event of the marriage failing *for whatever reason*. And if that's equality, I'm a *crème brûlée*.

10

THE FUTURE OF MARRIAGE

In all affairs it's a healthy thing now and then to hang a question mark on the things you have long taken for granted.

(Bertrand Russell, *The Problems of Philosophy*)

This chapter covers:

- Love-based marriage is a failed experiment and must evolve
- Proposed government involvement and new legislation on premarital wedding preparation, prenuptial agreements, and asset division in divorce settlements
- Bertrand Russell's perspective on marriage and morals
- A German politician's logical solution to the 'seven-year itch'
- A second alternative form of marriage
- Reflections on how to make marriages happier in the modern era and thereby reduce the divorce rate

We have seen (pages 122-126) that romantic or passionate love is a temporary and 'necessary' madness which evolved to drive *Homo sapiens* to reproduce and thereby ensure the future of the species, often at the cost of the individual partners' happiness. Why do we expect – as we do in the modern era – that our marriages will last successfully for half a century or more, when they are based on the temporary madness of romantic love? At the very least we should perhaps settle for companionate love, and not expect our marriages in themselves to deliver much in the way of happiness in the long run. The fact that a small proportion of couples manage to be happy together for 50 years or more does not mean that we can all manage the same feat ourselves. Nor even, possibly, that we should try.

It should not surprise us that the 200-plus-year-old experiment of love-based marriage has been failing many people for many years. Would it not make more sense to modify the institution of marriage to suit modern people, rather than expect modern people to modify themselves to suit an institution that is religious in its design and purpose, and that evolved in an era when most women were economically powerless? The institution needs to better accommodate the nature of men, as it already does the nature of women. And it needs to better accommodate the increasing number of men and women who are becoming ever more independent-minded and individualistic.

Widespread marital unhappiness and the consequent high divorce rate and family breakdowns impose enormous costs on society, both financial and otherwise. Provision of social housing for newly single parents, and a great deal of depression and its treatment, for example. The taxpayer should reasonably expect that people wishing to marry demonstrate their fitness for the institution. So governments need to intervene, and being someone with a right-of-centre political leaning, that's not something I say lightly. For perfectly sound reasons we accept that potential car drivers have to demonstrate their driving ability in order to obtain a driving licence. We don't rely on their self-assessment of their ability. Why should self-assessment suffice for marriage?

Before issuing wedding licences governments should require that couples undertake lengthy premarital preparation, and then complete a test along the lines of the one in Jeffrey Larson's *Should We Stay Together?* (reproduced on page 145 of this book). Only if the couple attain a minimum score on the test should they be allowed to marry. The state would then no longer be endorsing marriages that have poor prospects of success.

In terms of new legislation I propose the following:

-   Premarital preparation should become mandatory, and the issuing of marriage licences conditional on proof of both the individual aptitude of partners and their mutual compatibility.
-   Prenuptial agreements need to become mandatory, and be constructed within defined guidelines; for example, upon divorce neither party should lose any of the financial resources they brought to the marriage.
-   Partners who take time off from their careers for the purpose of caring for children should be compensated for the loss of earnings at a pre-agreed rate (£x pa) from the joint financial resources.

- After taking account of the above, as well as the financial resources required to house one of the partners and the children until the children reach the age of majority – and no longer – any remaining financial resources should be split between the partners *in line with the proportions they earned over the course of the marriage*. It follows that, when making financial settlements, consideration should no longer be given to the standard of living enjoyed by the couple before the breakdown of the marriage.

But of course marriage is about more than money, and the institution needs to change in ways that are beyond the reach of legislation. Which brings us to Bertrand Russell, one of the greatest thinkers – British or otherwise – of the late 19th and the 20th centuries. From the back cover of his book *Marriage and Morals*, first published in 1929:

> *Marriage and Morals* is a compelling cross-cultural examination of individual, familial and societal attitudes towards sex and marriage. By exploring the codes by which we live our sexual lives and conventional morality, Russell daringly sets out a new morality, shaped and influenced by dramatic changes in society such as the emancipation of women and the widespread use of contraceptives. From the origin of marriage to the influence of religion, Russell explores the changing role of marriage and codes of sexual ethics. The influence of this great work has turned it into a worthy classic.
>
> Bertrand Russell (1872–1970) was one of the most formidable thinkers of the modern era. A philosopher, mathematician, educational innovator, champion of intellectual, social and sexual freedom, and a campaigner for peace and human rights, he was also a prolific writer of popular and influential books, essays and lectures on an extensive range of subjects.

In 1950 Russell was awarded the Nobel Prize in Literature 'in recognition of his varied and significant writings in which he champions humanitarian ideals and freedom of thought'. So he was brighter than the average *Big Brother* contestant, it may safely be said. The following extract is from *Marriage and Morals*:

> When we look round the world at the present day and ask ourselves what conditions seem on the whole to make for happiness in marriage and what for unhappiness, we are driven to a somewhat curious conclusion: that the more civilised people become the less capable they seem of lifelong happiness with one partner. Irish peasants, although until recent times

marriages were decided by the parents, were said by those who ought to know them to be on the whole happy and virtuous in their conjugal life.

In general, marriage is easiest where people are least differentiated. When a man differs little from other men, and a woman differs little from other women, there is no particular reason to regret not having married someone else. But people with multifarious tastes and pursuits and interests will be apt to desire congeniality in their partners, and to feel dissatisfied when they find that they have secured less of it than they might have obtained.

The Church, which tends to view marriage solely from the point of view of sex, sees no reason why one partner should not do just as well as another, and can therefore uphold the indissolubility of marriage without realising the hardship that this often involves.

Another condition which makes for happiness in marriage is paucity of single women and absence of social occasions when married men meet respectable women. If there is no possibility of sexual relations with any woman other than one's wife, most men will make the best of the situation, and, except in abnormally bad cases, will find it quite tolerable. The same thing applies to wives, especially if they never imagine that marriage should bring much happiness. That is to say, a marriage is likely to be what is called happy if neither party ever expected to get much happiness out of it.

Fixity of social custom, for the same reason, tends to prevent what are called unhappy marriages. If the bonds of marriage are recognised as final and irrevocable, there is no stimulus to the imagination to wander outside and consider that a more ecstatic happiness might have been possible. In order to secure domestic peace where this state of mind exists, it is only necessary that neither the husband nor the wife should fall outrageously below the commonly recognised standard of decent behaviour, whatever this may be.

Among civilised people in the modern world none of these conditions for what is called happiness exist, and accordingly one finds that not many marriages after the first few years are happy. Some of the causes of unhappiness are bound up with civilisation, but others would disappear if men and women were more civilised than they are. . .

I think that uninhibited civilised people, whether men or women, are generally polygamous in their instincts. They may fall deeply in love and be for some years entirely absorbed in one person, but sooner or later sexual familiarity dulls the edge of passion, and then they begin to look elsewhere for a revival of the old thrill. It is, of course, possible to control this impulse in the interests of morality, but it is very difficult to prevent the impulse from existing.

With the growth of women's freedom there has come a much greater opportunity for conjugal infidelity than existed in former times. The opportunity gives rise to the thought, the thought gives rise to the desire, and in the absence of religious scruples the desire gives rise to the act.

Women's emancipation has in various ways made marriage more difficult. In old days the wife had to adapt herself to the husband, but the husband did not have to adapt himself to the wife. Nowadays many wives, on grounds of woman's right to her own individuality and her own career, are unwilling to adapt themselves to their husbands beyond a point, while men who still hanker after the old tradition of masculine domination see no reason why they should do all the adapting.

This trouble arises especially in connection with infidelity. In old days the husband was occasionally unfaithful, but as a rule his wife did not know of it. If she did, he confessed that he had sinned and made her believe that he was penitent.

She, on the other hand, was usually virtuous. If she was not, and the fact came to her husband's knowledge, the marriage broke up. Where, as happens in many modern marriages, mutual faithfulness is not demanded, the instinct of jealousy nevertheless survives, and often proves fatal to the persistence of any deeply rooted intimacy even where no overt quarrels occur.

There is another difficulty in the way of modern marriage, which is felt especially by those who are most conscious of the value of love. Love can only flourish as long as it is free and spontaneous; it tends to be killed by the thought that it is a duty. To say that it is your duty to love so-and-so is the surest way to cause you to hate him or her. Marriage as a combination of love with legal bonds thus falls between two stools. . .

There can be no doubt that to close one's mind on marriage against all the approaches of love from elsewhere is to diminish receptivity and sympathy and the opportunities of valuable human contacts. It is to do violence to something which, from the most idealistic standpoint, is in itself desirable. And like every kind of restrictive morality it tends to promote what one may call a policeman's outlook upon the whole of human life – the outlook, that is to say, which is always looking for opportunities to forbid something.

For all these reasons, many of which are bound up with things undoubtedly good, *marriage has become difficult, and if it is not to be a barrier to happiness it must be conceived in a somewhat new way* [Author's emphasis]. One solution often suggested, and actually tried on a large scale in America, is easy divorce. I hold, of course, as every humane person must, that divorce should be granted on more grounds than are admitted in the English law, but I do not recognise in easy divorce a solution of the troubles of marriage.

Where a marriage is childless, divorce may be often the right solution, even when both parties are doing their best to behave decently; but where there are children the stability of marriage is to my mind a matter of considerable importance. I think that, where a marriage is fruitful and both parties to it are reasonable and decent, the expectation ought to be that it will be lifelong, but not that it will exclude other sex relations. A marriage which begins with passionate love and leads to children who are desired and loved ought to produce so deep a tie between a man and woman that they will feel something infinitely precious in their companionship, even after sexual passion has decayed, and even if either or both feels sexual passion for someone else.

This mellowing of marriage has been prevented by jealousy, but jealousy, though it is an instinctive emotion, is one which can be controlled if it is recognised as bad, and not supposed to be the expression of a just moral indignation. A companionship which has lasted for many years and through many deeply felt events has a richness of content which cannot belong to the first days of love, however delightful these may be. And any person who appreciates what time can do to enhance values will not lightly throw away such companionship for the sake of new love.

It is therefore possible for a civilised man and woman to be happy in marriage, although if this is to be the case a number of conditions must be fulfilled. There must be a feeling of complete equality on both sides; there must be no interference with mutual freedom; there must be the most complete physical and mental intimacy; and there must be a certain similarity in regard to standards of values. (It is fatal, for example, if one values only money while the other values only good work.) Given all these conditions, I believe marriage to be the best and most important relation that can exist between two human beings. If it has not often been realised hitherto, that is chiefly because husbands and wives have regarded themselves as each other's policemen. If marriage is to achieve its possibilities, husbands and wives must learn to understand that whatever the law may say, in their private lives they must be free.

Those words were first published in 1929. I find them insightful, wise, and humane. And as valid today as they were 80 years ago.

Maybe it's because I've been a businessman for 30 years, but the whole idea of lifelong contracts is strange to me. In the commercial world most contracts for the supply of goods and services are of beween one and three years' duration. I propose that we adopt John Cleese's excellent proposal of fixed-term marriage contracts. At the end of the contract the marriage will automatically expire unless renewed for a new fixed term by the partners. And why not make those renewals conditional upon agreement of new postnuptial agreements each time, or renewal of the previous one if circumstances have not changed markedly in the interim?

A German politician proposed the idea of fixed-term marriage contracts before John Cleese. And so it is that we turn to Dr Gabriele Pauli. From the *Times Online* website, 21 September 2007, an article by Roger Boyes, 'How to cure the seven-year itch? Limit marriage to seven years':

Marilyn Monroe would have approved. The Seven-Year Itch, argues Germany's most glamorous politician, could be cured by making marriage vows valid for only seven years, thus legislating away what is regarded as the most unstable phase of a relationship.

The proposal to turn marriage into a kind of time-share arrangement has shocked Germany. It comes from Gabriele Pauli, who is running to become head of the Bavarian conservative Christian Social Union (CSU) party. 'Many marriages survive only because people think it gives them security,' Dr Pauli told a news conference in Munich. 'But only love should count.'

Her idea would apply only to civil marriages. Vows sworn on the altar, 'till death us do part', would not be amended. Civil marriages would be regarded as a limited seven-year contract. 'After that initial period each partner would have to say "yes" again in order to prolong the marriage,' she said. 'If they do, there is no reason why marriage should not end up as a lifelong partnership, but in the meantime we will have saved the financial and emotional cost of many divorces.'

The Seven-Year Itch – the supposed urge to stray into adultery – was a fixture of advice columns long before Billy Wilder made his 1955 film of the same name starring Marilyn Monroe as the blonde temptress of a bored husband. The subject matter was deemed so sensitive by Hollywood that the extramarital romance was played out only in the head of the protagonist, acted by Tom Ewell.

Since then agony aunts have also identified the Two-Year Bloat (when complacent husbands start to put on weight), the Fourth Year Slip (when office co-workers start to look more attractive than one's partner) and any year after the birth of a child as being as perilous to marriage as the seven-year restlessness.

Johann Reisel, head of Catholic marriage counselling in Bavaria, said: 'It sounds to me like renewing a mobile phone contract,' he said. 'This is just a random number; statistics show that marriages tend to last either three or four years, or significantly longer than seven years.'

Although conventional wisdom is that every third marriage in Germany ends in divorce, the reality is worse. By one calculation, 43% of marriages in western Germany (including Bavaria) end in divorce. In 1970, only 15% ended this way.

Catholic bishops called yesterday for Dr Pauli to be thrown out of the CSU. So too did Edmund Stoiber, who is head of the party and prime minister of Bavaria until next month. Mr Stoiber is standing down from both posts after a campaign by Dr Pauli. Her rivals have seized on her comments as evidence that she is unfit for office.

Dr Pauli is determined to shake up the party, which has ruled Bavaria for the best part of six decades. She posed for a magazine as a dominatrix, and is often photographed on her motorbike. She has been married twice. Her second marriage ended in divorce last February. It lasted seven years.

Dr Pauli has cracked the problem. A veritable triumph of German logic. *Two* types of marriage contract. One suitable for couples seeking a traditional and/or religious paradigm, another for couples seeking a more modern and/or secular paradigm.

I would go even further than Dr Pauli. We have seen that the divorce rate peaks at around four years of marriage. It would therefore make more sense to have marriage contracts expire after four years rather than after seven years. Combined with an initial prenuptial agreement and postnuptial agreements agreed every four years, we would have a sound base for the second marriage form. Not a 'romantic' notion, but perhaps all the better for that.

Husbands and wives tend to take one another more and more for granted as the years roll by. The prospect of their marriages ending in four years or less might lead them to have more consideration for their partners. Now wouldn't that be a good thing?

I leave you with a number of further reflections aimed at improving the prospect of happiness in marriage in the modern era:

1. If marriage licences were granted only to people with good personal aptitude for marriage *and* good compatibility with their partners, the number of new marriages would surely and speedily fall, and the number of divorces along with it.

2. Introverted spouses should be given as much 'personal space' as they ask for. Their happiness and even their mental health may depend on it. They should not be criticised when they decline to spend as much time with their partners – and their families – as might be deemed 'normal' by extraverts.

3. Introverts need to accept that their partners, if extraverts, are intrinsically more likely to have sex with other partners than they themselves are.

4. Both sexes need to accept that their partner – whether an introvert or an extravert – might occasionally desire or need sexual relations with another person, and the partner should be at liberty to satisfy this desire or need without fear of ending the relationship.

5. More couples need to appoint one of the partners as the main decision maker of the household, to reduce the frequency of the battles of will that damage so many marriages.

6. Marriage partners of differing religious convictions (or none) should resist the temptation to persuade their partners to share their convictions.

People sometimes ask me if I might ever consider marrying again, even after they've read this book. I always reply that I wouldn't, because I'm clearly so unsuited to marriage, and I see nothing to be gained by marrying again and thereby adding to the world's tally of unhappily married people.

But I might be prepared to make an exception for one of my favourite film actresses, either Cameron Diaz or Nicole Kidman, as long as she didn't insist on a prenuptial agreement. Either would surely make any man's life an altogether more pleasant affair, at least for a time. Taking this fantasy to its logical conclusion, if I were married to both of them at the same time, that would be bigamy. *Very* bigamy.

Until the next time.

APPENDIX 1

THE LETTER TO
THE CHIEF EXECUTIVE OF RELATE

Claire Tyler
Chief Executive
Relate Central Office
24–32 Stephenson Way
London SE22 8PU

19 November 2008

Dear Claire,

I am a businessman and author of three books, and am currently working on a fourth book which is about marriage in the modern era (excerpt attached). I wondered if I might meet with you or colleague(s) to explore a number of the book's themes, including the following:

- People entering the state of matrimony are woefully unaware of, and therefore unprepared to successfully manage, the principal problems that are likely to emerge in lengthy one-to-one relationships.
- The state should sponsor premarital preparation.
- Many people (and more over time) are constitutionally unsuited for lengthy one-to-one relationships.
- Rising divorce levels in the modern era are symptomatic not of relationships becoming less satisfying, but of individuals (particularly women) exercising increasing opportunities to divorce, rather than staying in unhappy relationships. Accordingly, divorce is not intrinsically 'a bad thing'.
- The paradigm of long-term one-to-one relationships and indeed marriage being intrinsically 'a good thing' is driven by religions and the majority of women, and thereby excludes the views of

both the non-religious (who are now in the majority in the UK) and a significant number of men.

- The extent of feminisation of Western society during my lifetime (I'm 51) has been truly astonishing, but women's tendency to acquire resources through their relationships with men, and emotional manipulation of men, has not abated. Susan Pinker in her excellent book *The Sexual Paradox* finally nails the lie that women are under-represented in some fields because of sex discrimination.

- There is no data available (as far as I am aware) that shows a cause and effect link between being married and being good parents, as opposed to people who are inclined to be good parents being more likely to marry.

I know from my own attempts to secure a publisher for my second and third books how dominant women are in the publishing industry. I think this is important because they thereby control the information fed to society about relationship expectations and norms, and so much else.

In conclusion, I should be grateful for a meeting with either yourself or colleagues to discuss the themes I have raised.

Yours etc.

Response from Mrs Tyler's personal assistant:

'Mrs Tyler is too busy to meet.'

APPENDIX 2

THE LETTER TO
THE RT HON HARRIET HARMAN QC MP

The Rt Hon Harriet Harman QC
Member of Parliament for Camberwell and Peckham, Deputy Leader of
the Labour Party, Labour Party Chair, Minister for Women and Equality,
Leader of the House of Commons, and The Lord Privy Seal
House of Commons
London SW1A 0AA

26 April 2009

Dear Ms Harman,

I am writing a book about marriage in the developed world in the modern
era. In this book, I reflect that marriage is but one of the ways in which
women advantage themselves at the expense of men, aided and abetted by
a number of groups with vested interests. This has always been the case,
and presumably will remain so while women campaign effectively for
'women's interests', and men fail to campaign for *their* own interests.

The purpose of this letter is to request a meeting to discuss what I see as
one of the more contentious aspects of New Labour policy, namely the
move from seeking equality of opportunity for women (which I applaud)
to equality of outcome (which I believe no government should try to
dictate). Women are 'under-represented' at senior levels in many walks of
life though exercising *choices*, as outlined so well by Susan Pinker in her
book *The Sexual Paradox*. Government policy completely disregards this
reality, and it's about time it didn't.

I should like to (audio) record an interview with you on these matters –
half an hour should suffice. I would, of course, be happy to meet you at a
time and location of your choosing. I attach an excerpt from my book on
this matter.

Yours etc.

EXCERPT FROM BOOK

When you look for it, it's not difficult to find examples of women working together to advance their interests at the expense of men. Let's start with The Rt Hon Harriet Harman QC, Member of Parliament for Camberwell and Peckham, Deputy Leader of the Labour Party, Labour Party Chair, Minister for Women and Equality, Leader of the House of Commons, and The Lord Privy Seal. She must have the largest business card on the planet.

In the foreword of the paper *Women's Changing Lives: Priorities for the Ministers for Women – One Year On Progress Report*, presented to Parliament in July 2008, Harriet Harman wrote the following:

> A modern democracy must be fair and equal. The government has fought for equal representation and it's because of this that we have record levels of women MPs, as well as more black and Asian MPs and councillors than ever before. But we need more women and more black, Asian and minority ethnic MPs and councillors to make our democracy truly representative.
>
> That's why in March I announced that political parties will be able to use all-women shortlists for the next five elections. . .

Wow. So through government diktat, for the next 22 or so years I – and every other man in the United Kingdom – could be stopped from becoming a prospective MP *solely on the grounds of gender*, regardless of our fitness for the office. And the least competent female candidate would *automatically* be deemed more worthy of public office than the most competent otherwise electable male candidate.

Response from Harriet Harman's assistant diary secretary:

'Unfortunately the Minister will not be able to grant your request due to heavy diary commitments at the time.'

APPENDIX 3

THE SEEKERS: A CASE STUDY OF COGNITIVE DISSONANCE

From Joel Cooper's book published in 2007, *Cognitive Dissonance: Fifty Years of a Classic Theory*.

An article that appeared in a Minneapolis newspaper gave Festinger and his students an ideal opportunity to study inconsistency in a real-world setting. The article reported on a group of west coast residents who were united in a belief about a significant event: the belief that the Earth was going to be annihilated by a cataclysmic flood on December 21, 1955. All of the people would perish in the cataclysm except for those who believed in the prophecies emanating from the planet Clarion; they alone would be saved from the flood.

Festinger reasoned that if Earth survived December 21, then the people in the little group, dubbed The Seekers by Festinger, Riecken, and Schachter (1956), would face a considerable amount of inconsistency on the next morning. While the rest of the world awoke to just another day, The Seekers would face a calamitous amount of inconsistency. The world's very existence would be inconsistent with their belief that the world as we know it was to have ended on the previous evening.

The Seekers was a serious group: this was not a collection of individuals who had a mild premonition of the world's demise. Their beliefs were specific and strong. As the December day approached, Seekers members sold their possessions and quit their jobs. Some, whose spouses did not share their beliefs, divorced. The Seekers members were united in their support of their leader, Mrs Marion Keech, who believed she was the medium through whom the unearthly beings on the planet Clarion communicated their wishes. She received her messages through automatic writing – a paranormal belief that a person's hand is seized by the spirits in another world and is used to communicate messages from the Great Beyond.

Clarion was specific. The group was to gather at Mrs Keech's home on the evening of December 20. They were to await the arrival of a spaceship that would come to Earth and whisk the group away from danger.

The Seekers were not publicity hounds. They sought no attention for their beliefs or their prophecy. When the reporter whose story appeared in the Minneapolis newspaper attempted to interview them, they grudgingly gave only the briefest interview. Publicity was not their goal; protecting themselves from the cataclysmic end of the Earth was.

As a social psychologist, Festinger saw the immediate relevance to the theory he was generating. If people are driven to deal with inconsistency, how would Marion Keech and her followers react to the morning of December 21 when the sun rose, the sky brightened, and the spaceship from Clarion failed to appear? The clear and specific anticipation of the world's demise, the elaborate preparations for the group to be saved, the broken marriages and other personal sacrifices, all would stand in stark contrast to the world's having made just another turn around its axis. Festinger and his colleagues predicted that the dramatic inconsistency would create the state of cognitive dissonance and the group would be driven to find some way to reduce it. They would need to find some way of restoring consistency to their mental maps of the cosmic events.

One of the researchers, Stanley Schachter, infiltrated the group. He carefully observed the group's preparations and specifically observed the events as they unfolded just after midnight on December 20. The group gathered near midnight, waiting for the arrival of the spacecraft. Tension and excitement were high. They had followed the Clarions' instructions meticulously. Mrs Keech's grandfather clock ticked the final seconds to midnight. No spacecraft.

Someone in the group checked his watch and saw that his watch still read only 11:55. All watches were reset. At 12:05, even by the ticking of the newly set watches, there was still no spacecraft. Another member of the group suddenly realized that he had not fulfilled all of the instructions given by the Clarions. They had insisted that all metal objects be removed from the human space travellers. Thus, they came with no zippers, belt buckles, or bra straps. But now a Seeker realized that he had a metal filling in a tooth. He removed it. [Author: I imagine that at this point some of the other Seekers 'forgot' they too had metal fillings.] Still, no spacecraft.

There followed a terrible few hours following the midnight disconfirmation of the prophecy. People sobbed and wept. Had they been abandoned by the Clarions? Had they been wrong all along, just like their more cynical spouses and former friends had told them? Shortly past 4:00 am, Mrs Keech received her final message from Clarion. The message provided the answer to their questions, and also provided the opportunity to restore consistency between their doomsday beliefs and their observation that the spaceship had not come and there had been no Earth-destroying cataclysm.

The Clarions' final message was brilliant. Through Mrs Keech's trembling hand, it said:

> This little group, sitting all night long, has spread so much goodness and light that the God of the Universe spared the Earth from destruction.

So that was it. The beliefs had not been wrong after all. God had been planning to destroy the Earth. All of the preparations for the cataclysm had not been in vain. In fact, it was precisely and only because of the preparations, sacrifices, and faith of the group that the Earth still existed on the morning of December 21. The sun still shone because of them; people went to work because of them; people still had homes to return to and families to love them . . . all because of the determination of the small group of Seekers.

Before December 21, Festinger et al (1956) had made a prediction. They hypothesised that The Seekers, who shunned publicity and notoriety, would take their cause to the public following the disconfirmation. And The Seekers did that with gusto. As soon as their new belief was in place – as soon as they had generated the story that their actions had saved the world – they took their case to the public. They looked for social support for their story. They desperately wanted others to see that their actions had not been in vain, that their prophecy had not been disconfirmed, that there was no inconsistency between their belief in the cataclysm and the bright sunny day that had dawned on December 21.

The premise of dissonance theory is that people do not tolerate inconsistency very well. The Seekers had found a way, post hoc, to make their actions feel consistent to themselves and they now sought validation in having the world believe them. They printed flyers, called newspapers and magazines, offered to talk on radio programs, all in an effort to bolster their new found consistency.

There are probably many factors that influenced the group of Seekers in their actions. Who can guess what had initially influenced these individuals to believe in the prophecy and the automatic writing? Who can guess what motives each individual may have had in the wake of the disconfirmed prophecy? But one thing seems certain. Caught in a major inconsistency among their beliefs, behaviours, and observations of reality, The Seekers did just what Festinger and his colleagues predicted they would do: they were driven to find a way to restore their consistency – driven to find a new belief that would make sense of what they had done and driven to convince a sceptical world of the truth of their new position.

APPENDIX 4

PERSONALITY TYPES AND THE MYERS-BRIGGS TYPE INDICATOR ®

The most widely-used psychometric test in the world is the Myers-Briggs Type Indicator (MBTI). Naomi Quenk is a clinical psychologist and author or co-author of numerous books on psychological types. The following is from her book published in 2000, *Essentials of Myers-Briggs Type Indicator Assessment*. The book is a well-written guide to the use and assessment of the tool, for mental health professionals.

HISTORY AND DEVELOPMENT

Jung's *Psychological Types* (1921) was translated into English in 1923. Interest in the work was generally limited to Jungian and psychoanalytic circles in both Europe and America. It was fortuitous, if not remarkable, that two women, Katharine Cook Briggs and her daughter, Isabel Briggs Myers (neither of whom had credentials in Jungian analysis or psychological test development), read Jung's work, spent 20 years studying it, and devised an instrument – the *MBTI* – to assess typology. Their years of intensive reading of Jung and careful observation of individual behaviour led to their conclusion that typology could provide a useful way of describing healthy personality differences and, importantly, that such assessment could be put to practical use in people's lives.

Jung's interest in types emerged from his observation of consistent differences among people that were not attributable to their psychopathology. At first he believed that two basic *attitude types* – extraverts and introverts – adequately explained the differences he found. Further observation convinced him that other differences must be at work and that his two-category typology was inadequate. He subsequently added opposite *mental functions* to his descriptive system: two opposite functions of perception, sensation (called Sensing in the *MBTI*) versus intuition, and two opposite functions of judgment, thinking versus feeling.

Briggs's early interest had been in the variety of ways that people achieved excellence in their lives. Prior to discovering Jung's work, she had studied biographies in an effort to develop her own typology. In addition to opposites similar to those described by Jung, she observed that individuals differed in the way they habitually related to the outside world. Her early observations ultimately led to the addition of a fourth pair of opposites to Jung's system, a Judging versus a Perceiving attitude toward the outer, extraverted world. Although Jung did not explicitly identify this pair of opposites, Briggs and Myers found it to be implicit in his writings.

Published forms of the *MBTI* have been in existence since 1956. Until 1975, when its publication moved from Educational Testing Service to

Consulting Psychologists Press, it was used primarily by a small number of enthusiastic researchers. Consulting Psychologists Press made the *MBTI* available to all professionals who were qualified to purchase Level B instruments. Since 1975 over 30 million people have taken the Indicator, more than 10 million in the past 5 years. About 2 million people fill out the *MBTI* annually, making it by far the most widely used instrument for assessing normal personality functioning. . .

THEORETICAL FOUNDATION OF THE *MBTI*

The Jung/Myers theory of psychological types is a way of describing and explaining certain consistent differences in the ways that normal people use their minds. The *MBTI* purports to identify these differences through a 93-item, self-administered, paper-and-pencil questionnaire. Results show the respondent's preferences on each of four pairs of opposite categories, which are called dichotomies. According to the theory, all eight categories, or preference poles, included in the *MBTI* are used at least some of the time by every person. However, individuals have an innate disposition toward one category (pole) of each dichotomy. The goal of *MBTI* assessment is to accurately identify preferences by sorting respondents into the categories to which they are already disposed. To elicit preferences between categorical poles rather than the degree of liking for or use of each opposite pole, all items are presented in a forced-choice format. This question format requires the respondent to choose between two mental functions or two attitudes in order to identify which is naturally preferred. If respondents were instead asked to indicate their use of or liking for each pole separately (as with a Likert-type rating scale), preference for one over the other could not be readily distinguished. Forcing respondents to choose between two legitimate ways of using their minds most directly and clearly elicits a preference.

The mental functions and attitudes that are the basic elements of the Jung/ Myers theory follow.

The Opposite Functions of Perception: Sensing and Intuition

Sensing perception uses the five senses to become aware of facts and details occurring in the present. When Sensing perception is being used, the perceiver is grounded in and trusting of the evidence of the senses, focusing on concrete reality and the gathering of facts and details. There is trust in what is known and can be verified. With little conscious effort, a person who prefers Sensing has a memory that is specific, detailed, literal, and complete. Without exercising considerable conscious effort, he or she is less likely to give credence and be interested in hypotheses, the unknown, and future possibilities. Sensing is a process that avoids inferences and conjecture and prefers instead to make decisions based on verifiable facts. People who prefer Sensing can experience any requirement to speculate on an unknown future as a pointless distraction from what is important.

Intuitive perception looks at patterns, meanings, and future possibilities that are believed to be implicit in current reality. When Intuition is being used, the perceiver focuses on concepts, ideas, and theories, inferring connections among diverse pieces of information. With little conscious effort, Intuitive perception moves quickly and easily from what is present in the here and now to what is implied and possible in the future. Without exercising considerable conscious effort, a person who prefers Intuition has difficulty memorising and using facts without putting them into an interesting context. Intuition is a process that is less experienced and interested in acquiring, remembering, and using facts and details for their own sake. People who prefer Intuition can experience such a focus as inhibiting to their free flow of ideas and as a pointless distraction from what is important.

The Opposite Functions of Judgment: Thinking and Feeling

Thinking judgment applies specific criteria and principles in a linear, logical analysis of Sensing or Intuitive information. The goal is to arrive at the objective truth or a reasonable approximation of truth. When Thinking judgment is being used, the person making the judgment takes an objective and dispassionate approach to the available data. With little conscious effort, individuals who prefer Thinking can maintain an objective stance and personal distance by keeping issues of their own and others' personal values and well-being separate from their decision making. Typically, only after a Thinking conclusion has been arrived at can conscious effort be devoted to considering issues of welfare and harmony.

Feeling judgment applies specific, usually personally held values to assess the relative importance of the Sensing or Intuitive information available. When Feeling judgment is being used, there is concern for the impacts and consequences of a decision on individuals or groups of people. The goal of a Feeling decision is to maximise harmony and well-being for people and situations. Without conscious effort, people who prefer Feeling take into account their own and others' feelings, values, and welfare. They use personal connections and empathy with the people affected by a decision to arrive at a conclusion. People who prefer Feeling can readily recognize logical principles and objective criteria for decision making. However, without exercising considerable conscious effort, they avoid using such criteria if harm and disharmony will result.

The terms chosen by Jung and retained by Myers for these two opposites have some unfortunate potential 'surplus meanings.' Therefore it is important to recognize that in the *MBTI* Thinking judgment does imply the absence of emotion but rather an automatic setting aside of value considerations for the sake of impartiality and objectivity. Feeling judgment does not refer to the experience and expression of emotion. Emotion is separate from Feeling judgment in that emotion is accompanied by a physiological response that is independent of decision making. Thinking types and Feeling types can be equally passionate about a favoured position in spite of contradictory evidence that violates certain logical principles (for Thinking types) or certain values (for Feeling types).

Similarly, a Thinking judgment is not more intelligent or correct than a Feeling judgment. In the Jung/Myers theory, Thinking and Feeling describe rational processes that follow laws of reason; that is, they evaluate data using definite criteria – logical principles for Thinking and personal values for Feeling.

The Opposite Attitudes of Energy: Extraversion and Introversion

Extraversion as an attitude directs psychic energy to and receives energy from the outer world of people, things, and action. When in the Extraverted attitude, a person interacts with the environment, receives energy through actively engaging with people and activities, and takes a trial-and-error approach to acquiring new experiences and skills. People who prefer Extraversion tend to think most effectively when interacting and talking to others and it takes little conscious effort for them to approach others and explore the outer world. Without conscious effort, it is hard for them to think only internally, since they often become aware of what they are thinking only when they are verbalising. Spending too much time without external activity can result in fatigue and low motivation.

Introversion as an attitude directs psychic energy to the inner world of ideas, reflection, and internal experiences and is energised by operating in that realm. When in the Introverted attitude, a person spends time reflecting on and reviewing ideas and experiences, and observes and thinks about whether or not to interact with new people or try new outside activities. People who prefer Introversion tend to think internally before expressing their thoughts to others. It takes little conscious effort to keep what they are thinking to themselves. Without conscious effort, it is uncomfortable and difficult for them to express their thoughts without first reflecting on them. Spending too little time alone and too much time interacting with people and the environment can result in fatigue and low motivation.

The Two Opposite Attitudes Toward the Outside World: Judging and Perceiving

A Judging attitude involves the habitual use of one of the judging functions, Thinking or Feeling, when interacting with the outer world. When a Judging attitude is being used, there is a desire to reach a conclusion (use judgment) and make a decision as quickly and efficiently as possible. Without conscious effort, individuals who prefer a Judging attitude are organised, structured, effectively work within schedules, and begin tasks sufficiently early so that deadlines can be comfortably met. Without exercising considerable conscious effort, they resist putting off decision making, working without a set plan, and operating in an environment where there are frequent interruptions and diversions.

A Perceiving attitude involves the habitual use of one of the perceiving functions, Sensing or Intuition, when interacting with the outer world. When a Perceiving attitude is being used, there is a desire to collect as much information (ie, perceive) as possible before coming to a conclusion. Without conscious effort, a person who prefers a Perceiving attitude is flexible, adaptable, and spontaneous when operating in the outside world, works comfortably and effectively when there is pressure of an imminent deadline, and welcomes interruptions and diversions because they stimulate new energy and may provide additional useful information. Without considerable conscious effort, it is difficult for him or her to start on tasks very far in advance of a deadline, operate within set schedules, and be orderly and methodical in pursuing desired goals. . .

An individual's preferences can be summarised in a four-letter code, each letter standing for one of the eight preferences, such as ISTJ for Introverted, Sensing, Thinking, Judging or ENFP for Extraverted, Intuitive, Feeling, Perceiving. All possible combinations of preferences yield 16 different types. All 16 types are seen as valid and legitimate ways of being psychologically healthy, adapted, and successful, though their interests, talents, and general outlooks are likely to be quite different.

Quenk offers mental health practitioners the following advice in relation to 'societal and gender expectations and biases':

Awareness of some general societal biases toward particular preferences or whole types can also be helpful in understanding and helping a client cope with specific issues. For example, many Introverts struggle with such labels as 'shy' 'unsociable' 'cold' or 'uncommunicative.' Even though the national representative sample indicates about an equal frequency of people reporting a preference for Extraversion and those preferring Introversion, our culture in general clearly favours extraverted qualities over introverted ones. It should be noted that many earlier estimates of the prevalence of Extraversion and Introversion in the United States suggested that there were three to four times as many Extraverts as Introverts. These estimates were based on various samples that were not representative of the population at large, such as Myers and McCaulley's (1985) high school student sample.

Another source of bias comes from gender expectations, particularly in confusing Thinking judgment with masculinity and Feeling judgment with femininity – exacerbated by mistakenly defining Thinking as hard-headed or unfeeling and Feeling as emotional. A lesser expectation is that women are by nature extraverted and men introverted. In fact, the T–F dichotomy is the only one of the four that has consistently shown a gender difference prevalence. In the national representative sample, about 57% of men identify Thinking and 43% Feeling as their preference; about 25% of women identify Thinking and 75% Feeling as their preference. It is interesting that compared with earlier, less carefully drawn samples, a greater percentage of both men and women identify Feeling as their preference. Also in contrast with earlier samples, slightly more women prefer Extraversion (52%) and somewhat more men prefer Introversion (54%).

Regardless of actual prevalence in the population, it is important to differentiate natural preferences for Thinking or Feeling from legitimate gender differences and to help clients understand and evaluate the impact that a confusion of type and gender may have on their lives. For example, women who prefer Thinking and men who prefer Feeling are judged differently – and often negatively – relative to women who prefer Feeling and men who prefer Thinking. Another frequent error is the assumption that all women 'should' be Feeling types and all men 'should' be Thinking types. Men and women who deviate from this expectation can be seen as deficient in masculinity and femininity when the distinctive qualities of the two judging functions are mistakenly fused and confused with gender qualities.

APPENDIX 5

QUOTATIONS ABOUT LOVE, SEX, MARRIAGE . . .

(Sorted alphabetically by the surname of the speaker or the writer, or by the title of a show.)

'Passion, sexual passion, may lead to marriage, but cannot sustain marriage. The purpose of marriage is the raising of children, for which patience, not passion, is the necessary foundation.'
Edward Abbey

'Marriage, in life, is like a duel in the midst of a battle.'
Edmond About

'Mrs Merton' to Debbie McGee: 'But what first, Debbie, attracted you to millionaire Paul Daniels?'
Caroline Aherne, *The Mrs Merton Show*

'Sex without love is an empty experience, but as empty experiences go it's one of the best.'

'My wife was an immature woman . . . I would be home in the bathroom, taking a bath, and my wife would walk in whenever she felt like it and sink my boats.'
Woody Allen, 'I Had a Rough Marriage'

'Alcestis had exercised a mysterious attraction and then an unmysterious repulsion on two former husbands, the second of whom had to resort to fatal coronary disease to get away from her.'
Kingsley Amis

'After a while marriage is a sibling relationship, marked by occasional, rather regrettable, episodes of incest.'
Martin Amis

Lady Astor:	If you were my husband, Winston, I'd put poison in your tea.
Winston Churchill:	If you were my wife, Nancy, I'd drink it.

'I married beneath me. All women do.'
Nancy, Lady Astor

'There is not one in a hundred of either sex who is not taken in when they marry. Look where I will, I see that it *is* so; and I feel that it *must* be so, when I consider that it is, of all transactions, the one in which people expect most from others, and are least honest themselves.'
Jane Austen, *Mansfield Park*

'Whatever you do, keep clear of thin women. They're trouble.'
Alan Ayckbourn, *A Small Family Business*

'Spouses are impediments to great enterprises.'
Francis Bacon

'Marriage must incessantly contend with a monster that devours everything: familiarity.'
Honoré de Balzac

'I thought I told you to wait in the car.'
Tallulah Bankhead, greeting an ex-lover after several years

'Love is just a system for getting someone to call you darling after sex.'
Julian Barnes, *Talking It Over*

'You may marry the man of your dreams, ladies, but 14 years later you're married to a couch that burps.'

'Husbands think we should know where everything is – like the uterus is a tracking device. He asks me, "Roseanne, do we have any Cheetos left?" Like he can't go over to that sofa cushion and lift it himself.'

'My husband complained to me. He said, "I can't remember when we last had sex." And I said, "Well I can, and that's why we ain't doing it." '
Roseanne Barr

'Love . . . the delightful interval between meeting a beautiful girl and discovering that she looks like a haddock.'
John Barrymore

'People keep asking me if I'll marry again. It's as if after you've had one car crash you want another.'
Stephanie Beacham

'My notion of a wife at forty is that a man should be able to change her, like a bank note, for two twenties.'
Warren Beatty

'The big difference between sex for money and sex for free is that sex for money usually costs a lot less.'
Brendan Behan

'Never marry a man who hates his mother, because he'll end up hating you.'
Jill Bennett

'People shop for a bathing suit with more care than they do for a husband or wife. The rules are the same. Look for something you'll feel comfortable wearing. Allow for room to grow.'
Erma Bombeck

'It is ridiculous to think you can spend your entire life with just one person. Three is about the right number. Yes, I imagine three husbands would do it.'
Clare Boothe Luce

'It is so far from being natural for a man and woman to live in a state of marriage, that we find all the motives which they have for remaining in that connection, and the restraints which civilised society imposes to prevent separation, are hardly sufficient to keep them together.'
James Boswell, *Life of Samuel Johnson*

'Love is an obsessive delusion that is cured by marriage.'
Dr Karl Bowman

'Marriage is the most advanced form of warfare in the modern world.'

'The whole point of marriage is to stop you getting anywhere near real life. You think it's a great struggle with the mystery of being. It's more like being smothered in warm cocoa. There's sex, but it's not what you think. Marvellous, for the first fortnight. Then every Wednesday. If there isn't a good late-night concert on the Third. Meanwhile you become a biological

functionary. An agent of the great female womb, spawning away, dumping its goods in your lap for succour. Daddy, daddy, we're here, and we're expensive.'
Malcolm Bradbury

'People marry for a variety of reasons, and with varying results; but to marry for love is to invite inevitable tragedy.'
James Branch Cabell

'I love it when my period comes round. I can really be *myself* again.'

'My ex-boyfriend came round last night which was a bit weird, because I didn't even know he was in a coma.'
Jo Brand

'Sex, on the whole, was meant to be short, nasty and brutish. If what you want is cuddling, you should buy a puppy.'
Julie Burchill, *Sex and Sensibility*

'I was married by a judge. I should have asked for a jury.'
George Burns

'It was very good of God to let Carlyle and Mrs Carlyle marry one another and so make only two people miserable instead of four.'
Samuel Butler, letter of 21 November 1884

Cliff Clavin: How's married life treating ya? Quite a change, huh?
Frasier Crane: Well, Lilith and I did live together for a year before we wed, so other than the fact that I now see it stretching endlessly before me until I die rotting in the grave, there's no real difference.
John Ratzenberger and **Kelsey Grammar**, *Cheers*

'It's only adultery if you get caught!'
Thunderin' Paul Carrington

'You know what the difference is between a wife and a terrorist? You can negotiate with a terrorist.'
Frank Carson

'If variety is the spice of life, marriage is the big can of leftover Spam.'
Johnny Carson

Sam Malone:	You know . . . you know I always wanted to pop you one? Maybe this is my lucky day, huh?
Diane Chambers:	You disgust me. I hate you.
Sam:	Are you as turned on as I am?
Diane:	More.

Ted Danson and **Shelley Long**, *Cheers*

'The trouble with some women is that they get all excited about nothing – and then marry him.'
Cher

'The pleasure is momentary, the position ridiculous, and the expense damnable.'
Lord Chesterfield on sex

'Marriage is an adventure, like going to war.'
GK Chesterton

'Many a man has fallen in love with a girl in a light so dim he would not have chosen a suit by it.'
Maurice Chevalier

'My wife and I were married in a toilet. It was a marriage of convenience.'
Tommy Cooper

'That married couples can live together day after day is a miracle the Vatican has overlooked.'
Bill Cosby

'I've sometimes thought of marrying, and then I've thought again.'
Noel Coward

'My wife and I were happy for 20 years. Then we met.'

'When it comes to sex, at my age I like threesomes. In case one of us dies.'

'We sleep in separate rooms, we have dinner apart, we take separate vacations – we're doing everything we can to keep our marriage together.'
Rodney Dangerfield

'I'd marry again if I found a man who had 15 million dollars and would sign over half of it to me before the marriage, and guarantee that he'd be dead within a year.'

'I should never have married, but I didn't want to live without a man. Brought up to respect the conventions, love had to end in marriage. I'm afraid it did.'
Bette Davis

'My wife is a sex object. Every time I ask for sex, she objects.'

'Last year my wife ran off with the fellow next door and I must admit, I still miss him.'
Les Dawson

'The difficulty with marriage is that we fall in love with a personality, but must live with a character.'
Peter Devries

'The feminist movement seems to have beaten the manners out of men, but I didn't see them put up a lot of resistance.'
Clarissa Dickson Wright, *Mail on Sunday*, 24 September 2000

'I have always though that every woman should marry, and no man.'
Lothair

'It destroys one's nerves to be amiable every day to the same human being.'
Benjamin Disraeli

'I've married a few people I shouldn't have, but haven't we all?'
Mamie van Doren

'Any intelligent woman who reads the marriage contract, and then goes into it, deserves all the consequences.'
Isadora Duncan

'They say marriages are made in heaven, but so are thunder and lightning.'
Clint Eastwood

'Men marry women with the hope they will never change. Women marry men with the hope they will change. Invariably they are both disappointed.'
Albert Einstein

'I would not marry God.'
Maxine Elliott, in a telegram denying rumours of her marriage

'We were happily married for eight months. Unfortunately, we were married for four and a half years.'
Nick Faldo, on his ex-wife

'I will not sulk about having no boyfriend, but develop inner poise and authority and sense of self as woman of substance, complete *without* boyfriend, as best way to obtain boyfriend.'
Helen Fielding, *Bridget Jones's Diary*

'Sex was for men. Marriage, like lifeboats, was for women and children.'
Carrie Fisher

Niles Crane: Are you *quite* finished undressing him with your eyes?
Roz Doyle: Oh, *please*. I'm already looking for my stockings and trying to remember where I parked my car.
David Hyde Pierce and **Peri Gilpin**, *Frasier*

'How strange. I usually get some sign that Lilith is in town: dogs forming into packs, blood weeping from the walls.'
Niles Crane (David Hyde Pierce), *Frasier*

'He taught me housekeeping; when we divorce I keep the house.'

'A man in love is incomplete until he is married. Then he is finished.'

'I want a man who's kind and understanding. Is that too much to ask of a millionaire?'

'I never hated a man enough to give him back his diamonds.'

'A girl must marry for love, and keep on marrying until she finds it.'
Zsa Zsa Gabor

'I cannot see myself as a wife. Ugly word.'
Greta Garbo

'If love means never having to say you're sorry, then marriage means always having to say everything twice.'
Estelle Getty

'By god, DH Lawrence was right when he said there must be a dumb, dark, dull, bitter belly-tension between a man and a woman, and how else could this be achieved save in the long monotony of marriage?'
Stella Gibbons, *Cold Comfort Farm*

'Love is an ideal thing; marriage is a real thing. A confusion of the real with the ideal never goes unpunished.'
Johann Wolfgang von Goethe

'Women are frightening. If you get to forty as a man, you're quite battle-scarred.'
Hugh Grant

'Women say they want a man who knows what a woman's worth. That's a pimp.'
Rich Hall

'Marriage is like the witness protection programme: you get all new clothes, you live in the suburbs, and you're not allowed to see your friends anymore.'
Jeremy Hardy

'Pitt the Younger was a great British Prime Minister. He saved Europe from Napoleon, he was the pilot who weathered the storm. I don't know whether he'd have done it any better or quicker had he been married.'
Edward Heath

'If you want to sacrifice the admiration of many men for the criticism of one, go ahead. Get married.'
Katharine Hepburn

'In a few years, no doubt, marriage licences will be sold like dog licences, good for 12 months.'
Aldous Huxley, *Brave New World*

'I have learned that only two things are necessary to keep one's wife happy. First, let her think she's having her way. And second, to let her have it.'
Lyndon B Johnson

'Men and women. Women and men. It will never work.'
Erica Jong

'Only choose in marriage a woman whom you would choose as a friend if she were a man.'
Joseph Joubert

'Seldom or never does a marriage develop into an individual relationship smoothly and without crisis. There is no birth of consciousness without pain.'
Carl Jung

'Any woman who still thinks marriage is a fifty-fifty proposition is only proving that she doesn't understand either men or percentages.'
Florynce Kennedy

'I'm against gay marriage. I think marriage is a sacred union between a man and a pregnant woman.'
Craig Kilborn

'I love being married. I was single for a long time and I just got sick of finishing my own sentences.'
Brian Kiley

'The honeymoon is over when he phones to say he'll be late for supper and she's already left a note in the refrigerator.'
Bill Lawrence

'Not all women give most of their waking thoughts to the problem of pleasing men. Some are married.'
Emma Lee

'We do not squabble, fight or have rows. We collect grudges. We're in an arms race, storing up warheads for the domestic Armageddon.'
Hugh Leonard

'Women do not find it difficult nowadays to behave like men, but they often find it extremely difficult to behave like gentlemen.'
Compton Mackenzie, *Literature in My Time*

'I'm glad I'm not bisexual. I couldn't stand being rejected by men as well as by women.'
Bernard Manning

'We declare that love cannot exist between two people who are married to each other. For lovers give to each other freely, under no compulsion; married people are in duty bound to give in to each other's desires.'
Marie, Countess of Champagne

'I believe that sex is one of the most beautiful, natural, wholesome things that money can buy.'
Steve Martin

'Politics doesn't make strange bedfellows – marriage does.'
Groucho Marx

'I never mind my wife having the last word. In fact, I'm delighted when she gets to it.'
Walter Matthau

'No married man's ever made up his mind until he's heard what his wife has got to say about it.'
Sheppey

'Dullness is the first requisite of a good husband.'
W Somerset Maugham, *Lady Frederick*

Wife: Mr Watt next door blows his wife a kiss every morning as he leaves the house. I wish you'd do that.
Husband: But I hardly know the woman!
Alfred McFote

'We were making love in the back of a truck and we got carried away.'
Spike Milligan

'I would like to be like my father and all the rest of my ancestors who never married.'
Molière

'Husbands are chiefly good as lovers when they are betraying their wives.'
Marilyn Monroe

'I have never had any great esteem for the generality of the fair sex, and my only consolation for being of that gender has been the assurance it gave me of never being married to anyone amongst them.'
Lady Mary Wortley Montagu, letter to Mrs Calthorpe of 7 December 1723

'A good marriage, if there is such a thing, rejects the company and conditions of love. It tries to imitate those of friendship.'
Michel de Montaigne

Eric: She's a lovely girl . . . I'd like to marry her, but her family objects.
Ernie: Her family?
Eric: Yes, her husband and four kids.
Eric Morecambe and **Ernie Wise**

'It's very slow. My favourite position is called "The Plumber". You stay in all day, but nobody comes.'
John Mortimer, on Tantric sex

'It has been said that a bride's attitude towards her betrothed can be summed up in three words: Aisle, Altar, Hymn.'
Frank Muir, *Upon My Word!*

'One doesn't have to get anywhere in a marriage. It's not a public conveyance.'
Iris Murdoch, *A Severed Head*

'To keep your marriage brimming,
With love in the loving cup,
Whenever you're wrong, admit it;
Whenever you're right, shut up.'
Ogden Nash

'Marriage is based on the theory that when a man discovers a brand of beer exactly to his taste he should at once throw up his job and go to work in a brewery.'
George Jean Nathan

'If married couples did not live together, happy marriages would be more frequent.'

'At the beginning of a marriage ask yourself whether this woman will be interesting to talk to from now until old age. Everything else in marriage is transitory: most of the time is spent in conversation.'
Friedrich Nietzsche

'Feminism is the result of a few ignorant and literal-minded women letting the cat out of the bag about which is the superior sex.'
Modern Manners

'There are a number of mechanical devices which increase sexual arousal, especially in women. Chief among these is the Mercedes-Benz 380SL convertible.'

'Staying married may have long-term benefits. You can elicit much more sympathy from friends over a bad marriage than you ever can from a good divorce.'
PJ O'Rourke

'Women: you can't live with them, and you can't get them to dress up in a skimpy Nazi uniform and beat you with a warm squash.'
Emo Philips

'Love is a reciprocity of soul and has a different end and obeys different laws from marriage. Hence one should not take the loved one to wife.'
Alessandro Piccolomini

'Marriage is really tough because you have to deal with feelings and lawyers.'
Richard Pryor

'My sex life has gone from bad to pathetic. My G spot stands for godforsaken.'
Joan Rivers

'There are some good marriages, but practically no delightful ones.'
Francois de La Rochefoucauld

'Sex is like art. Most of it is pretty bad, and the good stuff is out of your price range.'

'There's only one problem with wife swapping. You get another wife.'
Scott Roeben

'I think every woman is entitled to a middle husband she can forget.'
Adela Rogers St John

'Passion and marriage are essentially irreconcilable. Their origins and their ends make them mutually exclusive. Their co-existence in our midst constantly raises insoluble problems, and the strife thereby engendered constitutes a persistent danger for every one of our social safeguards.'
Denis de Rougemont

'Marriage is the only thing that affords a woman the pleasure of company and the perfect sensation of solitude at the same time.'
Personally Speaking

'A husband is what is left of a lover, after the nerve has been extracted.'
A Guide to Men

'Before marriage, a man declares that he would lay down his life to serve you; after marriage, he won't even lay down his newspaper to talk to you.'

'In olden times sacrifices were made at the altar – a practice which is still continued.'
Helen Rowland

'I love being married. It's so great to find that one special person you want to annoy for the rest of your life.'

'My boyfriend and I broke up. He wanted to get married and I didn't want him to.'
Rita Rudner

'Marriage? It's like asparagus eaten with vinaigrette or hollandaise, a matter of taste but no importance.'
Françoise Sagan

'In our part of the world where monogamy is the rule, to marry means to halve one's rights and double one's duties.'
Arthur Schopenhauer

'What God hath joined together no man shall put asunder: God will take care of that.'

'Changeable women are more endurable than monotonous ones. They are sometimes murdered but seldom deserted.'

'It is most unwise for people in love to marry.'

'The fickleness of the women I love is only equalled by the infernal constancy of the women who love me.'
The Philanderer

'The ideal love affair should be conducted by post.'
George Bernard Shaw

'Even under the best of circumstances men are hard creatures to trap. Women who flatter themselves into thinking they've trapped one are like people who believe they can get rid of the cockroaches in their kitchen. They're in for a big surprise late one night when they turn on the light.'
Harry Shearer

'A system could not well have been devised more studiously hostile to human happiness than marriage.'
Percy Bysshe Shelley, Notes to 'Queen Mab'

'Nothing anybody tells you about marriage helps.'
Max Siegel

'Take care of him. And make him feel important. And if you can do that, you'll have a happy and wonderful marriage. Like two out of every ten couples.'
Neil Simon, *Barefoot in the Park*

Marge Simpson:	Homer, is this how you pictured marriage?
Homer Simpson:	Yeah, pretty much, except we drove around in a van and solved mysteries.

The Simpsons

'For millions of years, we men have been able to get away with being useless fathers, doing nothing around the house, and being terrible in bed. Now we're expected to be brilliant at all those things. It's so unfair.'
Arthur Smith

'I'd like to get married because I like the idea of a man being required by law to sleep with me every night.'
Carrie Snow

'Women: you can't live with them, you can't live without them. That's probably why you can rent one for the evening.'
Jim Stark

'We are becoming the men we wanted to marry.'
Gloria Steinem, *Ms*

'The most memorable is always the current one. The rest just merge into a sea of blondes.'
Rod Stewart

'Venus, a beautiful, good-natured lady, was the goddess of love; Juno, a terrible shrew, the goddess of marriage: and they were always mortal enemies.'
Jonathan Swift

'If love is the answer, could you rephrase the question?'
Lily Tomlin

'There is no road to wealth so easy and respectable as that of matrimony.'
Anthony Trollope, *Doctor Thorne*

'You can't bring logic into this. We're taking about marriage. Marriage is like the Middle East. There's no solution.'
Shirley Valentine-Bradshaw (Pauline Collins), *Shirley Valentine*

'When once a woman has given you her heart, you can never get rid of the rest of her body.'
John Vanburgh, *The Relapse*

'I feel sure that no girl could go to the altar, and would probably refuse, if she knew all.'

'The Queen is most anxious to enlist every one who can speak or write to join in checking this mad, wicked folly of 'Woman's Rights', with all its attendant horrors, on which her poor feeble sex is bent, forgetting every sense of womanly feeling and propriety.'
Queen Victoria, letter to Theodore Martin of 29 May 1870

'Take it from me, marriage isn't a word. It's a *sentence*.'
King Vidor

'He is dreadfully married. He's the most married man I ever saw in my life.'
Artemus Ward, *Artemus Ward's Lecture*

Interviewer: Aren't you forgetting you're married?
Mae West: Hmmm – I'm doing my best.

'Marriage is a great institution, but I'm not ready for an institution.'
Mae West

'Whatever women do they must do twice as well as men to be thought half as good. Luckily, this is not difficult.'
Charlotte Whitton, *Canada Month*

'Marriage is a bribe to make a housekeeper think she's a householder.'
Thornton Wilder

'Women: you can't live with them . . . end of sentence.'
Jack McFarland (Sean Hayes), *Will and Grace*

'In Hollywood, all the marriages are happy. It's trying to live together afterwards that causes all the problems.'
Shelley Winters

'Chumps always make the best husbands. When you marry, Sally, grab a chump. Tap his forehead first, and if it rings solid, don't hesitate. All the unhappy marriages come from the husbands having brains.'
The Adventures of Sally

'I was in rare fettle and the heart had touched a new high. I don't know anything that braces one up like finding you haven't got to get married after all.'
PG Wodehouse, *Jeeves in the Offing*

[Author's note: PG Wodehouse, creator of the aristocratic Bertie Wooster and his butler Jeeves among much else, was one of the finest humorous writers in the English language. To my mind *the* finest. He wrote almost 100 books, numerous short stories, 250 lyrics for 30 musical comedies, and 15 plays. All this in the era of manual typewriters. They don't make them like PG Wodehouse any more.

He was, by all accounts, an *extremely* introverted man. After he and his wife moved to New York he asked her to start looking for apartments to buy, but insisted that she only look at ground floor apartments. When she asked him why, he replied, 'Because I never know *what* to say to the lift boy!']

'He had been building one of those piles of thought, as ramshackle and fantastic as a Chinese pagoda, half from words let fall by gentlemen in gaiters, half from the litter in his own mind, about duck shooting and legal history, about the Roman occupation of Lincoln and the relations of country gentlemen with their wives, when, from all this disconnected rambling, there suddenly formed itself in his mind the idea that he would ask Mary to marry him.'
Virginia Woolf

'I have certainly seen more men destroyed by the desire to have a wife and child and to keep them in comfort than I have seen destroyed by drink or harlots.'
WB Yeats

'Do you know what it means to come home at night to a woman who'll give you a little love, a little affection, a little tenderness? It means you're in the wrong house, that's what it means.'
Henny Youngman

QUOTATIONS:
INDEX OF WRITERS AND SPEAKERS

REFERENCES AND FURTHER READING

Andreae, Simon (2000), *The Secrets of Love and Lust* (London: Abacus).

Barrett, Louise, and Dunbar, Robin, and Lycett, John (2002), *Human Evolutionary Psychology* (Basingstoke and New York: Palgrave).

Boyer, Pascal (2002), *Religion Explained: The Human Instincts that Fashion Gods, Spirits and Ancestors* (London: Vintage).

Briggs Myers, Isabel, and Myers, Peter B (1980), *Gifts Differing: Understanding Personality Type* (Consulting Psychologists Press Inc.).

Browne, Anthony (2006), *The Retreat of Reason: Political Correctness and the Corruption of Public Debate in Modern Britain* (London: The Institute for the Study of Civil Society [Civitas]).

Coontz, Stephanie (2000), *The Way We Never Were: American Families and the Nostalgia Trap* (New York: Basic Books).

Coontz, Stephanie (2005), *Marriage, a History: From Obedience to Intimacy, or How Love Conquered Marriage* (New York: Viking).

Cooper, Joel (2007), *Cognitive Dissonance: Fifty Years of a Classic Theory* (London: Sage Publications).

Dawkins, Richard (2006), *The God Delusion* (London: Black Swan).

Doyle, Laura (2001, first published 1988), *The Surrendered Wife: A Step-by-Step Guide to Finding Intimacy, Passion and Peace with Your Man* (London: Simon & Schuster).

Duffell, Nick (2000), *The Making of Them: The British Attitude to Children and the Boarding School System* (London: The Lone Arrow Press).

Gantt, Donna A (2002), *Marriage is Ministry not Misery (A Wife's Handbook)* (1st Books Library).

Goleman, Daniel (1995), *Emotional Intelligence: Why It Can Matter More Than IQ* (London: Bloomsbury).

Gottman, John (2007), *Why Marriages Succeed or Fail and How to Make Yours Last* (London: Bloomsbury).

Gray, John (1993), *Men Are From Mars, Women Are From Venus* (New York: HarperCollins).

Harman, Harriet (1993) *20th Century Man, 21st Century Woman: How Both Sexes Can Bridge The Century Gap* (London: Vermillion)

Helgoe, Laurie (2008) *Introvert Power: Why Your Inner Life is Your Hidden Strength* (Naperville, Illinois: Sourcebooks Inc.).

James, Oliver (1998), *Britain on the Couch: Treating a Low Serotonin Society*, (London: Arrow Books).

Jeffries, William C (1991), *True to Type: Answers to the Most Commonly Asked Questions About Interpreting the Myers-Briggs Type Indicator* (Charlottesville, Virginia: Hampton Roads Publishing Company Inc.).

Jung, Carl G (1989; first published 1921), *Psychological Types* (London: Routledge).

Laney, Marti Olsen (2002), *The Introvert Advantage: How to Thrive in an Extravert World* (New York: Workman Publishing).

Larson, Jeffry H (2000), *Should We Stay Together? A Scientifically Proven Method for Evaluating Your Relationship and Improving its Chances for Long-term Success* (San Francisco: Wiley).

Litvinoff, Sarah (2001), *Better Relationships: Practical Ways to Make Your Love Last (Relate Guides)* (London: Vermillion).

Moxon, Steve (2008), *The Woman Racket* (Exeter: Imprint Academic).

Nettle, Daniel (2007), *Personality: What Makes You the Way You Are* (Oxford: Oxford University Press).

Onedera, Jill D (ed) (2008), *The Role of Religion in Marriage and Family Counselling* (Abingdon: Routledge).

Pearman, Roger R, and Albritton, Sarah C (1997) *I'm Not Crazy, I'm Just Not You: The Real Meaning Of The 16 Personality Types* (Mountain View, California: Davies-Black Publishing).

Pinker, Steven (1997), *How the Mind Works* (London: Penguin).

Pinker, Steven (2003), *The Blank Slate: The Modern Denial of Human Nature* (London: Penguin).

Pinker, Susan (2008), *The Sexual Paradox: Men, Women, and the Real Gender Gap* (New York: Scribner).

Quenk, Naomi L (2000), *Essentials of Myers-Briggs Type Indicator Assessment* (John Wiley & Sons Inc.).

Rufus, Anneli (2003), *party of one: the loners' manifesto* (New York: Marlowe & Company).

Russell, Betrand (2009; first published 1929), *Marriage and Morals* (Routledge).

Seligman, Martin E P (2007), *What You Can Change . . . and What You Can't: The Complete Guide to Successful Self-Improvement* (London: Nicholas Brealey Publishing).

Simring, Steven and Sue (2001), *Making Marriage Work For Dummies* (Indianapolis: Wiley Publishing).

Steinberg, Robert J, and Weis, Karen (eds) (2006) *The New Psychology of Love* (Yale University Press).

Storr, Anthony (1997), *Solitude* (London: HarperCollins) (first published in Great Britain by André Deutsch Ltd in 1988, under the title *The School of Genius*).

Tallis, Frank (2004), *Love Sick* (Arrow Books).

INDEX OF CITED PUBLICATIONS

SUBJECT INDEX